Manifested in the Flesh

Manifested in the Flesh:
How the Historical Evidence of Jesus
Refutes Modern Mystics and Skeptics

Joel McDurmon

AMERICAN VISION
POWDER SPRINGS, GEORGIA

AMERICAN VISION

A BIBLICAL WORLDVIEW MINISTRY

THE MISSION OF AMERICAN VISION, INC. IS TO PUBLISH AND DISTRIBUTE BOOKS
THAT LEAD INDIVIDUALS TOWARD:

A personal faith in the one true God: Father, Son, and Holy Spirit

A lifestyle of practical discipleship

A worldview that is consistent with the Bible

An ability to apply the Bible to all of life

Cover design: James Talmage, Byron, Georgia

American Vision, Inc.

3150 Florence Road, Suite 2

Powder Springs, Georgia 30127-5385

www.americanvision.org

1–800–628–9460

Library of Congress Cataloging-in-Publication Data

McDurmon, Joel
  Manifested in the Flesh: / Joel McDurmon—1st ed.
  Includes bibliographical references and index.
  ISBN: 0–915815–61–3

To four pastors who have seen me along:

The Rev. David Wacker,
The Rev. Jerry Underwood,
The Rev. Paul Sagan,
and
The Rt. Rev. David Hicks

Table of Contents

APPENDICES

Foreword

TODAY'S CLIMATE OF attack on Christianity has reminded many of the parallels between the hostile pagan environment of the early church and ours today. The analogies are very real, including outright persecution of Christians in some areas of the world. But there is one stark difference: ancient infidels might almost be forgiven in view of their totally pagan background, whereas modern antagonists against the faith—many of them educated in a Christian culture and with all the evidence for the reliability of Christianity at their disposal—nevertheless choose the path of apostasy almost in defiance of the evidence.

Whatever their motives—sensationalism and its monetary rewards, rebellion, or honest conviction—theirs is a sorry lot. As the pages of this important book will demonstrate, they try to divorce Jesus and his following from history itself, twist the history that survives, and draw mistaken conclusions regarding the origins of the faith. In the process they will madly search for parallels with ancient mystery cults and heretical Gnostic sects, and finally exercise bad judgment in trying to add a sheen of credibility to what are ultimately worthless arguments.

Is such language excessive? Or justified? Those who read these pages should have a delightful time determining which is the case. But who are these foes against the faith today? They come in two basic categories: popular sensationalizers and more serious scholars. Our present horizon is cluttered with the former. They are the writers of articles, books, novels, and screenplays who, along with radio, television, motion-picture, and DVD producers, know the sure-fire formula for best-sellerdom and sales success: *create controversy* by presenting a radical recasting of previously-accepted truths. Controversy has always been the mother's milk of sales, so it was hardly surprising that when Dan Brown distorted the facts regarding the greatest statistical phenomenon in the history of the world—the holy Christian church—the controversy resulting (and of course the sales) of his *The Da Vinci Code* were correspondingly huge. At least thirty-five such titles that preceded the *Code* and since its publication could be listed here.

The other category is comprised of more serious authors for whom the bottom line is less significant than their conviction that through their research in various forms, they have arrived at a fuller understanding of how Christianity came to be. They want to share their findings with the world in the name of emancipating the public from "errors of the past" when it comes to Christian origins.

Manifested in the Flesh takes on this group in particular, and author Joel McDurmon does so with careful scholarship, dispassionate research, compelling logic, graceful prose, and even dashes of humor. He easily identifies the methodological chinks in the armor of the attackers and cuts through the tissues of misrepresentation on which they rely so heavily. As for the ancient pagan mystery cults (which, they claim, so heavily influenced Christianity), McDurmon lays bare the excessive, almost frantic search by such critics in trying to find parallels between the cults and early Christian practices, as well as how they warp the results of that search. (This malady has well been called "Parallelomania" in Komoszewski's *Reinventing Jesus*.)

Their attacks against Christianity range from the ridiculous—"There never was a historical person named Jesus of Nazareth"—to the basic claims underlying most of these revisionists: "Jesus may have existed, but he's not who you think he was." But their case dies before it even has a chance to be born, since their attempt to sunder Jesus from history fails at the outset. All the founding heroes and heroines of the ancient mystery cults had little or nothing to do with factual history, so if Christianity drew from these cults, Jesus must necessarily be pared away from history as much as possible.

This, however, is *not* possible. Instead we have a colossal paradox today: just at a time when our media are offering us caricatures of Christ and the church that he founded, his *genuine* portrait is becoming ever clearer when the secular resources of ancient history and archaeology provide fascinating additional confirmations of the biblical record. Christian apologetics—how to defend the faith—has never been easier!

These pages, then, provide a wealth of information not only on why the current critics of Christianity are wrong, but why our faith is right. In the cluttered welter of world religions, parareligions, cults, and spiritual fantasies, two and only two religious systems are totally anchored to the proven facts of the past, that is, to history: our parent Judaism and Christianity. This is not to deny that the founders of other faiths were not historical—certainly there was a Gautama Buddha, a Muhammed, a Mary Baker Eddy, a Joseph Smith— but one looks in vain for any solid correlations between what is claimed in their holy books and the history of the contextual world of their time.

Christianity, on the other hand, delights in how intertwined the Gospels and Epistles are with the world of their day—with solid history. Many Christians assume that because *their* faith is so well grounded in fact, that all other religions must have similarly strong links with the past. Alas, that is far, *far* from the case. For that reason alone, *Manifested in the Flesh* is *very* significant reading for our time.

Paul L. Maier
Professor of Ancient History
Western Michigan University, and
author of *In the Fullness of Time*

Preface

The foolishness of man perverteth his way: and his heart fretteth against the LORD (Prov. 19:3).

Let the proud be ashamed; for they dealt perversely with me without a cause: but I will meditate in thy precepts (Ps. 119:78).

WHEN I ORIGINALLY sat down to begin this project, I expected to write only a couple of chapters on the mystery religions for the publisher to use in a multi-part book about recent attacks on the Christian faith. As I wrote, however, the work took on a much different look and developed its own force. The decision was made to publish it as a stand-alone volume.

Such a development occurred, I believe, because atheism is not merely an intellectual position relegated to one discipline of study; it is a *worldview*. Worldview issues by nature spread into every area of human thought and action. So, when I began to respond to the mystery religions, I entered an historical study. But this historical study soon morphed into a theological study. From there it went into comparative religion, biblical studies, apologetics, and so on. All of the issues inseparably intertwine. In order to answer the critics faithfully, the student must get underneath the surface arguments, address the presuppositions, and then see how the different areas of knowledge interact with core beliefs.

Responding to atheist attacks reminds me of the old arcade game "Whac-a-mole" where a "mole" quickly pops up through one of several holes, and the player must whack it with a big mallet before it darts back down. Kids get so frustrated at the varmint that they keep feeding quarters to the machine so they can get one more whack at it. At that point, they have been suckered in. The mole gets away, and it gets away with their money. The way to beat it is not to keep feeding money to the enemy but to pull the plug and scrap the machine. The same goes for atheism: You cannot waste your time responding to the flurry of trifling arguments and sarcastic slanders that atheists and critics toss at you. By the time you take a swing, they have popped up and down again in three other places. Instead, you have to get behind the source of their power: pull the plug and demolish the framework.

For these two reasons—the nature of the subject as a worldview, and the shotgun style of particular attacks—this book comes to you in the form it is in. It incorporates an overarching worldview apologetic against atheism and mysticism and simultaneously ties together several academic disciplines to answer specific attacks. Readers should keep both in mind as they read through the chapters. The attacks to which this book responds fail because they have an incoherent worldview behind them, and they therefore produce convoluted arguments about history, theology, and scholarship.

This book upholds the traditional Christian doctrine of the historical Incarnation of Jesus Christ against recent attacks by atheists, humanistic scholars, and New Age mystics. Christ came in the flesh—fully man and fully God. The attacks, however, have come in the "Whac-a-mole" fashion, and thus the response must avoid the trap of responding to every little critique. My approach is as follows:

My Introduction first pulls the plug on the pagan worldview: The attacks of the atheists and the mystics all follow the same lie that the serpent told Eve in the garden. The lure of satanic religions is always the promise of enlightenment apart from God's Word, the denial of God's power in history, and the promise of divinization for man. If we understand this as we come to the recent attacks on the Gospel, as well as the ancient versions of "mystery religions" to which modern critics appeal, we will see the satanic criteria clearly as the power source for all of them.

Chapter 1 seeks to show how this fallen criteria have remained the same for the modern critics, the ancient mystery religions, as well as every atheistic and mystical critic in between. There is nothing new under the sun. The modern attacks on the faith are in reality just old fables in new dress. But the fact that the arguments tend to recur in history shows that they have a powerful pull on the fallen human heart, and they must therefore be confronted. It is important to see the rise of such "intellectual" denials of the faith since the nineteenth century and the development of academic response to that endeavor.

Chapter 2 begins the meat of the specialized applications of the apologetic. There I explore the critics' claim that there were several ancient religions that believed in a "dying and rising god" who sacrificed himself to save the world and that Christianity was just one more version of this pagan motif which happened to win the day. As I walk through the most significant of the ancient mystery religions in this chapter, the reader can see that they in reality have very little in common with Christianity. An analysis drives the point home.

Chapter 3 answers the criticism that the early Church fathers had no answer for the alleged similarities between the mystery religions and Christianity. Following the historical study in Chapter 2 that shows that there were actually very few similarities, this chapter makes the point by—and hold on for this one—actually reading the early Church fathers. The fathers practically ridiculed the idea. They treated the mystery religions as any other idolatry and relied solely on the Old and New Testaments for their understanding of Jesus Christ.

Chapters 4 and 5 make up a section of biblical study which refutes the critics' view of the Apostle Paul. Chapter 4 answers the question of Paul's view of and relation to Jesus Christ. Critics argue that Paul's letters reveal that he believed in only a mystical Christ not an historical person. The argument is nonsense. While Paul does seem to write about the spiritual aspects of Christ much more than the historical, the epistles do explicitly reveal the opposite as well. The rebuttal is that simple. Nevertheless, this chapter affords an opportunity for a wonderful Bible study that highly enriches the answer to the question.

Chapter 5 continues the biblical study by answering the criticism that Paul was primarily a pagan thinker, drawing from his pagan surroundings (especially the mystery religions) in order to form a new religion that we call Christianity. This chapter benefits from the latest of New Testament scholarship which now sees what it should have understood all along: Paul was steeped in Old Testament theology, and the religion that he promoted was not tainted by pagan mysteries but was traditional Old Testament theology with the resurrected Christ as the fulfillment of the Messianic promises.

Chapters 6 and 7 change gears slightly in order to look at how underlying beliefs can drive how people do scholarship. Both believers and unbelievers have underlying presuppositions which affect how they view evidence and indeed what they even consider as evidence. These chapters essentially apply apologetics to the very types of criticisms that the atheists and mystics rely on themselves. Chapter 6 turns the critics' own question on them: Who can you trust? I explore one criticism in depth to show how trust in unbelief exists in the unbeliever's heart *before* he examines the evidence and drives how he answers the question. Chapter 7 does the same thing, but with a broader perspective, across several issues. It relies on a very scholarly article published by Bruce Metzger in 1955. Metzger's reply to the mystery religion proponents is powerful and timeless, and this chapter is an attempt to bring his expert analysis into more accessible language.

With these specific questions answered, Chapters 8 and 9 intend to relate the truth that the critics are reacting so violently against: the truth of Jesus Christ. The truth about the Incarnation of our Lord is too glorious to be summed up in twenty pages, but I have given enough to communicate the traditional understanding of the doctrine as well as how that doctrine refutes every pagan conception of humanity. Especially at issue, since the topic of this book is the true humanity of Jesus, is the doctrine of the perfect man as put forth by both pagans and Christians. Since the atheist and mystic critics deny that God's Son took on human flesh and revealed Himself as perfect humanity, they look for a perfect man in other places and ways: pagan places and pagan ways. Both Chapters 8 and 9 show the contrast and show the destructive and tyrannical results of looking for divine perfection among fallen men.

The concluding Chapter 10 pulls the several strands of historical studies, biblical studies, theology, and apologetics, back together into the overall worldview endeavor. The issue: idolatry. I rehearse the main points covered throughout the book and then end with a needed motivational appeal to educate ourselves and our posterity as an organic Church.

I have included four appendices on related subjects. These expand ideas touched on in the text, and the titles are self-evident. Appendices I and II expand on the idea of how prior religious beliefs drive the practice and results of scholarship. Appendix I shows this across the board in New Testament studies, Appendix II illustrates this in the legacy of one very influential scholar who appears to have turned out badly wrong.

Appendix III picks apart one of the main books which has promoted the mystery religion theory behind Christianity. I hold the book up to the high standard it claims for itself and expose the work for the farce that it is. Despite bold claims and relentless "evidences," the mystic's case crumbles under its own weight.

Appendix IV is a reproduction of one of the earliest written Christian apologetics. Aristides is an unfamiliar name to most Christians—even pastors and seminary students—despite being readily available today. I have included his brief work against pagan religions for several reasons: First, because it is a brief and easily readable work; second, it shows that the earliest of the early Church that we have records of did respond quite soundly to paganism of all sorts; third, I want to encourage believers to read and study what the early fathers of the Church wrote. Their works have lasted throughout the centuries for good reason—they are good works—and Aristides provides a relevant and practical place to start.

The scholarship in this area continues to grow. Many books have appeared within the last years, and a few other fairly recent works have come to my attention. Notable among these are the works of Larry Hurtado, in particular his books *How on Earth did Jesus Become a God?: Historical Questions About Earliest Devotion to Jesus* (2005), his massive *The Lord Jesus Christ: Devotion to Jesus in Earliest Christianity* (2003), and *The Earliest Christian Artifacts: Manuscripts and Christian Origins* (2006). Likewise, I have not been able to draw from a very recent work of N. T. Wright, *Paul: In Fresh Perspective* (2006), nor from the broad tome by Richard Bauckham, *Jesus and the Eyewitnesses: The Gospels as Eyewitness Testimony* (2006). These wonderful works of scholarship contain valuable insights into biblical Theology and early church history which would add much to the discussion in this book. I recommend them all for further study.

Many acknowledgments are due. Thanks to Gary DeMar for his professionalism and guidance. His desire for apologetics and Bible studies that are relevant to the modern reader and which confront modern skeptics head-on, has been the force behind this project. Likewise, the talented staff at American Vision, which has turned out so many quality textual, audio, and visual productions to date, has crafted my bare manuscript into a beautiful presentation pleasing to the eye. For this I am grateful and blessed. Very Special thanks to Gary North, who provided me with a thorough critique and helpful suggestions, many of which I have adopted. His comments helped me streamline what was a loose collection of academic essays into a more accessible and coherent presentation to laymen (something he himself has always excelled at). Those areas of the work which may come across as a bit dry, are places where I probably have not taken North's advice. Thank you also to Dr. Paul Maier, who has provided an insightful Foreword, along with some helpful suggestions, as well as a very cheerful and encouraging correspondence. His passion for early Christianity has further inspired mine. Finally, I thank my wife, Lori, who has borne the strains of seminary life upon our family, with the added stress of me working on this book nearly every night for a good while. Her patience and endurance during this time has been a source of inspiration and motivation.

While I have tried to be thorough in this work, the very nature of the questions leads into fields far more vast than can be presented here. Aside from providing what is necessary to refute the critics squarely, I hope this effort opens many doors to further reading and pushes pastor, student, and scholar alike to pursue biblical studies—historical, theological and apologetic—as a lifetime pursuit. At thirty-two years old, Lord willing, my pursuit has only begun.

Joel E. McDurmon
Flourtown, PA
November 2006

Introduction

Could it be that the story of Jesus was actually yet another version of the myth of Osiris-Dionysius?[1]

What is more plausible than to posit the gradual evolution of spiritual ideas, with Christianity emerging from the ancient Pagan Mysteries in a seamless historical continuum?[2]

Yea, hath God said? (Gen. 3:1)

The fool hath said in his heart, There is no God (Ps. 14:1).

S<small>T. PAUL TELLS</small> us that Jesus Christ, the Son of God, "Was made of the seed of David according to the flesh" (Rom. 1:3), and that this "mystery of godliness" was "manifested in the flesh" (1 Tim. 3:16). The coming of Christ in the flesh to save His people is the focal point of human history, and the heart of Christian belief and practice. But this fundamental belief of the historic truth of Jesus Christ has come under intense attack in recent times. New groups of radicals are working hard to popularize the belief that a historical Jesus never walked the earth. Some want to read Christianity as a mere myth under the mystical umbrella of New Age "spirituality," others deny the faith and the existence of God altogether. But as our Lord was truly "manifested in the flesh," so must the

---

[1]Timothy Freke and Peter Gandy, *The Jesus Mysteries: Was the "Original Jesus" a Pagan God?* (New York: Three Rivers Press, 1999), 62.

[2]Freke and Gandy, *The Jesus Mysteries*, 12.

foolishness of these modern pagans be revealed in open light: "for their folly shall be manifest to all men" (2 Tim. 3:9).

Pagan religions have many faces but one folly that originated in the Garden of Eden, when the serpent prompted Eve to ask the question, "Hath God said?" When Eve stepped onto this unholy ground of radical skepticism, and made it the foundation for her interpretation of the world, she adopted the religion of foolishness. She suspended in her heart and mind the truth that God had revealed—which she knew to be true—in order to rely solely upon her own ability. She traded God's sure revelation for her own limited understanding. From that point on it did not matter how she answered, for she had already denied God by her reliance upon herself. This legacy of assuming that man can submit God's Word for testing and analysis is the basis of man's fall, the original sin, and the continuing force behind all pagan religion.

The serpent's question has surfaced again today in several places, exemplified by a book entitled *The Jesus Mysteries*. The two authors of this New-Age propaganda have drawn from ancient paganism as well as the most radical of modern scholarship, in order to rephrase the serpent's question in a slightly new way. They query, "Could it be that the story of Jesus was actually yet another version of the myth of Osiris-Dionysius?"[3] Along these same lines, another recent attack on the historical Jesus, the atheist documentary film *The God Who Wasn't There*, claims to reveal that "Jesus Christ is likely a fictional character, a legend never based on a real human."[4] Both of these works attained best-seller status. With such harmful ideas becoming popular to the degree that they have, it is time that their core claims be refuted.

The refutation begins by understanding the serpent's loaded question, "Hath God said?" With this query the devil initiated the first "mystery religion"—a quest for hidden truth—the very same religion that undergirds the modern attacks on the faith. The serpent deceived Eve

---

[3] Freke and Gandy, *The Jesus Mysteries*, 62. "Osiris" and "Dionysius" are the names of two pagan gods whom we shall meet in a later chapter. The important point here is that the authors put Jesus on the same level as *mythological* gods.

[4] Claim taken from the back of the DVD cover of Brian Flemming, *The God Who Wasn't There: A Film Beyond Belief* (Beyond Belief Media, 2005).

into a quest for "truth," though God had already given her the truth. In taking the first step on that quest, Eve denied God's revelation (and therefore His grace as well). Tied to this rejection of God's revealed truth was the denial of God's historical sanction: "Ye shall not surely die" (Gen 3:4). In other words, what God said was true for *history*, the serpent relegated to *mythology*. The companion temptation to this rejection of God's Word and sovereignty was the lure of secret knowledge and special enlightenment. The serpent promised, "your eyes shall be opened, and ye shall be as Gods" (Gen. 3:4). These aspects of the serpent's approach characterize all of the pagan mystery religions from the Garden to today. The program includes the following elements:

> 1. The quest for secret, hidden, or "mystery" knowledge: "Hath God said?"
> 2. The outright rejection of God's sovereignty in history: "Ye shall not surely die."
> 3. The promise of enlightenment by the quest: "Your eyes shall be opened."
> 4. The promise of becoming divine (or divinization): "Ye shall be as gods."

The serpent has hissed the same questions all throughout history, and in every clash between biblical religion and its false parodies, God's representatives triumph by relying upon God's revelation of Himself in history. When Moses confronted Pharaoh, his message was, "Thus saith the LORD God of Israel" (Ex. 5:1). Pharaoh replied, "Who is the LORD, that I should obey his voice?" (5:2). When God responded through Moses with miracles and plagues, Pharaoh had his magicians imitate them (7:11, although they could not always do so). Similarly, when Elijah confronted the priests of Baal at Mt. Carmel, the issue was, "How long halt ye between two opinions? If the LORD be God, then follow him: but if Baal, then follow him" (1 Kings 18:21). The pagan priests relied on their own versions of sacrificial rituals: yelling, dancing, cutting their own flesh (we shall see more of this behavior in the later mystery religions). Elijah relied on God's word: "I have done all these things at thy word"

(18:36). In another example, the three Hebrew children, Shadrach, Meshach, and Abednego, opposed the decree of the pagan king Nebuchadnezzar (Dan. 3:10) in the name of their God (3:17). As a result, God saved the children in the fiery furnace and, "changed the King's word" (3:28). In all of these cases God's people trusted the Word of God while pagans used every possible means to challenge that divine revelation.

The serpent still hisses today. Modern proponents of the so-called "Jesus Mysteries Thesis" try to tempt us with the same old twisted story. Their approach exactly parallels that of the serpent. They propose the quest for hidden truth: "Could it be that the story of Jesus was actually yet another version of the myth of Osiris-Dionysius?"[5] They reject the divinely revealed history: "The Jesus story is a perennial myth . . . not merely a history of events that happened to someone else 2,000 years ago."[6] Then, exactly as the serpent, they promise enlightenment and divinization: "The Jesus story is a perennial myth with the power to *impart saving Gnosis,*[7] which can *transform us into Christ.*"[8] Sound familiar?

The authors of *The Jesus Mysteries* and many like them wish to overturn centuries of traditional understanding with such loaded questions and promises. They want us to adopt their destructive approach of radical skepticism: to rely upon our own feelings and our own limited perspective, as if these were the real test of truth. But to do so would be to hold God's revelation in question, and thereby deny it from the outset. In questioning the truth revealed in Christ we deny it by placing ourselves, as Eve did, in the position of the ultimate Judge.

What Exactly is a Mystery Religion?

The mystery religions of the ancient world were a vast array of cults that offered initiates secret knowledge through which they promised en-

---

[5]Freke and Gandy, *Jesus Mysteries,* 62.
[6]Freke and Gandy, *Jesus Mysteries,* 13.
[7]"Gnosis" is the Greek word for "knowledge." Here it refers to the secret knowledge that the mystery religions claimed would enable a person to transcend the world and become divine. This was the core belief that distinguished the early heretics called "Gnostics" as well as the pagan mystery cults from New Testament Christianity.
[8]Freke and Gandy, *Jesus Mysteries,* 13.

lightenment and divinity. In each case, the "knowledge" given revolved around myths told about certain gods and goddesses. The mystery-cults spanned several centuries and usually had two faces: one public and one private. The public side was watered-down and usually served the interests of the pagan States. These were accompanied by regular ceremonies with great pageantry and often coincided with the alleged divinity of the Emperor. In contrast, the private rituals varied greatly. Some were ascetic, some sinister. A few promoted a quiet life of retreat from society; some engaged in human sacrifice. Almost all employed bizarre rituals to dazzle the senses: "No means of exciting the emotions was neglected."[9] These emotion-driven secret meetings were attended by primarily women. These displays and their accompanying hero stories downplayed historical reality and emphasized the mythology of their gods as a basis for understanding life.

The early Church fathers—in fact, some of the earliest from whom we have records[10]—confronted the pagan mystery cults of their time and refuted them squarely. Scripture indicates that the apostles themselves had to deal with very similar attacks, probably from pagans who belonged to mystery cults, or who otherwise knew various pagan mythologies. We see Peter, for example, urging that, "We have not followed cunningly devised fables . . . but were *eyewitnesses* of his majesty" (2 Pet. 1:16). The apostle responded to the charge that Christianity was just another myth by referring to a distinct historical event that he had *eyewitnessed.* The New Testament writers always emphasized their physical witness of the Lord (Luke 1:1–3; John 19:35–6; 21:24; 1 Cor. 15:5–8; 2 Pet. 1:16–18; 1 John 1:1–3). By their accounts, the original Jesus was indeed an historical figure. Likewise, the apostle Paul often speaks of Jesus as the historical person that He was. Paul purposefully *warns against mythology* several times. In fact, the words "myth" or "fable" (from the Greek

---

[9]Samuel Angus, quoted in Freke and Gandy, *Jesus Mysteries*, 19.

[10]See Appendix IV, "The Apology of Aristides," which reprints one of the earliest (that we have) Christian responses to pagan foolishness.

word *mythos*) only appear in the New Testament in the context of warning or condemnation (1 Tim. 1:4; 1:14; 4:7; 2 Tim. 4:4; 2 Pet. 1:16).[11]

The only way, therefore, to get around the claims of the New Testament and the early Church fathers is to create a hypothesis in which the apostles were liars, and in which the New Testament is unreliable. Not surprisingly, this is exactly what the modern "Jesus Mysteries" do: they want so badly to present Jesus as one more religious myth or fable, that they go to great lengths to reject (with much twisting and contorting) every possible reference to a truly historical Jesus. The last thing they would ever want is for their mythical "god-man" belief to become a historical reality. For them, *they* will become gods; *they* will become incarnate deities. If Jesus Christ were the One True God manifested in the flesh, it would spoil the mystics' whole parade: they would then be forced to acknowledge the One higher than all.

This Side of the Fig Leaf

The belief that Jesus never existed in history is nothing more than an intricately sewn fig-leaf covering for sin. It is the attempt by atheists and New Age proponents to hide their guilt before God. Unlike Eve, who at least had the advantage of innocence when the serpent confronted her, we live in a fallen world with fallen hearts and minds. We must deal with our sinful dispositions daily. If we do not accept the covering that God has provided in the historical blood of Jesus Christ, then we will try to manufacture our own, just as Adam and Eve sewed together fig-leaves for themselves. Often in history those fig leaves have taken the form of the wilted petals of man's intellectual ingenuity. The mystery religion theory of Christian history is merely an intellectual excuse for rejecting Christ, and it will hold up about as poorly as the original fig leaves did. Can you imagine standing before God on Judgment Day

---

[11]An interesting case appears in the inter-testamental Apocryphal book of Baruch (3:23). The passage warns against "myth-tellers" (Greek—*mythologoi*) and "inquisitors of understanding," saying, "They have not found the way to wisdom, or remembered its paths." Written probably in the second-century B. C., this Apocryphal book most likely testifies to a Jewish-minded rebuttal of typical pagan idolatry. The groups in question could well have been mystery cults offering myths and secret knowledge.

with the excuse, "God, I couldn't determine whether the Gospels actually portrayed an historical person or not!" But above all, fallen man
wants to escape this final judgment of God, and in the attempt to run,
man will do or say the most ridiculous things: he will claim that God
does not exist, and he will reject as myth the most important parts of
history that God has revealed.

But the Bible cannot honestly be read as anything but real, factual
history. The Gospels, Paul and the other apostles all write in the light of
an historical figure and His historical death and resurrection. No matter
how hard you try, you cannot divorce Jesus Christ from history and reality. Even mystery-religion theorists sometimes unwittingly refute themselves in this regard. Alan Dundes, one of the mystery-theory scholars
interviewed in *The God Who Wasn't There*, does just that. He scoffs, "[I]f
you take away the folklore from the Bible you don't have a heck of a lot
left, except begat, begat, begat, begat." But notice the obvious point that
he misses: it is the "begat, begat, begat," that *ties Jesus Christ to an historical setting.* The very part of the Bible that the scholar ridicules provides the details which refute his theory. Jesus was the promised Seed
of David and Seed of Abraham, and the "begat's" tie Him to history in a
way that the pagan gods would never imagine. Those gods had their genealogies, too, but they were always obviously mythological: Chaos gave
birth to Kronos, and Kronos to Zeus; then Athena burst forth from the
brow of Zeus! With Jesus we find a much different story: He is a direct
descendent of earthly figures, chronicled in a Jewish genealogy in the
way that the Jews had always done in the Old Testament (Matt. 1:1–17;
Luke 3:23–38). St. Paul wrote to Timothy to avoid "fables and endless
genealogies, which minister questions, rather than godly edifying which
is in faith" (1 Tim. 1:4). It could very well be that Paul wrote these words
in response to a problem Timothy was having with local mystery cults.
Paul rejected those mythological tar-babies, because he trusted the historical lineage of Jesus Christ, the "seed of David" (Rom. 1:3). The core
of the Christian faith is historical versus the mythology of the mystery
religions. Even when scholars such as Dundes try to cut out everything

from the Bible that they can distort as mythology, there still exists a core of material that is distinctly and unmistakably *historical.*

This book seeks to promote that historical reality, and to refute the modern serpentine hiss that Jesus was a mythological figure derived from the pagan mystery religions. It exposes mystery-religion scholarship as a fig-leaf for sin, and shows that the Christian faith—especially the background of the apostle Paul—found everything it needed in the Old Testament revelation of God in the light of Jesus Christ the Messiah. Furthermore, it contrasts the mythical nature of pagan religions with the historical reality of Christ's incarnation. While this "mystery of godliness" is indeed great, I do not shrink the fact that "He was manifested in the flesh."

The critics, however, do get one thing right: "Contemporary Christians are largely ignorant of the origins of their religion."[12] Books like this one that you are reading face the uphill challenge of a disinterested or complacent Christian world. Christians do not study the historical creeds of their *own* faith, let alone things like obscure mystery cults and early Church confrontations with pagans. If we are to stop the influence of New-Age and atheistic attacks on our culture, then we must educate our families and our flocks. That education can begin with the next chapter.

---

[12]From the back cover of Flemming's DVD, *The God Who Wasn't There.*

Fads and Myths,
Old and New

*You shall not follow the crowd toward evil, nor sway a controversy
by leaning after the crowd* (Ex. 23:2)[1]

A N OLD PROVERB says, "Those who can talk Latin may always find their
way to Rome." You can get anywhere you want to go if you know
the right language. Mystery religions speak the language of the fallen
human heart. As long as they stay hidden in their dark corner of history
and do not intrude into popular religion, they cause little problem; but
when they become militant and seek to dominate the culture around
them, they propose an offense. In Christianity's confrontation with
cults, in ancient times as well as now, the Gospel of Jesus Christ clashes
with basic desires of depraved human nature: exclusive knowledge, escape from human problems, and the illusion of becoming divine. Fallen
man has no problem convincing himself that whatever way he desires
is the right way, especially when that way is wrapped in the glamour of
big-screen production and professional cover-art. Following the crowd
to do evil has never been easier. The Bible, however, specifically tells
us not to follow a mob. We are not to let popular movements pervert
the truth and lead us into a lie. The command not to bear false witness

---

[1]My translation.

means that we must stand against the tide, even when it means unpopularity or even persecution. Contrary to the atheists and humanists who ridicule Christians for having a "herd" mentality—blindly following our leaders and unable to think for ourselves—the Bible teaches us to reason against the waves and fads of popular religion.

The proponents of today's fads and myths about Jesus constitute just such a mob. For well over a century, in the darkest corners of popular religion, a trend has lurked which recently has exploded into the popular imagination. The so-called "mystery religions" of the ancient world have gained new popularity through certain novels, films, and websites that take a militant stance against the traditional understanding of Jesus Christ and Christian history. The resultant chaos has led to what one Christian scholar calls "junk food for the mind—a pseudointellectual meal that is as easy to swallow as it is devoid of substance."[2] The spiritual famine that has lead to this craze is an opportunity to educate hungry Christians and non-Christians alike with the true bread of Christ and the early fruit of that faith. For some this will mean a change of appetite for both heart and mind. The task of feeding these hungry souls falls to pastors, deacons, elders, seminary professors, Christian high-school and college teachers, home-schoolers, and most importantly, parents.

Once we examine the modern mystery-religion fad for ourselves, we find that like many trends it merely rehashes another old and forgotten ones. It is nothing less than the corpse of long-dead paganism washed up far downstream. A quick glance through the bibliography for this book will reveal that the dates of relevant works range from the nineteenth century to the present—the point being that scholarship has dealt extensively with the questions of the historical Jesus, Paul, and the pagan mystery cults for well over a hundred years. Despite the fact that many critics present their spiel as if no one before them had ever heard it, or as a detective story in which suppressed "truths" are gradually discovered by the probing author, this is not cutting edge stuff. In fact,

---

[2]J. Ed Komoszewski, M. James Sawyer, and Daniel B. Wallace, *Reinventing Jesus: What the Da Vinci Code and Other Novel Speculations Don't Tell You* (Grand Rapids, MI: Kregel Publications, 2006), 222.

it goes back much further; the first scholarly treatment of mystery religions was written in 1614 by the Puritan scholar Isaac Casaubon.[3] Not only this, but the earliest apologists in the second century addressed the ancient mysteries as well. Contrary to the claim of some atheists, Christian scholars have always known of the old pagan myths and have studied them to death. Nothing has changed to date. The mystery religions of pagan gods such as Osiris, Cybele, Mithra, etc.,[4] give us no surprise and no cause for panic.

The Descent of Foolishness

The strongest case for the influence of mystery religions upon early Christianity was made during the late nineteenth and early twentieth centuries by liberal German scholars, who were following in the tradition of "Higher Criticism."[5] The higher critics applied the doctrine of evolution[6] to the study of history, arguing that every religion has evolved from previous ones. The idea continues today. For example, the authors of *The Jesus Mysteries* ask, "What could be more plausible than to posit the gradual evolution of spiritual ideas, with Christianity emerging from the ancient Pagan Mysteries in a seamless historical continuum?"[7] When they engage in this kind of questioning they assume the doctrine of evolution in the same way as Darwin did in relation to nature. Just as Darwin would have us see the *Descent of Man* from primitive life forms, the critics of Jesus would have us see the descent of Christianity from primitive pagan religions. In reality, no such descent can be shown. Just as unbelieving archaeologists scrape together fragments

---

[3]In his *De rebus sacris et ecclesiasticis exercitationes*. Bruce M. Metzger, "Methodology in the Study of Mystery Religions and Early Christianity," in *Historical and Literary Studies: Pagan, Jewish, and Christian*. New Testament Tools and Studies, ed. Bruce M. Metzger, 8:1–24 (Leiden: E. J. Brill, 1968), 1 note 1.

[4]See the next chapter for explanations of the various pagan gods.

[5]On Higher Criticism, see Gary North, *The Hoax of Higher Criticism* (Tyler, TX: The Institute for Christian Economics, 1989) and George Eldon Ladd, *The New Testament and Criticism* (Grand Rapids, MI: Eerdmans, 1984), 1967.

[6]The original higher critics derived their doctrine of evolution from the philosophy of G. W. F. Hegel. Darwin later applied the idea to science.

[7]Timothy Freke and Peter Gandy, *The Jesus Mysteries: Was the "Original Jesus" a Pagan God?* (New York: Three Rivers Press, 1999), 12.

of bones—sometimes found great distances apart, sometimes non-existent—in order to present the appearance of primate descendants of man, so the mystery theorists do the same with selective pieces of religious history. A few pieces exist here and there, the rest is the writer's imagination. The heritage of paganism simply rejects God's revelation, God's history, and therefore God Himself. As "the fool hath said in his heart, there is no God" (Ps. 14:1), the heritage of paganism—the alleged descent of man, as well as descent of religion—is in reality, the decent of foolishness.

In the scholarly world, this approach has often been seen for the foolishness that it is. Even the strongest attempts by the critics were immediately challenged, severely crippled by the 1930s, had all visibly failed by the 1950s, and were pretty much given up on by the 1970s. Today, only the most radical among liberal scholars and the most crazed among unscholarly occultists take the mystery religion hypothesis even remotely seriously. Now, after the competition and contradiction of liberal scholars among themselves, and with the rise of more serious study of Palestinian Judaism as it was at the time of Christ and the apostles, scholars are now seeing Paul and the early Church as they rarely have before.[8] New Testament studies have progressed to a point where nearly all of the conclusions and supposed "scientific" guesses of the nineteenth century—especially those concerning the mystery cults—amount to an embarrassment.

One simple reason for this is that no evidence of interaction between Jesus or Paul and the mysteries has ever turned up. The paucity of evidence, which could have been seen as well then as now, liberal scholars simply filled in using their imaginations. As a result, their hypotheses fail to hold intellectual water, and they provide us with little more than an example of what to avoid. New Testament scholar Scott Hafemann explains:

---

[8]That is, historically speaking. The ancient lectionaries (which are books composed of sections of scripture arranged for reading and study), not to mention St. Paul himself, show that the church made many Old Testament connections *biblically* from the earliest days of Christian liturgy and worship. The ancient church always saw the New Testament message as growing out the Old Covenant promises and prophecies. Scholars today are just catching up in their historical understanding.

The inconclusive and internally contradictory history of Pauline studies since Baur[9] has demonstrated that the temptation to re-construct some grand hypothesis based on isolated fragments and "catch words" from Paul's letters, which are then filled out by recourse to distant parallels, must be resisted. For the simple fact is that there is no direct evidence from any of Paul's opponents themselves. . . .[10]

This recognition, however, comes a bit late in one regard. So much time and energy was spent creating a body of scholarship—the object of which was to replace the supernatural truth of Jesus with naturalistic explana-tions—that honest scholars today must hack through the dense under-brush of modern biblical studies in order to get down to the presupposi-tions of past failures. This means lots of scholarly machete work.

The Jungle of Mystery-Cult Scholarship

The scholarly tangle that we have to clear away grew out of the world-views of evolution and naturalism.[11] From these ultimate presupposi-tions, an entire jungle of scholarship twisted and overshadowed every-thing that came before. In hindsight, the arguments and books produced at the time betray an ideological bent so obvious that reading them seri-ously takes a good bit of emotional discipline. Well-fixed philosophical starting points govern their conclusions and give much of their scholar-ship a clear circularity.[12]

For example, trying to stack the deck in favor of the mystery-cult theory, they emphasize and rely upon the claim that the Gospels did not

---

[9]Ferdinand Christian Baur of Tübingen University was one of the foremost propo-nents of higher criticism who applied the doctrine of evolution to Christian history. He made as great an impact upon Pauline Studies and New Testament Studies in general as anyone in his era.

[10]S. J. Hafemann, "Paul and His Interpreters" in *Dictionary of Paul and His Letters: A Compendium of Contemporary Biblical Scholarship*, eds. Gerald F. Hawthorne, Ralph P. Martin, and Daniel G. Reid (Downers Grove, IL: InterVarsity Press, 1993), 671.

[11]Hegel's evolutionary philosophy, which included both spiritual and historical evo-lution, had tremendous impact on the early German scholars, and still does upon a few today; but most of their higher critical work was carried out upon strictly naturalistic assumptions.

[12]See the appendix, "Presuppositions and New Testament Studies."

appear until at least forty years after the events took place. They believe that this gap of time allows for stories about the historical Jesus to be told and retold until blown up into tall tales and myths about a super-natural guy who walked on water, healed people, and raised the dead. Never mind that not a single fiber of manuscript evidence has been dis-covered to support their theory. Arguments by atheists that promote the claim usually echo the serpent, "Could it be? Can't you imagine it?" The supposition conveniently allows disbelievers to reject the earliest written records of the life of Christ as mythology.[13]

But a survey of recent New Testament scholarship shows that later dates for the Gospels belong to a minority position. There is some evidence that places the Gospel of Mark as early as A.D. 40, not long after the resur-rection of Christ. Mid-50s to early 60s is almost certain.[14] Likewise, Acts was certainly written before A.D. 62, and Luke's Gospel, being the "former treatise" which he mentions in Acts 1:1, must have come before that date.[15] Arguments for later dates, especially for Luke, must deal with the fact that Acts does not mention the fall of Jerusalem (A.D. 70), the persecution of Christians under Nero (A.D. 64), or the martyrdoms of Paul (A.D. 64–65) or James the brother of Jesus (A.D. 62), although he does mention the martyr-dom of James the son of Zebedee (A.D. 44). All of these important events should certainly have found their way into an official history of the apos-tolic church. Their absence is telling. Those who ignore the weight of these considerations—among the thousands of facts compiled since the original higher critics began their attack—in order to believe that the Gospels came much later, are obviously pursuing some ideological agenda. Indeed, it is well known—if it is not often stated—that late dates are generally only pro-moted by axe-grinding radicals whose intellectual precommitments (and endowed chairs at liberal universities) drive their work.

---

[13]For some who argue for Jesus as just one more mystery-religion figure, this sup-position becomes part of their evidence!

[14]D. A. Carson, Douglas J. Moo, and Leon Morris, *An Introduction to the New Testament* (Grand Rapids, MI: Zondervan, 1992), 96–99. See also Donald Guthrie, *New Testament Introduction* (Downers Grove, IL: InterVarsity Press, 1973), 72–76.

[15]Carson, Moo, and Morris, *An Introduction to the New Testament*, 116–117 and Guthrie, *New Testament Introduction*, 340–348.

Once they have brushed the Gospel records aside, they claim that a great historical gulf exists between the Jesus who lived in history and the one who came to be immortalized in the Gospels. I am reminded of a verse: "He that diggeth a pit shall fall into it" (Eccl. 10:8). The only official records that existed, they assume, between roughly A.D. 30 and 75–90, came from the Apostle Paul. From this basis, they argue that Paul, not Jesus, was the founder of Christianity as we know it. And the Paul they want us to see is quite a different character as well. They emphasize the fact that Paul originally came from Tarsus (funny: they have no problem with the historicity of this claim of the Bible), which was a known center of Greek philosophy and mystery religions. Growing up as a young radical, Paul must have assimilated lots of ideas from the abundant mystery religions—ideas he later transformed into the Christian teachings we know today.

From here the story gets really strained: Paul, some claim, did not believe that Jesus was ever human. It is argued that he never mentions the humanity of Jesus; he never mentions Mary, Joseph, Bethlehem, Herod, Pilate, Jesus' earthly ministry or miracles; and he never actually quotes Jesus. Since he mentions none of these things, then Paul's Jesus was not an historical but a mythological figure. The only events of Jesus' life that Paul knows are the crucifixion, resurrection, and ascension. These he constantly harps on, but only as heavenly, mythological events which he derived from the ancient mysteries. The argument runs that because he only speaks of these heavenly events, and not the historical, therefore he certainly did not know about or believe in the historical. If I only mentioned the general word "breakfast" in my writings, and nothing else about it, then it would prove to some that I knew nothing about ham and eggs.

I will deal with the gratuitous biblical oversights involved with this argument in later chapters; here I just intend to introduce the problem as modern writers have presented it. From their perspective, Paul created Christianity from the mystery cult myths with the divinized character of Jesus as the hero. This was certainly the view of the leading liberal scholar of the twentieth century, Rudolf Bultmann, who thought that

Paul could "easily interpret the death and Resurrection of Jesus in terms of the mysteries and their sacramentalism," and as a "Gnostic conception."[16] Then writers after Paul created the Gospels as mere works of literature by rationalizing the life of Jesus and infusing it with the folklore and mythology of Paul's precedent. The critics point to "parallels" between practices in the mystery religions and key elements of the Christian faith. The latter, it is uncritically assumed (yet confidently asserted), stole from the mysteries which came before.

Today, in the world of scholarship, this belief is almost dead. It survives only in a few liberal American universities where fundamentalist-bashing still earns fellowships and chairs. But it has seen a recent revival in popular works of fiction, movies, and atheist documentaries—all works by modern-day gnostics who want to rewrite the history of the church for their purposes. Since their theory has failed the tests of scholarly peer-review, scrutiny, and debate, it has retreated to the world of popular media. Like many bad theological ideas, its only safe haven is in the world of fiction and imagination.

Yet there is a certain danger to letting such ideas, ridiculous as they may be, circulate and propagate unchallenged. As much as I would prefer to watch them fizzle out unaided, they have a tendency to produce an audience through propaganda or through some unforseen agent. For example, the immediate precursor to the type of scholarship I have described was the work of Ferdinand Baur and his followers at Tübingen University in the early nineteenth century. They followed a hard-line method of anti-supernaturalism, denying every possibility of miracle or divine intervention in history. Their historical-critical product soon gained wide recognition for devastating the faith of many people. With this visible result the work was readily adopted as the oppressive tool of an atheistic government. Communist revolutionary Maxim Gorky wrote to Joseph Stalin,

> It is essential to put the propaganda of atheism on solid ground. . . .
> Every quotation of a believer is easily countered with dozens of

---

[16]Rudolf Bultmann, *Primitive Christianity: In Its Contemporary Setting*, trans. R. H. Fuller (Cleveland, OH: The World Publishing Company, 1965), 197.

theological quotations which contradict it. We cannot do without an edition of the Bible with critical commentaries of the Tübingen school and books on criticism of the biblical texts, which could bring a very useful confusion into the minds of believers.[17]

This same danger continues today. It signals a battle over souls, and over the proper ordering of both society and eternity. In this battle, the enemies of God love "a very useful confusion," propaganda, and stilted scholarship. Christians must counter the lies and knock the stilts down to earth.

Why Now?

Why have mystery religions become a public issue at this point in time? The answer presents an ominous parallel to the early Church era, when the apologists had to defend the Scriptures against pagan attacks. Charles Norris Cochrane gives the classic account of the decline of the Roman Empire from the earliest of the Caesars who allowed himself to be worshipped as a political god.[18] From this point the seeds of "barbarism and superstition," which the Empire claimed to eliminate, "were enshrined at the very heart of the system itself in the worship of the divinized sovereign."[19] The State grew progressively more powerful in its lust to play a Messianic role in the earth. The military grew, civil law expanded, private law fell to the State, and taxation skyrocketed. Religion, philosophy, and culture became subservient as well. The arid heritage of Graeco-Roman philosophy and religion presented the people with only *fate* or *chance* as ultimate principles. Religion was, therefore, depersonalized, and the people forced beneath the press of a merciless and purposeless world. As with all Messianic states, "It was, in a word, the tragedy of men who, being required to play the part of gods, descended to that of beasts."[20] That such a state of affairs would inevitably lead to

---

[17]Quoted in Alister E. McGrath, *The Future of Christianity* (Oxford: Blackwell Publishers, 2002), 134.

[18]Charles Norris Cochrane, *Christianity and Classical Civilization: A Study of Thought and Action from Augustus to Augustine* (Oxford: Clarendon Press, 1940), 115ff.

[19]Cochrane, *Christianity and Classical Civilization*, 160.

[20]Cochrane, *Christianity and Classical Civilization*, 129.

decline was foreshadowed when one of the earliest of the Caesars, Tiberius, said, "After me: the deluge."[21]

Into this environment entered, especially by military travels, an influx of Eastern mystery religions. These secretive cults presented emotional rituals and myths that involved personal gods. They met the needs of an overly-rationalized populace who longed to escape the coldness of the State religions. The cults emphasized cyclical history, drawing from the cycles of nature, to assure members that the decline of society that they saw around them simply belonged to the grand scheme of the natural evolution and fall of civilizations. These remained secluded and underground for the most part—in some cases they were even persecuted—until the late second to early third centuries. At that point, when the roots of the classical republic had all but eroded away, and, "The voice of Greek and Latin literature . . . was almost stilled," then, "Orientalism in its grosser forms broke in wave after wave upon the capital."[22] This "orientalism" was nothing less than the extravagant—and often bloody—ritualism of the mystery religions.

The appearance of the mystery religions in great numbers, therefore, corresponded to the final stages of the decaying Messianic State. At a time of impersonal beliefs and failed political saviors, the mystery religions provided the personalism, sense of participation and purpose in the cosmos, and emotional stimulation that so many people wanted. It should not surprise us then to see the same recurrence in our day. On the heels of Darwinism, which denies the Hand of the personal Creator and Sustainer in the universe, we have a critical era of religious, philosophical, and political apostasy. Many in main-line denominations have abandoned the Scriptures and endorsed every pagan idea imaginable, homosexuality being only one of the most talked about. "Philosophy" as well, that two-headed snake, has once again hung itself at a fork in the road: one side devolves every question into its most minute "analytical" fragments of grammar and syntax, the other ignores technicality almost completely in favor of passion, emotion, images, symbols, and intuition.

---

[21]Cochrane, *Christianity and Classical Civilization*, 129. I have added the semicolon.
[22]Cochrane, *Christianity and Classical Civilization*, 154.

Meanwhile, the State continues to assume more power as it tries to address every perceived crisis in every area of life. Militaristic police and bureaucrats multiply: "For the transgression of a land many are the princes thereof" (Prov. 28:2). Our time is little different from the failed Roman Empire of the early Christian era,[23] and the influx of religions offering escapism, secret knowledge, and transcendence above history draws as big an audience now as it did then.

Conclusion

It is time that a concise apologetic be written which encompasses the worldview issues established in the nineteenth century, while accounting for the popular appeal of New-Age mystery-religion thought (for the two work hand-in-hand). We must revive the tradition of biblical learning and godly passion of the early Church apologists, and yet account for the attacks of today (which are actually less substantial than their second-century cousins). Our Lord Jesus Christ, who was "manifested in the flesh," and the apostolic tradition which He founded, provide us with the fullest and truest possible understanding of a personal, historical, sovereign, gracious, and loving God. No mythical counterfeits can come close.

For those today, including the menagerie of liberal scholars, outspoken atheists, and radical critics, who insist on dragging up the long-dead theory that Christianity borrowed its beliefs and practices from ancient mystery cults, I offer the critique that follows. The mystery-cult theory rests upon three great faults: (1) a distorted representation of what the mystery cults believed and practiced; (2) a poor understanding of what the Bible itself says; and (3) highly selective, fanciful and perhaps dishonest methods of reconstructing the two together. In short, the mys-

---

[23]Martin Van Creveld sees the modern nation-state as an institution in decline. He argues that it is a failed form of government that will soon be replaced by another that is more international and yet more decentralized. This herald of the doom of the modern institution parallels the situation of ancient Rome, as the State sees itself as a Messiah and yet cannot control the inner contradiction of playing god while acting as a beast. (Martin Van Creveld, *The Rise and Decline of the State* [Cambridge: Cambridge University Press, 1999]).

tery cult theory presents *bad history, bad theology,* and *bad judgment.* The following chapters will expand these three critiques.

One word of warning: some of the ancient mysteries included vulgar and violent practices, and I include reports of some of these in what follows. Parents should give some consideration as to whether their children should have unguarded access to the next few chapters.

Myths about Myths

The ancient Pagan Mysteries did not die. They transformed into something new—into Christianity.[1]

Early in 1926 the hardest boiled of all the atheists I ever knew sat in my room on the other side of the fire and remarked that the evidence for the historicity of the Gospels was really surprisingly good. "Rum thing," he went on. "All that stuff of Fraser's about the Dying God. Rum thing. It almost looks as if it had really happened once."[2]

Every bit of historical investigation, whether it be in the directly biblical field, archaeology, or in general history is bound to confirm the truth of the claims of the Christian position. . . . [E]very fact is and must be such as proves the truth of the Christian theistic position.[3]

To BEGIN WITH, the mystery religion theory—promulgated by the old "history-of-religions school" and carried on by a handful of pros-

---

[1]Timothy Freke and Peter Gandy, *The Jesus Mysteries: Was the "Original Jesus" a Pagan God?* (New York: Three Rivers Press, 1999), 255.

[2]C. S. Lewis, *Surprised by Joy* (New York: Harcourt, Brace & World, 1955), 223–224. Quoted in John Warwick Montgomery, *Where is History Going?: Essays in Support of the Historical Truth of the Christian Revelation* (Minneapolis, MN: Bethany Fellowship, [1969] 1972), 54.

[3]Cornelius Van Til, quoted in Greg L. Bahnsen, *Van Til's Apologetic: Readings and Analysis* (Phillipsburg, NJ: Presbyterian and Reformed, 1998), 639.

elytizing atheists—can perpetuate itself only with a lot of historical ingenuity. And a lot of it they have. They often claim that several "dying and rising gods" preceded Christ, and that the mystery cults had
a "sacramental meal" and "baptism," all of which Christianity allegedly
stole. If this were not enough, there are mentions of empty tombs, blood
sacrifice, being "born again," and more. Some go so far as to class Christianity as just one more among all the ancient mysteries;[4] and one of
the most widely published historians of the twentieth century, whose
volumes have circulated in the millions, concurred: "Christianity was
the last great creation of the ancient pagan world."[5]

But what exactly does history reveal? Do we find the alleged parallels
and precursors to the Christian faith? Or have some imaginative writers
overstated their case? The following section will show that the mystery-cult
theory constitutes *bad history* because the myths themselves do not say
what the critics claim they say, and the supposed similarities are no greater
than the same old forms of paganism recorded in the Old Testament.

Dramatis Personae
Introducing the Mystery Religions[6]

No one has any idea exactly how many mystery religions there were,
how much influence they truly had, or how much individual cults
changed over time, let alone much of what actually went on in their
meetings. This is less true of the earlier cults which had public rituals
and state support. Later cults grew more private, emphasized the "mystery" in mystery religion, and, like some fraternal organizations today,
only passed on their knowledge to initiates who bound themselves by

[4]Joscelyn Godwin, *Mystery Religions in the Ancient World* (San Francisco, CA:
Harper and Row, 1981), 90–97.

[5]Will Durant, *Caesar and Christ: A History of Roman Civilization and of Christianity from their Beginnings to A.D. 325* (New York: Simon and Schuster, 1944), 595.

[6]For other introductions see Everett Ferguson, *Background of Early Christianity*, 3rd
ed. (Grand Rapids, MI: Eerdmans, 2003), 251–300; Jane Ellen Harrison, *Prolegomena
to the Study of Greek Religion* (Princeton, NJ: Princeton University Press, [1903] 1991),
363–571; Marvin W. Meyer, ed., *The Ancient Mysterie: A Sourcebook—Sacred Texts of
the Mystery Religions of the Ancient Mediterranean World* (San Francisco: Harper &
Row, 1987); Ronald H. Nash *Christianity and the Hellenistic World* (Grand Rapids, MI:
Zondervan/Probe, 1984), 115–199.

oath. Due to the secrecy, all we know about them is what can be gained from archaeology: caves, inscriptions in stone, sculptures, mosaics, etc. The amount of evidence has greatly increased over the last 150 years since the big wave of excitement about early church history began. But the flood of knowledge has tended to disprove the outrageous claim of Christian-borrowing by sharpening the image of what the mystery religions were actually like. After just a bit of knowledge gathering, the alleged parallels of "dying and rising Gods," "sacramental meals," and "baptism"[7] all fall away, and a powerful contrast arises between Christianity and an incoherent collage of pagan myths.

Local and Early Greek Cults

Most of the Greek mysteries were tied to the cycle of nature and related to the unpredictable aspects of human life such as reproduction, safety, and food production. Gods, goddesses, and myths were created to explain the continual dying and rebirth of vegetation during the year. These served as direct powers over planting and harvest, as well as analogies to human fertility and prosperity. The earliest of the mysteries display these basic characteristics and were generally limited to particular regions. One such mystery, belonging to a local family of Eleusis, eventually opened to the public and quickly became a popular movement. From this popularization mystery religions soon took on a more universal character.

The Eleusian cult revolved around the familiar myth of Demeter, goddess of grain and agricultural fertility. She fell into the misfortune of having her daughter Kore (or Persephone) kidnapped by Hades, the god of the underworld. After a long and vain search by Demeter, Zeus intervened and Hades agreed to share: Kore could spend eight months a year with Demeter, and four months underground with him. Thus it follows that plants grow for eight months while Kore resides with Demeter

---

[7]Rudolf Bultmann, *Primitive Christianity: In Its Contemporary Setting*, trans. R. H. Fuller (Cleveland, OH: The World Publishing Company, 1965), 157–159. Bultmann's use of Christian language to describe the pagan religions is deceptive, though it is standard fare among sympathizers.

and die when she returns to Hades. The cult had two sides: one open
to the public with public rituals, another private, expensive, secret and
with many degrees of brotherhood. Nothing is known of the content of
the private rituals.[8]

Another widespread and early cult was that of Dionysus (called Bac-
chus by the Romans). He was the offspring of Zeus and a human mother
who died at her own wish in an encounter with her Olympian lover.
Dionysus descended and rescued his mother from the underworld; he
was associated with vegetation and also became an educator of mankind, giving them above all things the gift of wine. This gift was made
ready use of in his worship as groups of mainly women would fast and
then gorge themselves into drunken orgies. In the height of their mania,
they would kill a wild animal, eat its raw flesh, and drink its blood. This
consumption they believed would infuse them with the nature of their
god.[9] With a belly-full of wine and raw meat, they might have doubted
their religion the next morning.

The Dionysian cult received protection from the State and was wildly
popular with the public through State-supported art. "Travelling guilds
of actors that presented plays throughout the empire were organized
as a religious association dedicated to Dionysus. They were considered
'sacred' and granted immunity and special protection by the rulers."[10] A
real force behind the myth seems to have been a primitive, if corrupt,
spiritual hunger among the people coupled with the popular media
of the day. Dionysus prospered "partly through people's desire for the
more personal experience of the Mysteries . . . partly through the popularity of the theater and the prevalence of guilds and actors dedicated
to him."[11] What? A welfare state and a pagan entertainment industry

---

[8]Bultmann, *Primitive Christianity*, 256–258.

[9]Bultmann, *Primitive Christianity*, 261; Nash, *Christianity and the Hellenistic
World*, 134–135.

[10]Bultmann, *Primitive Christianity*, 263.

[11]John Ferguson, *The Heritage of Hellenism: The Greek World from 323 to 31 BC*. History of European Civilization Library, ed. Geoffrey Barraclough (Harcourt Brace Jovanovich, 1973), 133.

producing a drunken, sex-crazed, bloodthirsty, irrational culture? Some things never change.

Dionysian worship later morphed into a very similar myth featuring Orpheus. This cult appears to have promoted a myth which was itself created by the practitioners of the Dionysian myth. Orpheus was supposed to have been a Dionysian priest who was killed and eaten in the same way as the sacrifice he made—ripped apart and eaten by female worshipers.[12] This violent feast was central to both the cult of Dionysius and Orpheus, and drew the disgust and horror of the early Church fathers.[13] On certain occasions the Dionysian-Orphic ladies would replace the bull with a human sacrifice, and there is evidence for even the sacrifice of children.[14]

Isis and Osiris

The cult of Osiris and Isis originated in ancient Egypt and was the earliest and most popular among foreign mysteries in the Greek world. According to the myth,[15] Osiris' brother Set tricked and murdered him and sank his casket into the Nile. Isis, who was both sister and wife to Osiris, searched for and recovered the body. Set again nabbed the corpse and this time hacked it into pieces, which he scattered throughout the land. Isis searched again to retrieve the pieces and was successful with the exception of his unmentionable part. In its void, Isis placed a golden image which later played a central role in the cult's worship. Despite being reclaimed in body by his wife/sister, Osiris continued in the underworld and in one version of the story, gained power over it. From his position he was able aid his son Horus against the murderer Set.

When introduced to the Greek world, the cult figure mixed extensively with other personas among the native gods. In various cases, the

---

[12]Harrison, *Prolegomena to the Study of Greek Religion*, 454–455, 460–461.

[13]Harrison, *Prolegomena to the Study of Greek Religion*, 483–485. Clement of Alexandria, *Exhortation to the Heathen* 2, recounts the incest, mutilation, and infanticide featured in the myth; Tatian, *Address of Tatian to the Greeks*, 29, condemns the "effeminate" cultists whose gods are "delighting in human gore and the blood of slaughtered men."

[14]Harrison, *Prolegomena to the Study of Greek Religion*, 487–491.

[15]See Ferguson, *Background of Early Christianity*, 270, for the following account.

Greeks identified Isis with Demeter or Aphrodite, and Osiris with Apis. The latter mixture resulted in an entirely new deity, Serapis. The vast amount of syncretism creates as much doubt as to the actual names, places, origins, and versions of the myth. In fact, the best sources seem to be late and post-Christian. In all cases, though, the cult had elaborate and ornate ceremonies which captured much attention, but like its Greek counterparts, it also had two faces, private and public. It provided displays and processions for the masses but reserved its secrets for those who could endure its tedious initiations. The public side, however, held great importance in that the cult was closely linked to the expansion of the State during the second-century B.C. It was made a official civic cult in 180 B.C. and served as a central myth for the spread of the Ptolemaic empire.[16] This may have been its place as early as the ancient Pharaohs.

Astarte and Adonis

While the influential cult of Isis and Osiris came from Egypt, dozens of local deities arose in various parts of the Graeco-Roman world. Among these, the fertility goddess Astarte gained wide recognition in ancient Phoenicia but was Hellenized and adopted into Greek mythology by the time of Christ. As a result, little is known of the original mystery. The later Greek version identifies Astarte with Aphrodite and finds her in love with the beautiful young male deity Adonis. The lad, however, is killed in a hunting accident (gored by a boar), and he fades to the underworld. There he falls under the eye of Persephone who becomes a rival lover to Aphrodite. In an unusual moment of cooperation between Greek deities (usually known for their carousing, conniving, and killing), the girls agree to share. The time split between the upperworld and the underworld by Adonis—another god of vegetation—agrees with the cycle of nature, just as the myth of Persephone herself.

The myth was not exclusive to the Phoenician tradition, but had close counterparts in other places. Syrians called the goddess Atargatis,

---

[16]Ferguson, *Background of Early Christianity*, 266.

but she played a similar role there as goddess over nature and fertility. The Syrian cult was widely advertised[17] by her traveling priests called "galli," who had devoted themselves to her by castration. The gruesome act is summarized by Everett Ferguson:

> While the pipes were wailing and the men were dancing, frenzy seized many of them. The man who was seized stripped off his clothes, grabbed a sword, and castrated himself. He ran through the city and threw what was cut off into any house he chose and took from the house women's apparel. Thereafter he belonged to the goddess and wore woman's clothes.[18]

While the men abused themselves, young women followers would serve the goddess through prostitution in her temple. Whether to Astarte, Atargatis, or Aphrodite, ritual prostitution continued into the New Testament era, and almost certainly underlies the harlotry and gender strife St. Paul had to deal with in Corinth (see 1 Cor. 6:18–20; chap. 11).

Cybele and Attis

The cults just mentioned in which a mother-wife goddess mourns her lover's departure find a very influential repetition in the mystery of Cybele and Attis. As one of the earliest eastern cults and one of the most popular, it endures with great variation.[19] Cybele—"The Great Mother," or "The Mother of the Mountain"—fell in love with the youthful mortal Attis. Some versions say that when Attis was pledged to marriage, a rival love interest ended his courtship by causing him to castrate himself. Another claims that Cybele made Attis pledge chastity to her. When he later denied his vow in lust for a nymph, Cybele drove Attis mad as punishment, and Attis in a rage castrated himself. The castration is usually said to be fatal, but other versions say Attis actually died in a hunting accident, either from a friend or an animal.

---

[17]Ferguson, *Background of Early Christianity*, 280.
[18]Ferguson, *Background of Early Christianity*, 281.
[19]Ferguson, *Background of Early Christianity*, 281ff, for here and following; also Nash, *Christianity and the Hellenistic World*, 138ff.

In any case, the outstanding features of the cult were its troop of eunuch priests, just as with Atargatis, along with another bloody ritual called the *taurobolium*. I have already presented the first of these two. The latter comes to us through late second-century sources,[20] but liberal scholars have placed great importance upon the ritual as a precursor to Christian baptism. I disagree, but since liberal scholars are so well credentialed, I defer to the reader's judgment:

> The person receiving the rite entered a deep underground pit that was covered with a wooden lattice work. A garlanded bull was brought to the planks covering the pit and killed with a spear. The blood ran through the openings and showered the initiate below, who held up his face so that the blood covered it and so that he could drink some. He was then exhibited to the worshipers, who praised him. The rite apparently meant the transfer of the energy of the bull to the person undergoing it or to the one for whom he performed it.[21]

There you have it: Christian baptism plain and clear. Right? You can see it, can you not? If the logic of liberal scholarship continually fails, its ingenuity never does. Creativity has kept it going for 150 years now. The more I study the more I see that the dominant myths of our day have not come from ancient mysteries but from creative writers in certain religious studies departments.

Mithraism

Mithraism deserves special treatment for two important reasons. Some scholars give it more attention than other cults as a possible influence on the Christian sacraments. Also, it has undergone a recent academic revolution which has overturned decades of misguided scholarship and therefore it provides us with an insight into the nature of modern New Testament studies.[22]

---

[20]Ferguson, *Background of Early Christianity*, 285
[21]Ferguson, *Background of Early Christianity*, 285.
[22]See the Appendix on Mithraism and Cumont.

Differing theories of Mithraism connect it to either ancient Persia or Greece itself. By far the most influential have been the opinions of Franz Cumont, which held sway in the academic world from 1896 until recent times. His theory stood unchallenged and his two-volume work on the issue exerted considerable influence on succeeding generations of scholars. Cumont found the seeds of Mithraic faith in ancient Iran and India. There, Mithra drew worship as an associate of Varuna, the lord of light and goodness. Varuna, or Ahura-Mazda, engaged his forces in a perpetual cosmic war against the opposing forces of darkness lead by Ahriman. Myths featuring a bull factor only in a very few obscure Indian versions, where both the bull's blood and semen appear to have significance for the fertility of plant life in the earth. Details of this aspect are scant and vague.[23]

Cumont's theories have come under intense scrutiny in recent times due to many outstanding elements of Greco-Roman Mithraism, which find no counterpart in the Persian myths. Central among these is a bull-slaying scene (called the "tauroctony"), which pervades Mithraic art.[24] Following key critiques of other scholars, David Ulansey has presented a thorough alternative which finds the origins of Mithraism in Greco-Roman astral religions. Considering the keen interest in astrology by the Stoic philosophers[25] of the era and contemporary advances in astronomy, an astrology-based religion would have found a sizeable audience. More importantly, several figures recur in the tauroctony—a bull, a scorpion, a snake, a raven, a dog and a lion—which each represent constellations, and in much of the art a zodiac accompanies the scene. Directly above the bull, Taurus, in the "star map" we find the constellation Perseus, wielding a dagger and traditionally depicted as wearing a Phrygian cap.[26] The astrologers believed Perseus' slaying of the bull to have "cosmic significance, indicating the end of the Age of Taurus, when

---

[23]David Ulansey, *The Origins of the Mithraic Mysteries: Cosmology and Salvation in the Ancient World* (New York and Oxford: Oxford University Press, 1989), 13–18.

[24]Ulansey, *The Origins of the Mithraic Mysteries*, 8.

[25]Ulansey, *The Origins of the Mithraic Mysteries*, 67–76.

[26]Ulansey, *The Origins of the Mithraic Mysteries*, 25–7.

the spring equinox occurred in the constellation of the Bull, and beginning a new age when the spring equinox entered Aries."[27]

Whichever theory of origins is more true, the cult permeated the
Roman Empire in the second century. Dozens of Mithraic sanctuaries
have been discovered from Turkey and the Middle East all the way to
the western shores of Spain, and from Scotland to North Africa.[28] The
greatest concentration of these Mithraea occur in places of high military occupancy, for example, the Danube River, the eastern frontiers,
sea ports, and the vicinity of Rome itself.[29] Even the Emperor Commo-
dius, at the end of the second century, was an initiate, and Julian the
Apostate strongly promoted the cult.[30] The concentration of Mithraic
activity, however, occurred near military hot-spots and Imperial icons,
and did not affect the Middle East or Greek-speaking world in general.
Due to this concentration of artifacts and to its second to third century
rise, most scholars now admit that the idea that Mithraism influenced
Christian doctrine appears largely impossible.[31]

Mithra had no difficulty commanding the allegiance of soldiers.
Militaristic aspects of the cult included a strictly regimented lifestyle,
taking of oaths, and the exclusion of women. "The Mithraic cult was a
form of military service; life on earth was a campaign led by the victori-
ous god."[32] The graduated levels of initiation found in the mystery no
doubt appealed to minds bent on rank and order. Furthermore, upon
Ulansey's construction of Mithraic origins, we could easily understand
the idea of the dawn of a New Age to fuel the expanding pride of Roman
Imperialism. Cult brainwashing and empire always work well together.

---

[27]Ferguson, *Background of Early Christianity*, 290.

[28]Ulansey supplies a map showing the great number and vast distribution of the
sanctuaries, 5.

[29]M. J. Vermaseren, *Mithras, the Secret God* (London: Chatto & Windus, 1963), 30.

[30]Ferguson, *Background of Early Christianity*, 290.

[31]D. E. Aune, "Expansion and Recruitment among Hellenistic Religions: The Case of
Mithraism" in *Recruitment, Conquest, and Conflict: Strategies in Judaism, Early Chris-
tianity, and the Greco-Roman World*, eds. Borgen, Robbins & Gowler (Atlanta, GA:
Scholars Press, 1998), 42–3, 52; Ferguson, E., 291; Nash, *Christianity and the Hellenistic
World*, 136–8.

[32]Vermaseren, *Mithras, the Secret God*, 30.

Many of the details of Mithraic practices[33] remain hidden from us for the same reasons that its origins do, with the added obstacle of the cult's secrecy. The traditions in Mithraism, as in any secret society, were no doubt transmitted orally, under oath of secrecy[34] and never written down. We do have some references from Christian apologists such as Justin Martyr, Origen, and Jerome, but we have no guarantee of the accuracy of their sources or accounts. The cult was secret and therefore properly earned the title of a "mystery" religion. Those who so desired had to submit to initiation to gain Mithraic knowledge. The inductions took place in designated caves or cave-like structures and, judging from both inscriptions and descriptions, involved bizarre and humiliating rituals that included nudity, disorientation and a noose placed around the initiate's neck.[35]

Whatever knowledge initiates received, we do know that it included seven levels or degrees and apparently revolved around the tauroctony. The bull-slaying scene dons every known Mithraic cave. Ulansey's "star map" theory explains the Mithraic cave as an "image of the cosmos." The initiates would have seen themselves as players in the cosmic drama of Perseus ushering in the age of Aries. This larger drama would easily find a smaller counterpart in a personal spiritual journey. "The central focus of the cult was the preparation for astral salvation which would be realized upon death when the soul would ascend through the seven planetary spheres to the place of its origin."[36]

A "Pan-mystery-religion"

With all of the similarities between the various mystery religions, it is not unreasonable to inquire if they have some common background in history. Whether the commonalities come from an earlier historical source that branched out through different cultures and arose in several

---

[33]This section relies on Aune, "Expansion and Recruitment among Hellenistic Religions," 44–8.

[34]Vermaseren, *Mithras, the Secret God*, 131.

[35]Aune, "Expansion and Recruitment among Hellenistic Religions," 48; M. J. Vermaseren, *Mithras, the Secret God*, 131–7.

[36]Aune, "Expansion and Recruitment among Hellenistic Religions," 46.

myths during the Graeco-Roman era, or whether they have some ready source deep in the bosom of fallen human nature, we cannot settle at this time. The truth is probably a combination of both.

Many details, however, of each myth reappear within different mysteries although they were separated by time and space. The emasculation that went on for Cybele and Atargatis would make sense also as a part of the Osiris cult in which the fallen god himself had been so mutilated. His castrated worshipers would then be imitating their god, and thus identifying with him as he lived on in the underworld. But we find such ritual castrations only in the Eastern cults and not in the Egyptian. What is mythology in Egypt appears as literal ceremony in Syria and Phoenicia. This leads one to speculate that the two waves of mysteries —Egyptian and Eastern—must have had some intermingling over time. But historical and archaeological data to date show that the eunuch tradition shared no such historical intercourse. Perhaps it was all a sad joke on posterity played by the Egyptians who seem to have gotten the better end of the deal.

For now, in order to see a common myth which may underlay the various lies, we either have to project the elements of the stories back onto those of a much earlier time in history, or look to the fabrications that have arisen in the twentieth century. The early Christian apologists caught onto the correct biblical explanation, which I explain below. *Historically*, however, we have no evidence from the time of the early church of the existence of, or an attempt to create, one mystery religion which summarized them all.[37]

Nevertheless, the apparent unity among the myths—female goddesses falling in love with young males who get slain, hunting accidents, love competitions, murders, along with gruesome bloody ceremonies and ornate parades—has led a few enterprising new-agers as well as a few scholars of our time to rally in support of a universal mythol-

---

[37]Even the liberal Helmut Koester says that there was no "homogenous phenomenon." In fact, many have argued that the mysteries cannot properly even be called religions. See Helmut Koester, *History, Culture, and Religion of the Hellenistic Age*, Introduction to the New Testament (Philadelphia: Fortress Press, 1982), 1:196–203.

ogy. The most famous of these was Joseph Campbell, a follower of the philosophy and psychology of Carl Jung and prolific writer of comparative mythology. Campbell is most famous for his book *The Hero with a Thousand Faces*, in which he argues that the plethora of religions throughout history, including Christianity, are all masks that play parts in a larger mythology derived purely from the life of humanity. For him the religions have nothing to do with God and everything to do with the story of human living. Of God he said, "That old man up there has been blown away."[38]

Campbell arranged his pan-mythology around what he called "the adventure of the hero." This "adventure"—itself a myth compiled by Campbell—follows a consistent pattern involving three phases in the life of the hero figure: separation, initiation, and return.[39] Campbell then begins to list several hero figures from history who fit the pattern: Prometheus, Jason (of Argonaut fame), Aeneas, Buddah. Of course, the three phases are so broad that they can encompass the life of any figure proposed for them. I got up this morning, left my apartment, went to work, and then came home. *That* fits the pattern. But you can get international awards and recognition if you apply this to religious studies. Campbell, perhaps sensing this vagary, added bullet-points within each section so that each phase contained multiple elements. He unfolded the whole structure of his arch-myth in seventeen subsections, each representing a stage in the hero's adventure.[40]

But the added definition did not enhance his prowess. Like so many myth-chasers today, Campbell spied so many parallels between religious traditions that he began to see them where they did not exist. For example, he describes a central myth of Buddhism in which Gautama (later Buddah) sits beneath the "the great Tree of Enlightenment, the Bo Tree" and enters a great conflagration with the god of love and death. The enemy hurls every imaginable cosmological terror at him including

---

[38]Quoted in K. C. Cole, "Master of the Myth: Joseph Campbell Followed His Bliss and Became a Legend After His Own Time," *Newsweek* (November 14, 1988), 61.

[39]Joseph Campbell, *The Hero With a Thousand Faces*, Bollingen Series XVII (Princeton, NJ: Princeton University Press, 1973), 30.

[40]Campbell, *The Hero With a Thousand Faces*, 36–37.

"thunder and flame" and "his razor-sharp discus," but the soon-to-be-Buddah dispels them all with the aid of the goddess Earth. From this victory he was led into "perfect enlightenment." The myth is entertaining enough to be related, but Campbell, with some wild leap of logic and effort of imagination, alleges a parallel to the Crucifixion of Christ. In his words the Buddah myth is

> the most important single moment in Oriental history, a counterpart to the Crucifixion of the West. The Buddah beneath the Tree of Enlightenment (the Bo Tree) and Christ on Holy Rood (the Tree of Redemption) are analogous figures.[41]

Campbell's analysis could use some help. A tree is a commonality, yes, but for Christ it was a man-made cross, not a mythical tree. Whereas the Buddah repelled the evil god and stood invincible before the tree, Christ accepted the full extent of punishment and torment of sin and died upon His tree, then conquered death itself through resurrection by His Father. Buddah refused to die; Christ died willingly, knowing He could triumph over even death. The Buddah myth is filled with every possible mythical element, and is told in such a way as to ensure its mythological status. The crucifixion of Christ is an historical event carried out by historical figures in the environment of the Roman Empire and by known Roman methods. In other words, the two stories have nothing in common except, in the most general terms, a hero, some form of wood and the hero's eventual triumph. But then again, this also describes every baseball game.[42]

Many other scholars attempt similar point systems for the alleged hero myth, but none with the success of Campbell. Interestingly, every other attempt differs with the next, which betrays the fictional aspect in them all. Nevertheless, in recent times some have laid great stress upon the number of points that any given heroic figure finds in common with the archetypal pattern. A higher score supposedly demonstrates that your religion partakes more heavily of the pan-mystery. One website

---

[41] Campbell, *The Hero With a Thousand Faces*, 33–37.
[42] Excepting those with aluminum bats, of course.

has taken the twenty-two point formula from Lord Raglan's *Study of Folklore* and tested several figures against it.[43] Jesus, according to their figuring, scored 16 out of 22. Moses 20. (Moses scored higher than Jesus?) Romulus, the founder of Rome, 21. How accurate could the test be? One internet author noted that her cat scored a 13.[44] The point being that the system is so vague that it allows plenty of wiggle room. Despite the precise sounding titles given to some points, such as "His mother was a royal virgin," when enthusiasts actually determine whether a figure matches the point, a lot of stretching and fudging in interpretation can go on. The language is obviously written for Jesus, but lots of scoundrels are allowed to slide their way in as well.[45]

But little stress has been put on the modern origin of the system itself. Obviously, when a composite myth is distilled from all possible heroes in history, the religions that have dominated history will most affect the synthesis. Therefore we should not be surprised, as some atheists pretend to be, when Christ scores on several points. The points were created with His influence in mind to begin with. It is like putting twelve spoonfuls of sugar into your coffee and then acting surprised that it is sweet. This type of "surprise" is that of the classic idolater who builds an idol out of wood with his own hands, and then pretends to discover in it a deity. "Oh my creation, thou hast made me!" (See Isaiah 44:9–20). The pan-mystery theory is simply an idol of twentieth century religious studies. Scholars created it by summarizing all of religious history and then worshiped it for encompassing all of religious history.

Campbell's and his followers' work is not a rare illumination of history nor an important synthesis of fragmentary mythology, but a grandiose expression of their own humanistic faith. They have simply set aside real history in order to promote their own mythology. Along these

---

[43]http://department.monm.edu/classics/Courses/Clas230/MythDocuments/HeroPattern/default.htm as of June 1, 2006.

[44]http://www.tam-lin.org/abby/raglan.html as of June 1, 2006.

[45]The internet apologist J. P. Holding has done an excellent job tracing the history of this type of mythological analysis. He arrives at similar conclusions as I, but covers a lot more material. I discovered his article after compiling my own work and do not see the need to expand. See his article "Ragland Reduced" at http://tektonics.org/copycat/raglan.html as of June 1, 2006. Holding has much more useful information besides.

lines, Joseph Campbell should be remembered only for his most important contribution to the twentieth century, which is not his scholarship: it is the fact that his own hero myth was the inspiration for the movie *Star Wars*. Perhaps his myth theory does hold some truth in another galaxy—far, far away.

Christian Reviews of the Evidence

The claim, as I have already stated, by some atheists and propagandists today is that the mysteries involved several motifs that Christianity (beginning with Paul) later stole. These include the idea of a baptism, a communal meal, and a dying and rising savior. But reread the myths for yourself. In fact, you may check the veracity of my versions by consulting the original sources for the mythologies. In the case of one compilation I have used—one which is standard for the purpose—the only place Christian-sounding ideas appear is in the editor's introductions.[46] Nowhere in any of the myths is there a genuine parallel to the Christian religion—either theological or historical. Where in the Osiris myth, for example, is there anything close to a bodily resurrection? The gathering together of his body parts by his wife did not bring him back to life. He remained in the underworld, separated from his body. The other myths are just as fuzzy. Everett Ferguson explains,

> There is nothing in the myth of Osiris that could be called a resurrection: the god became ruler over the dead, not the living. The myth of Attis contains no specific mention of a resurrection . . . The Adonis myth perhaps most clearly indicates the resuscitation of a god, but even here it is not strictly a resurrection. These beliefs are more closely allied to the cycle of nature . . . But insofar as paganism offered "dying and rising gods," these gods are a world apart from Christ's resurrection, which was presented as a one-time historical event, neither a repeated feature of nature nor a myth of the past.[47]

---

[46]Marvin W. Meyer, ed., *The Ancient Mysteries, A Sourcebook: Sacred Texts of the Mystery Religions of the Ancient Mediterranean World* (San Francisco: Harper & Row Publishers, 1987), which is a helpful compendium.

[47]Ferguson, *Background of Early Christianity*, 298.

The resurrection of Christ was and remains an unprecedented event in history, and foreshadowed only by a few passages in the Old Testament.[48]

The early Church father Athanasius (A.D. 295–373) saw the same lack of anything approaching the resurrection in the Greek myths. He wrote, "For although the Greeks have told all manner of false tales, yet they were not able to feign a Resurrection of their idols,—for it never crossed their mind, whether it be at all possible for the body again to exist after death."[49] For Athanasius, then, not only is a resurrection of the body absent from the mysteries, but it never even crossed their minds.

One obvious reason for this is that the idea of resurrection itself would have been repugnant, especially to the Greek mind. In the Greek traditions, the body was the prison house of the soul—a nasty, filthy, and corrupt vessel which fettered the immortal soul from escaping to its rightful heavenly abode. To the Greek, the body was mere "hair, mud and filth" which the youthful Socrates could not see as deserving of any connection to immortality.[50] Consequently, no Greek tradition presents the body as being something worthy of reclaiming after death. They were too happy to escape it. N. T. Wright notes that the pagan gods might have dwelt in their idea of heaven among the stars, but he adds,

> They had not, however, been raised from the dead. Cicero is quite clear, and completely in the mainstream of greco-roman thought: the body is a prison house. A necessary one for the moment; but nobody in their right mind, having got rid of it, would want it or something like it back again. . . . Resurrection was not an option. Those who followed Plato or Cicero did not want a body again; those who followed Homer knew they would not get one.[51]

The resurrection of Jesus Christ had no forerunners, not in the pagan world. Rather, the teaching grows naturally out of the Old Testament

---

[48]Ezekiel 37 to start. See Chapters 4 and 5.

[49]Athanasius, *On the Incarnation of the Word* in *The Nicene and Post-Nicene Fathers*, ed. Philip Schaff (Albany, OR: AGES Software, 1997), 4:337.

[50]The phrase appears in a discussion over what substances can be connected to Plato's ideal "forms" and can be found in his *Parmenides*, 130.

[51]N. T. Wright, *The Resurrection of the Son of God* (Minneapolis: Fortress Press, 2003), 60.

and was understood that way at the time of Christ. The Jewish background accounts for it; the pagan not only fails but hates the body too much to think about it.

Likewise the bloody bull-slaughtering rite of Cybele and Attis has not even the slightest comparison to the Christian sacrament of baptism as is claimed. Only by the wildest stretch could a scholar, or even a neo-pagan enthusiast, reach such a conclusion. None of the myths has any true parallel to Christian Baptism.

The same scenario exists for the Christian Eucharist. The mithraic rite of "communion," for example, involved an initiate eating bread and drinking water as part of joining the cult. Aside from the fact that eating and drinking are such fundamental parts of human life that they would surely have found their way into at least one pagan cult, the two cases are entirely different. The mithraist used water versus the Christian wine. It might well have been abominable to him to use anything else but pure water. For the mithraist the rite was initiatory and, as far as we know, only performed once. The Christian must have already received baptism (our initiation) in order to partake. The purpose for the Christian was "remembrance" of the Lord's death, confession of sin, and giving of thanks. The flesh-eating Orphic and Dionysian ritual had followers gorging themselves in order to absorb the qualities of the victim. This practice represents an old hold-out of ancient nature-magic—called "sympathetic magic"[52] (Voodoo is an example)—in which results come merely from taking part in the external ritual. This is nowhere close to what Christ meant when he spoke of eating His flesh (John 6:48–60). He was making an analogy of his flesh—which came from heaven and was to be sacrificed—as the manna the Israelites ate in the wilderness. There is simply nothing like this in the pagan world.[53]

The latest scholarship on the issue has basically shattered the dreams that critics imagined in the nineteenth century. Scholarship has progressed to the point where the influence of the earlier liberals is largely

---

[52]Harrison, *Prolegomena to the Study of Greek Religion*, 486–487.

[53]For more information see Ferguson, *Background of Early Christianity*, 297–300; Nash, *Christianity and the Hellenistic World*, 131–181.

overthrown. New Testament scholar G. R. Beasley-Murray comments on the situation: "For too long we have had to be content with the judgment of experts on these matters who have failed to provide the evidence on which their conflicting opinions were based."[54] The matter has changed, however, with two highly detailed studies: one by Günter Wagner[55] in 1967, another by A. J. M. Wedderburn[56] twenty years later.

Wagner concludes that the mysteries had absolutely no influence on the Christian doctrines of baptism and resurrection, and he sets out ten exegetical arguments against the idea.[57] Wedderburn refines Wagner's earlier work—allowing for a greater probability that Paul interacted with the practices of existing pagan cults—and still proves that the mystery-cult theory is impossible. At the end of his detailed analysis, he concludes of Paul and the mysteries that, "[W]e can no longer interpret either in the light of the other: the mysteries were not saying the same thing as Paul, nor was Paul borrowing his ideas from the mysteries."[58] In fact, Wedderburn figures to have "set a large warning sign at the entry to what I believe to be a 'dead end' in Pauline studies, the interpretation of Paul's doctrine of union with Christ as derived from the mystery-cults of his day."[59]

Table Guests and Conquests

The early Church did later adopt some *minor* practices from the pagans, but not until the early fourth century. This should not surprise us, for it has been a center of controversy regarding the purity of the Church throughout history. Those particular debates aside, the relevant ques-

---

[54]G. R. Beasley-Murray, "Foreword," in Günter Wagner, *Pauline Baptism and The Pagan Mysteries: The Problem of the Pauline Doctrine of Baptism in Romans VI. 1–11, in the Light of its Religio-Historical "Parallels,"* trans. J. P. Smith. (Edinburgh and London: Oliver & Boyd, 1967), ix.

[55]Wagner, *Pauline Baptism and The Pagan Mysteries,* ix.

[56]A. J. M. Wedderburn, *Baptism and Resurrection: Studies in Pauline Theology against its Graeco-Roman Background* (Tübingen: J.C. B. Mohr [Paul Siebeck], 1987).

[57]Wedderburn, *Baptism and Resurrection,* 283–285. Rehearsing the arguments here would take too much space. Advanced readers can pursue Wagner's work for themselves.

[58]Wedderburn, *Baptism and Resurrection,* 396.

[59]Wedderburn, *Baptism and Resurrection,* 396.

tion to answer is, "Why?" How much paganism did the Church adopt and why did it do it?

As to how much we have to include the tradition of patron saints (and praying to them), images of Mary holding the Christ child being used to replace those of the "Queen of Heaven" Isis holding her son-husband Horus, the practice of using certain fingers to motion a blessing, ornate processions with sacred objects on display, tonsures, and more.[60] Please note that none of these things relates to the essentials of baptism, Eucharist, salvation, the person of Christ, the nature of God, the nature of man, or any other essential doctrine of the Christian faith. At best, such adoptions could provide us only with a good Catholic-Protestant debate—certainly not the sort of radical claim made by critics that the mysteries constituted the basis of Christian doctrine. Furthermore, since these pagan appendages to Christian practice did not come along until the fourth century, they certainly speak of a certain idea of *evangelism*, and not of any of the earliest formative ideas of the Church.

This hits on the question of why Christianity later adopted certain pagan practices. The simple answer is that the Church remained immovable on essential doctrines, but quite flexible on the outward forms and expressions of worship. The leaders had no problem coopting pagan symbols and gestures where they could be reinterpreted without threatening the purity of the faith. Yale historian Roland Bainton explains that converts from pagan religions would tend to see parallels in parts of the Christian faith as well, because they would bring the baggage of the pagan mysteries with them and interpret Christian doctrine by their experience. He wrote that they would "tend to think of the resurrection as the rebirth of a nature god, and Easter would become a fertility rite centering on eggs and rabbits."[61] He continues,

---

[60]Metzger, "Methodology in the Study of Mystery Religions and Early Christianity," 4–6. See also Gordon J. Laing, "Roman Religious Survivals in Christianity," in John Thomas McNeill, Matthew Spinka, and Harold Willoughby, eds., *Environmental Factors in Christian History* (Chicago: The University of Chicago Press, 1939), 72–90, which is highly accurate when dealing with the tangential aspects of Christian practice (77ff), but woefully wrong in giving too much credence to pagan influence of Christian communion, regeneration, and life after death (74–77).

[61]Roland H. Bainton, *Early Christianity* (Princeton, NJ: D. Van Nostrand Company,

Against such misreadings the Church was required to be on guard. Her general principle was one of intransigence at the core and flexibility at the periphery. The cardinal doctrines could not be recast, but there was no objection to setting the celebration of the birth of Jesus on December 25, the winter solstice on Julian calendar, the birthday of the sun god Mithras. By setting the Christian festival on the same day, converts from Mithraism were preserved from relapsing on that occasion.[62]

Thus the practice was one of pastoral concern for new converts. It is quite possible that a convert would have been at a mithraic meal one week and then in Christ's kingdom the next. These people required special discipleship.

Add to this that the adoption of some practices was a mark of the triumph of Christianity over the pagan religion. One case in point, the Syrian versions of the Astarte and Adonis myth had its own regional peculiarities. Drawing from ancient Canaanite culture, their religion used the term "baal" to describe their gods. "Baal" appears commonly throughout the Old Testament as it was a general title meaning "lord" or "master." One false "baal" in the Old Testament is "Ashtaroth"[63] (also known by "Astarte" or "Ishtar"). From "Ishtar" it is quite evident that we derive the word "Easter,"[64] but we have no reason to gasp at such a fact. While atheists would love to point to it as "proof" that Christianity borrowed its religion from paganism, their simplistic understanding needs a bit of basic historical education. Christians did not adopt paganism, but conquered it by using its own symbols. The pagan mysteries are dead and gone for a reason. True, we may have a hard time fitting eggs and rabbits into any mental picture of Christian worship, but we do only think of Easter as a season of the Christian Church. The reason

---

1960), 33.

[62]Bainton, *Early Christianity*, 33.

[63]Judges 2:13, 10:6; 1 Samuel 7:3–4, 31:10; 1 Kings 11:5, 33; 2 Kings 23:12.

[64]The word "Easter" appears in the King James Version of the Bible only once, in Acts 12:4, where it is used to translate the Greek word "pascha." The word should be translated "Passover," which the context also makes clear (Acts 12:3). Nearly every modern translation of the Bible translates it correctly.

Astarte and Ishtar sound like strange names dug up out of obscure history books is because they are. Christ conquered what those false gods had hold of, and now they have long since gone down the memory hole. The only place they live on is in the fictional works of neo-gnostics and pagans who have to ignore or reinterpret the best parts of history in order to write their books.

Conclusion

In 1897, the Anglican clergyman Samuel Cheetham prefaced his published lectures on the mystery religions by complaining of "much wild theorising" that had characterized the writing on the subject. He closed his preface commenting on the claim of Christian borrowing. Though he did not completely deny the possibility, he ended saying, "It seems in some cases to have been pressed further than the evidence warrants."[65] Anglican clergyman are known for understatement.

Cheetham's conclusion shows that the nature of the mystery religion claim has not changed since the nineteenth century. From the historical perspective, evidence is "fragmentary and inconclusive," and, "According to the prepossessions with which they set out, different inquirers have arrived at the most curiously various results."[66] The same is true today. Modern pagans take the sparse evidence, add their own imagination, and then weave a tapestry of their own mythology. And yet for all of their fine-knitting, any amateur historian who sticks to the facts will begin to pull the threads apart one by one, reducing the mystery-religion theory to the pieces from which it came.

---

[65]S. Cheetham, *The Mysteries: Pagan and Christian*. The Hulsean Lectures, 1896–1897 (London: MacMillan and Co., 1897), xv. For the former quotation see page v.

[66]Cheetham, *The Mysteries: Pagan and Christian*, v.

3

The Early Church Response

Desperate to come up with an explanation, the Church fathers re-
sorted to one of the most absurd theories ever advanced. From the
time of Justin Martyr in the second century onward, they declared
that the Devil had plagiarized Christianity by anticipation in or-
der to lead people astray.[1]

By reason of these tales, O King, much evil has arisen among men,
who to this day are imitators of their gods, and practise adultery
and defile themselves with their mothers and their sisters, and by
lying with males, and some make bold to slay even their parents.
For if he who is said to be the chief and king of their gods do these
things how much more should his worshippers imitate him?[2]

And to me there is no doubt but that the earth abides through the
supplication of the Christians. But the rest of the nations err and
cause error in wallowing before the elements of the world, since
beyond these their mental vision will not pass. And they search
about as if in darkness because they will not recognize the truth;
and like drunken men they reel and jostle one another and fall.[3]

---

[1]Timothy Freke and Peter Gandy, *The Jesus Mysteries: Was the "Original Jesus" a Pagan God?* (New York: Three Rivers Press, 1999), , 28.

[2]Aristides, *The Apology of Aristides,* Ch. IX. In Ante-Nicene Fathers, Vol. X. eds. James Donaldson and Alexander Roberts (Albany, OR: AGES Software, 1997), 415–6. Aristides' work is the earliest philosophical defense of the faith against pagan religions that we have outside of the New Testament. It dates from around A.D.125.

[3]Aristides. *The Apology of Aristides,* Ch. XVI. In Ante-Nicene Fathers, Vol. X, 432.

WHAT WE ARE hearing today from the neo-pagans with their mystery-religion theories mirrors the situation of the early Church very closely. Apologists of the first few centuries of the Church had to ward off attacks by pagans who aimed for the heart of the Gospel. Pagan writers such as the very eloquent Celsus denied the resurrection of Christ as a fable and claimed that Christians had invented their whole religion. They pointed to the pagan cults—and pagan civilization for that matter—as preceding Christianity and claimed that the greater antiquity of the pagans exposed Christ as an innovation.[4] But the apologists stood ready to answer. They replied with what should have been obvious to any observer, that Christian doctrine grew naturally out of the Old Testament and thus had a greater antiquity than the hubris of the Greeks. For example, Tertullian (b. A.D. 155) pointed out that, "Moses and God existed before all your Lycurguses and Solons. There is not a single later age that does not derive from primitive sources."[5] Origen (A.D. 185–254) answered Celsus by arguing that, "Moses and the prophets . . . are not only earlier than Plato but also than Homer and the discovery of writing among the Greeks."[6] Moses was writing the truth before the Greeks could write at all. Though antiquity by itself does not prove truth, the apologists' thoughtful replies show that they were indeed prepared to give a reasoned defense against pagan attacks.

This lesson cries for attention today because many atheists and propagandists love to claim that the early apologists were at a loss to answer the pagan mysteries. Along these lines they quote one allegedly embarrassing quip from Justin Martyr, who after briefly explaining the Christian Eucharist with Christ's words of institution, adds,

> *Which the wicked devils have imitated in the mysteries of Mithras,*
> *commanding the same thing to be done. For, that bread and a cup*

---

[4]Jaroslav Pelikan, *The Emergence of the Catholic Tradition (100–600)*. The Christian Tradition: A History of the Development of Doctrine, vol. I (Chicago and London: The University of Chicago Press, 1975 (1971), 34.

[5]Tertullian, *Against Marcion*. 2.17.3, quoted in Pelikan, *The Emergence of the Catholic Tradition*, 35.

[6]Origen, *Against Celsus*. 6.7, quoted in Pelikan, *The Emergence of the Catholic Tradition*, 35.

of water are placed with certain incantations in the mystic rites of
one who is being initiated, you either know or can learn.[7]

The argument runs that the early Church was so void of explanation for the alleged obvious similarities between Christianity and the mystery religions that it had to resort to saying, "The devil knew what was coming and copied it in advance." Some even claim that this argument is still used today.[8] But this claim is the obvious product of an atheistic version of a "witch-hunt" in which any semblance of real scholarship is set aside; and the charge falls flat on two counts. First, it misrepresents the quote itself by adding the idea of "advance," as if the devil counterfeited the Christian claims ahead of time. Justin did not make this claim. All he argued was that the Mithraists "imitated" what had been handed down by the apostles in the Gospels. For all we know he was talking about the Mithraic cult as it existed *after* the Gospel of Christ was established. The cults did change over time and the modern critics cannot escape the possibility that the post-Christian versions did in fact mimic the rites of the rapidly growing Christian faith in order to keep from losing adherents. Borrowing could have gone both ways,[9] and it is more likely that pagans would engage in syncretism than Christians, whose Jewish roots would have decried pagan pollution.

Secondly, the atheists have pulled Justin's quotes out from the larger context in which he was arguing. He did not merely retort what amounts to, "The Devil did it and that is that!" To see this in Justin would be highly reductionistic and oversimplified. His claim was that Christians relied upon the Scriptures for doctrine, and those Scriptures, especially the Old Testament, provided essential material for the devil to duplicate in pagan lands. For example, just prior to the quotation above Justin had written, "For the apostles, in the memoirs composed by them, which are called Gospels, have thus delivered unto us what was enjoined upon

---

[7]Justin Martyr. *First Apology of Justin Martyr,* Chap. 66. *In Ante-Nicene Fathers,* Vol. I. eds. James Donaldson and Alexander Roberts (Albany, OR: AGES Software, 1997), 340–1.

[8]This is the unlearned claim made in Brian Flemming's DVD *The God Who Wasn't There.*

[9]Metzger, "Methodology in the Study of Mystery Religions and Early Christianity,"11.

them."[10] In other words, he was emphasizing historical continuity in Christian doctrine—from Christ to the apostles to him—against the corruptions of paganism. More to the point, in chapters 69 and 70 of his *Dialogue with Trypho*, Justin lays out his case more fully. He claims,

> I am established in the knowledge of and faith in the Scriptures by those counterfeits which he who is called the devil is said to have performed among the Greeks; just as some were wrought by the Magi in Egypt, and others by the false prophets in Elijah's days.[11]

Working from precedents in Old Testament history he lists several cases in which the mysteries could represent corruptions of traditions already written in Old Testament times, including a prophecy that pagan peoples would sate themselves with idolatrous versions of the true faith they could not understand. He then continues with a presentation about Messianic prophecies. The lengthy section is worth reproducing:

> And when those who record the mysteries of Mithras say that he was begotten of a rock, and call the place where those who believe in him are initiated a cave, do I not perceive here that the utterance of Daniel, that a stone without hands was cut out of a great mountain, has been imitated by them, and that they have attempted likewise to imitate the whole of Isaiah's words? For they contrived that the words of righteousness be quoted also by them. But I must repeat to you the words of Isaiah referred to, in order that from them you may know that these things are so. They are these: 'Hear, ye that are far off, what I have done; those that are near shall know my might. The sinners in Zion are removed; trembling shall seize the impious. Who shall announce to you the everlasting place? The man who walks in righteousness, speaks in the right way, hates sin and unrighteousness, and keeps his hands pure from bribes, stops the ears from hearing the unjust judgment of blood closes the eyes from seeing unrighteousness: he shall dwell in the lofty cave of the strong rock.

[10]Justin Martyr, *First Apology*, Ch. 66.

[11]Justin Martyr, *Dialogue of Justin Philosopher and Martyr with Trypho, a Jew*, Chs. 69–70. In Ante-Nicene Fathers, Vol. I. eds. James Donaldson and Alexander Roberts (Albany, OR: AGES Software, 1997), 447.

Bread shall be given to him, and his water [shall be] sure. Ye shall see the King with glory, and your eyes shall look far off. Your soul shall pursue diligently the fear of the Lord. Where is the scribe? where are the counselors? where is he that numbers those who are nourished,—the small and great people? with whom they did not take counsel, nor knew the depth of the voices, so that they heard not. The people who are become depreciated, and there is no understanding in him who hears.' Now it is evident, that in this prophecy [allusion is made] to the bread which our Christ gave us to eat, in remembrance of His being made flesh for the sake of His believers, for whom also He suffered; and to the cup which He gave us to drink, in remembrance of His own blood, with giving of thanks. And this prophecy proves that we shall behold this very King with glory; and the very terms of the prophecy declare loudly, that the people foreknown to believe in Him were foreknown to pursue diligently the fear of the Lord. Moreover, these Scriptures are equally explicit in saying, that those who are reputed to know the writings of the Scriptures, and who hear the prophecies, have no understanding. And when I hear, Trypho," said I, "that Perseus was begotten of a virgin, I understand that the deceiving serpent counterfeited also this.[12]

Justin was not just engaging in name-calling games or uncritical reaction, nor is he arguing that pagans had read the Old Testament and then created their own religion based on it; but he has a solid basis in claiming that *all* of paganism can be seen as a corruption of elements found in the only true Source of true religion. The Old Testament, he conveyed, could account for *both* the doctrines and practices of the Christian faith and the elements of the pagan mysteries.

The way in which the radicals today have tried to make Justin look uneducated, reactionary, and paranoid lines up with the character of the early attacks on Christianity. Johannes Quasten, the eminent patrologist, comments on the approach of the early critic Celsus. Quasten nails the tactic: "The aim of Celsus was to convert the Christians by

---

[12]Justin Martyr, *Dialogue of Justin Philosopher and Martyr with Trypho, a Jew*, 448– 449. The idea of Daniel behind the mithraic myth has even more plausibility when we remember that Daniel wrote during the Persian captivity of the Jews; and Persia is considered to be one of the likely sources of mithraism.

shaming them out of their religion."[13] Nothing has changed. Critics act as if by slandering the image of Christianity they can overturn it. But the facts are too strong, and the Bible speaks too loudly.

In fact the Bible speaks so clearly that Origen accuses Celsus of going to lengths—just as atheists do today—to obscure the importance of the Old Testament Scriptures. He complains, "I have made these remarks in reply to the charges which Celsus and others bring against the simplicity of the language of Scripture, which appears to be thrown into the shade by the splendor of polished discourse."[14] Elsewhere he criticizes Celsus for completely ignoring the Scriptures. While Origen and his students deal with, "the hard sayings, and of those passages in the law, and prophecies, and Gospels,"[15] he confronts Celsus that these Scriptures are they "which you have despised as not containing anything worthy of notice, because you have not ascertained the meaning which they contain, nor tried to enter into the aim of the writers."[16]

Once he ignored the Scriptures, like our critics today, Celsus turned to other sources in order to impugn the Christian faith. Reaching into obscure myths and mysteries, he claimed to find parallels to Christian teaching. Origen simply explains that the source for Christian doctrine could more easily be found in the Old Testament. One case in point refers to the nature of God and of heaven. To make his case, Celsus drags up the mystery religions. Origen writes:

> Celsus, desiring to exhibit his learning in his treatise against us, quotes also certain Persian mysteries, where he says: 'These things are obscurely hinted at in the accounts of the Persians,

---

[13]Johannes Quasten, *The Ante-Nicene Literature After Irenaeus.* Patrology, Volume II (4vol.) (Westminster, MD: Christian Classics, Inc. 1992), 52.

[14]Origen, *Againt Celsus,* 6.2. In Ante-Nicene Fathers, Vol. IV. eds. James Donaldson, Alexander Roberts, and A. Cleveland Coxe (Albany, OR: AGES Software, 1997), 1133.

[15]Origen, *Against Celsus,* 3.74. In Ante-Nicene Fathers, Vol. IV, 966.

[16]Origen, *Against Celsus,* 3.74. In Ante-Nicene Fathers, Vol. IV, 966. Modern atheists rarely even try to understand what the Scriptures and the fathers are saying. In some cases when they actually do quote the Bible it appears to be with such an undiscerning mentality that it must be fueled by hatred for God rather than a love of truth and scholarship.

and especially in the mysteries of Mithras, which are celebrated amongst them,"[17]

The quote continues with intricate descriptions of Mithraic nonsense which Origen rightly sees as irrelevant to the real issue. First of all, for his purpose Celsus has gone far afield to fetch one mystery—and that one was chosen poorly—to the neglect of many others. This passing by of the others Origen argued should have alerted him to pass over the less helpful one as well. Origen essentially asks, "Why not? Why strain over a gnat?" After this chide Origen offers a better answer for the source of Christian doctrine:

> If one wished to obtain means for a profounder contemplation of the entrance of souls into divine things, not from the statements of that very insignificant sect from which he quoted, but from books—partly those of the Jews, which are read in their synagogues, and adopted by Christians, and partly from those of Christians alone—let him peruse, at the end of *Ezekiel's prophecies*, the visions beheld by the prophet, in which gates of different kinds are enumerated, which obscurely refer to the different modes in which divine souls enter into a better world.[18]

He continues by sending the reader to the Revelation of John, and then to Moses in Numbers; the point being that Christian doctrine finds its vital roots in the Old Testament, not in strained and non-existent parallels with paganism. Christians did not get their ideas from a bad read of Plato, nor from the mysteries. Origen added, "neither do our prophets, nor the apostles of Jesus, nor the Son of God Himself, repeat anything which they borrowed from the Persians or the Cabiri."[19]

Another early apologist, Tertullian, also alludes to the mystery cults. He treats the mysteries like all other idolatry and heresy. In describing where we get the distortions of Scripture that lead to heresies, he writes, "By the devil, of course, to whom pertain those wiles which pervert the

---

[17]Origen, *Against Celsus*, 6.22. In *Ante-Nicene Fathers*, 4:1153.

[18]Origen, *Against Celsus*, 6.23. In *Ante-Nicene Fathers*, 4:1154. Italics added.

[19]Origen, *Against Celsus*, 6.23. In *Ante-Nicene Fathers*, 4:1155.

truth, and who, by the mystic rites of his idols, vies even with the essential portions of the sacraments of God."[20] The devil is the great distorter of doctrine, the great perverter of truth. Tertullian argues very similarly to Justin Martyr: the devil works through the distortions of what has already been revealed—in Old Testament Scripture or in history—and this through the efforts of misguided people. He proceeds by listing several instances in which the mysteries have alleged similarities to Christianity, and uses one cult leader as an example. He writes,

> Suppose now we revolve in our minds the superstitions of Numa Pompilius, and consider his priestly offices and badges and privileges, his sacrificial services, too, and the instruments and vessels of the sacrifices themselves, and the curious rites of his expiations and vows: is it not clear to us that the devil imitated the well-known moroseness of the Jewish law? Since, therefore he has shown such emulation in his great aim of expressing, in the concerns of his idolatry, those very things of which consists the administration of Christ's sacraments, it follows, of course, that the same being, possessing still the same genius, both set his heart upon, and succeeded in, adapting to his profane and rival creed the very documents of divine things and of the Christian saints—his interpretation from their interpretations, his words from their words, his parables from their parables.[21]

If anyone can be accused of copying, Tertullian argues, it is the mystery cults, not the Christians. The devil has a documented history of trying

---

[20]Tertullian, *The Prescription Against Heretics*. In *Ante-Nicene Fathers*, 4:40. eds. James Donaldson, Alexander Roberts, and A. Cleveland Coxe (Albany, OR: AGES Software, 1997), 475.

[21]Tertullian, *The Prescription Against Heretics*, 475–476. In another work, *De Corona*, Tertullian warns Christians against adorning themselves with crowns. He refers to an obscure rite of Mithraism in which the participant resists a crown on his head and rather places it upon his shoulder. This he argued should shame those Christians who seek the honor of a crown. He adds that the rejection of such an honor by the Mithraist (which Christians in reality often did as well) was another instance of the devil copying Christian piety. Unfortunately, Tertullian does not develop his argument here as he did in other places. See Tertullian, *De corona*, 15 (189). He does, however, as always, leave us with some beautiful rhetoric (chapter 14): "be not crowned with flowers at all, if you cannot be with thorns."

to copy God's every move throughout the Old Testament. Why should the pagan religions of the second century any different?

So, there exists no historical indication anywhere that the early Christian apologists considered the mystery religions as anything more than instances of pagan idolatry. They did not see the cults as threats, but viewed Adonis and Mithra just as they viewed Baal or Dagon from the Old Testament: as false gods and powerless statues.

Not only did the early apologists ably answer the pagan attack, their second and third-century answers have startling relevance for today. On Origen's work *Against Celsus*, Quasten explains, "In it we see the struggle between paganism and Christianity as in a mirror . . . Eusebius was so convinced of the force of Origen's refutation that he thought the author had answered the heresies of all centuries to come."[22] Eusebius may not have been too far off. The reason for this is that Origen had an underlying theology for his apologetic that took into account the fallen nature of man, and to address the problem of human nature in relation to God is to address all men, everywhere and in all times. The issue is not one of mere intellectual knowledge but of faithfulness and worship to God. Origen wrote,

> The truth, then, is verily held (in unrighteousness), as our Scrip-
> tures testify, by those who are of opinion that "the chief good
> cannot be described in words," but who assert that, "after long
> custom and familiar usage, a light becomes suddenly kindled in
> the soul, as if by a fire springing forth, and that it now supports
> itself alone."[23]

This he aimed at even those pagan writers who had a few good things to say; because while they might have arrived at certain points of truth, they refused to see the Creator and Author of that truth, and to give Him the worship He deserves. Instead, Origen charged, these so-called sophisticated and civilized Greeks would speak of wisdom and virtue

---

[22]Quasten, *The Ante-Nicene Literature After Irenaeus*, 56.
[23]Origen. *Against Celsus*, 6.3. In *Ante-Nicene Fathers*, 4:1135.

one minute and then fall into some ridiculous—even heinous—mystery cult the next. He said,

> Notwithstanding, those who have written in this manner regarding the "chief good" will go down to the Piraeus and offer prayer to Artemis, as if she were God, and will look (with approval) upon the solemn assembly held by ignorant men; and after giving utterance to philosophical remarks of such profundity regarding the soul, and describing its passage (to a happier world) after a virtuous life, they pass from those great topics which God has revealed to them, and adopt mean and trifling thoughts, and offer a cock to Aesculapius! And although they had been enabled to form representations both of the "invisible things" of God and . . . had no mean glimpses of His "eternal power and Godhead," they nevertheless became "foolish in their imaginations," and their "foolish heart" was involved in darkness and ignorance as to the (true) worship of God. Moreover, we may see those who greatly pride themselves upon their wisdom and theology worshipping the image of a corruptible man, *in honor*, they say, of Him, and sometimes even descending, with the Egyptians, to the worship of birds, and four-footed beasts, and creeping things![24]

Origen contrasted this behavior with the doctrine of the Bible which sees religion as a matter of purity of heart and of right living, and believes that God is not to be represented as a bull, a building, or a human. He wrote,

> *Our* wise men, however,—Moses, the most ancient of them all, and the prophets who followed him,—knowing that the chief good could by no means be described in words, were the first who wrote that, as God manifests Himself to the deserving, and

---

[24]Origen, *Against Celsus*, 6.4. In *Ante-Nicene Fathers*, 4:1135–1136. Italics in original. Plutarch made a very similar critique of the Stoic philosophers to whom Paul argued that God does not dwell in temples made with hands. Plutarch comments, "The Stoics, while applauding this as correct, attend the mysteries in temples, go up to the Acropolis, do reverence to statues, a place wreaths upon the shrines, though these are the works of builders and mechanics." Quoted in Richard J. Gibson, "Paul and the Evangelization of the Stoics" in *The Gospel to the Nations: Perspectives on Paul's Mission*. eds. Mark Thompson and Peter Bolt (Downers Grove, IL: InterVarsity Press, 2000), 320.

to those who are qualified to behold Him, He appeared to Abraham, or to Isaac, or to Jacob. But who He was that appeared, and of what form, and in what manner, and like to which of mortal beings, they have left to be investigated by those who are able to show that they resemble those persons to whom God showed Himself: for He was seen not by their bodily eyes, but by the pure heart. For, according to the declaration of our Jesus, "Blessed are the pure in heart, for they shall see God."[25]

Origen understood that the attack on Christianity was not the product of well-founded knowledge, nor of the acute observance of philosophers; rather it came from the embittered and prejudiced heart of unbelief, grasping at every possible straw of perceived evidence, twisting that evidence, selectively quoting and misrepresenting its opponents, doing everything it could to shame Christians from their religion.[26] Nothing has changed. Modern books and videos by angry atheists, new-agers, and liberal scholars adopt the exact same approach of shouting random lies while throwing dust in the air. It is a weak attempt at diversion and confusion.

In the overwhelming majority of the cases in which the early Christian apologists responded to attacks pertaining to the mystery religions their argument was the same: Christians had no need to look to the mysteries as a background to their religion; they had all they needed and more in the Scriptures of the Old Testament, especially as seen through the person of Jesus Christ. Critics have obviously seen the arguments of the apologists—since they have quoted them out of context—but they should further consider the force of the Old Testament prophetic background that the apologists promoted, for against this the mystery religion theory falls flat. More on that later.

Piercing the Mystery

Following the early Church's example, we can look to the Old Testament and find the historical roots of all religion—both true and pagan—in the Garden of Eden. Man is made in the image of God. Everything about

---

[25]Origen, *Against Celsus*, 6.4. In *Ante-Nicene Fathers*, 1136. Italics in original.
[26]Quasten's phrase; see Quasten, *The Ante-Nicene Literature After Irenaeus*, 52.

man will necessarily reflect that Image. This means that man is inescapably religious. Even his fallen attempts at religion will emphasize those aspects of life that God created as important: life, blood, survival, reproduction, and unfortunately death. It should not surprise us that on this side of the fall of man—where our minds, wills, hearts, emotions, and bodies are corrupted—religion without the benefit of the Bible or a specially revealed tradition will revolve around our depraved fears about life, blood, survival, reproduction and death. Looking at the pagan mysteries that is just what we see.

But looking at the mysteries a bit closer, especially those that feature a mother and son, we can find a very interesting parallel in the Old Testament. Immediately after the fall in Genesis 3, and after God curses the serpent, the Bible presents us with the famous "proto-evangel"—the first instance of the Gospel preached to mankind. In Gen 3:15, God says to the serpent, "I will put enmity between thee and the woman, and between thy seed and her seed; it shall bruise thy head, and thou shalt bruise his heel." This is taken by most scholars as the first prophecy of the coming Christ, the Sacrifice and Redeemer of mankind. It precedes the development of all religious thought, both Christian and pagan.

Noticing the characters in the story—the woman, her child and the serpent/enemy—do we not have the very elements of nearly every pagan myth? The seminal prophecy would have been passed on by oral tradition, and without the benefit of special revelation, the story would have soon been twisted and corrupted into many variations. Powerful leaders would likely have claimed—and convinced many—that they were the manifestation of the old prophecy. The twisted myth soon would have been a tool of empire and rule. As an historical possibility, it makes a lot of sense. Cain and Abel had the same knowledge of how to approach God, but Cain corrupted the practice through his own invention. He could be called the father of paganism. The problem is not one of proper knowledge, but obedience to the truth before us. Pagans simply distorted the proto-evangel and used it for their own purposes throughout history.

As for the practices of the mysteries the outstanding factors were most obviously control, empire, self-release, the promise of secret knowledge, and fear. The pagan mysteries were not for the faint of heart, just the bereft of moral sense. Their lack of courage shows not in a fear of pain or physical terror—obviously, if they could even castrate themselves—but in their fear to not belong. Closeness to divinity and the inner circle of knowledge are powerful draws upon the chords of fallen human nature, all belonging to the lust of the flesh, lust of the eyes, and pride of life (1 John 2:16). The deception of popular religion in these regards can lead men to the furthest reaches of insanity, vulgarity, and self-defacement. Well did Wisdom say, "He that sinneth against me wrongeth his own soul; all they that hate me love death" (Prov. 8:36). In the pursuit of pagan mysteries we have seen worshipers engage in drunkenness and orgies, eat the raw flesh and blood of animals, sacrifice humans and probably infants, mutilate and especially castrate themselves, and deny their manhood in the name of belonging to a female deity. Paganism, therefore, betrays an inherent love of death, and a stark denial of man's created purpose. Castration demonstrates a man's willingness to deny his very manhood for the sake of misguided religious devotion. The show of courage worked up in order to perform the act (aided by frenzy and drugs) is in reality the mistress of every fear and religious timidity that believes there is no way to move up in the world other than some irrational act. The early Church father Clement of Alexandria picked up on this important point as well. Noting God's law he said,

> And do you not see Moses, the hierophant of the truth, enjoining that no eunuch, or emasculated man, or son of a harlot, should enter the congregation? By the two first he alludes to the impious custom by which men were deprived both of divine energy and of their virility; and by the third, to him who, in place of the only real God, assumes many gods falsely so called,—as the son of a harlot, in ignorance of his true father, may claim many putative fathers.[27]

---

[27]Clement of Alexandria, *Exhortation to the Heathen,* chap. 2. In *Ante-Nicene Fathers,* 2:337.

For the pagan mind, however, the moral courage needed to stand against the draw of secret knowledge and promised divinity makes even self-mutilation appear to be the easy way out. The pagan cannot resist. He simply is not man enough, and in proving so he proves that he hates himself and his Creator as well.

Conclusion

This chapter has merely touched upon the thorough response of the early Church fathers to pagan attacks in the second century. A full review would probably take several books. One of the best ways to educate yourself against modern pagans and gnostics is to read the Church fathers for yourself. These days, their works are cheap and easy to find; many are free on-line. Once you enter into the depth of their philosophical arguments, and experience the richness of their biblical understanding of Jesus Christ, you will see, as you have seen in this chapter, that the modern characterizations of the fathers have no grounding in reality whatsoever.

The early Christians had no problem with the mystery religions. They saw the pagan cults as idolatry pure and simple. Far from needing the Greek myths to bolster their understanding of Jesus, the fathers knew the Old Testament, and continually returned to Moses, the Prophets, and the Psalms to find the roots of the promises which Jesus Christ fulfilled in the flesh. From their work, the early fathers understood the underlying history behind all religion, pagan and Christian. They knew paganism to be a corruption of the true Old Covenant line that led to Jesus. Unlike the critics today, the early Church fathers could tell myth from reality.

Paul's Jesus:
Mythical or Historical?

It is a completely remarkable fact, however, that Paul says nothing at all about the historical Jesus![1]

If Jesus was a human who had recently lived, nobody told Paul. . . Paul doesn't believe that Jesus was ever a human being.[2]

M OVING ON FROM the mystery religions historically considered, and the early Church's refutation of them, the most important part of the Christian defense comes from the Scriptures themselves. For all of the mystery-religion theory's bold claims about Jesus and the Apostle Paul, few if any of them resonate with what we actually find in Scripture. Perhaps this is because the critics begin by denigrating the value of Scripture to begin with, or ignoring it. But even their claims against the Bible itself will not hold up.

The radical claim that Paul created our Christian religion from a patchwork of mystery-religion practices relies on the beliefs 1) that Paul's teachings about Jesus are completely void of any reference to the

---

[1]Timothy Freke and Peter Gandy, *The Jesus Mysteries: Was the "Original Jesus" a Pagan God?* (New York: Three Rivers Press, 1999), 151.

[2]From Brian Flemming's film, *The God Who Wasn't There.*

earthly, historical figure of Jesus, presenting Him rather as a heavenly or mythological figure, and 2) that Paul was primarily a Hellenistic thinker, his mind bent and shaped by the Greek world, its philosophies and religions. With these two suppositions, the critics throw away the Old Testament, early church tradition, and Paul's Jewish education, and then begin to search every known Greek and Roman source from Homer forward hoping to find any fragment which they can describe in Christian language and then present as a forerunner to Christ. But what does the Bible reveal about Paul and Jesus? Will the critics' presuppositions pass a good double-checking?

Paul and the Historical Jesus

From a cursory reading of the New Testament you could possibly get the idea that Paul did not see the earthly and human side of Jesus, but you would have to glance over it pretty crudely. Even the casual reader will come across passages that show otherwise. For example, while the critics allege that Paul knew nothing of the birth of Jesus, the apostle writes in Galatians 4:4, "But when the fulness of the time was come, God sent forth his Son, made of a woman, made under the law."[3] Could it be any clearer that Paul sees Christ as an historical figure, born of a woman? If this were not clear enough, Paul explicitly says that Christ came in the flesh. He writes, "Concerning his Son Jesus Christ our Lord, which was made of the seed of David *according to the flesh*" (Rom. 1:3).[4] Elsewhere Paul writes, "We have known Christ after the flesh" (2 Cor. 5:16); but since Paul does not elaborate on that earthly life in the way that the Gospels do, and since these few verses do not enjoy the greater emphasis of the Pauline writings, the critics miss them, or pretend they are not there. But they are there, and they remind us very pointedly that Paul had in mind a human, earthly and historical Jesus Christ.

---

[3]This and most of the following instances are found in Joseph A. Fitzmyer, *Pauline Theology: A Brief Sketch* (Englewood Cliffs, NJ: Prentice Hall, 1967), 11–13. This little work of less that a hundred pages is one of the handiest resources on Pauline theology I have seen. It is a learned and insightful summary from a modern Roman Catholic.

[4]Italics added.

In fact, a study of Paul's letters with the incarnation of Christ in mind turns up more data yet. When speaking of the glory of the Jewish heritage and the blessings which God conferred through it, Paul adds, "Of whom as concerning the flesh Christ came" (Rom. 9:5). Paul sees Christ as an historical descendent of the Israelite race. Not only is He *a* descendent, but *the* promised seed of Abraham (Gal. 3:16–19). Even in those epistles in which Paul does stress the heavenly ascended position of Christ more strongly, he still makes reference to the historical aspect of Jesus. For example, when speaking of Christ's role in breaking down the barrier between Jew and Gentile, Paul states that Christ accomplished this by "having abolished in his flesh the enmity . . . by the cross" (Eph. 2:15–16). Likewise in his letter to the Colossians Paul preaches that reconciliation with God was accomplished by Christ, "In the body of his flesh through death" (Col. 1:21–22). "In him dwelleth all the fulness of the Godhead *bodily*" (Col. 2:9).[5] For Paul, Christ indeed was God incarnate, in the flesh, on the earth, in history. To Paul, the incarnation belongs to what is without question a great mystery, but this mystery includes the fact that "He was manifest in the flesh" (1 Tim. 3:16). So while he did not write a birth narrative like Matthew or Luke, nor a striking statement like that of John 1:14, the understanding of Christ as an incarnate person—real, physical, bodily and in the flesh—can be seen underlying the superstructure of Paul's doctrine of Christ.

The critics miss many other earthly details of Christ's life which the apostle records. He knows a Christ Jesus, "who before Pontius Pilate witnessed a good confession" (1 Tim. 6:13).[6] This reference to the historical occasion of Christ before Pilate is either unseen or ignored by the critics. Likewise Paul speaks of Christ's betrayal and His institution of the Eucharist (1 Cor. 11:23–5)—both historical events. Also, against the

---

[5] Italics added.

[6] A few critics would try to get around Paul's witness to the historical episode of Pilate by saying that the Epistle to Timothy was not written by Paul, but by someone else much later. This theory has very little to commend it. Guthrie, after a characteristically thorough review of the issues, concludes that the traditional view of Pauline authorship is not only quite possible, but much more likely than any of the alternatives. See Donald Guthrie, *New Testament Introduction* (Downers Grove, IL: InterVarsity Press, 1973), 620. For his extended discussion see 584–622.

claim that Paul only writes of an exalted and ascended Christ, an important point of Paul's theology is the crucifixion of Christ. In fact, when dealing with the extremes of Greek philosophy on the one hand and Jewish power-religion on the other, the apostle emphasizes to the Corinthian church that "we preach Christ crucified" (1 Cor. 1:23). "Christ crucified" is a recurring theme in Paul's letters to the Corinthians and to the Galatians,[7] and it corresponds to the same form of the early Gospel preached by Peter (Acts 2:23, 36; 4:10). So in these details not only does Paul show himself to believe in an historical Jesus, but stands in the same tradition preaching the same Jesus as the other apostles.

Paul and the Apostolic Tradition

Paul elsewhere makes it clear that he stood in that line of early tradition. A mere three years after his conversion, Paul traveled to Jerusalem and spent fifteen days with Peter (Gal. 1:18). Imagine the discussion! Surely, that which Paul received directly from the Lord (Gal. 1:12, 16) was reinforced and confirmed in his two-week dialogue with the other apostle. As a late-comer to the spreading religion,[8] Paul would have had a little catching up to do, especially in the area of whatever hymns and liturgies were developing, and his writings show a knowledge of such things. The Eucharistic formula, already mentioned (1 Cor. 11:23–5), shows that Paul knew the very words of Christ and the manner in which the early Church already conducted the Supper. The same seems to be true for early hymns, which Paul appears to use in his letters. Most scholars agree that the famous passage in Philippians 2:6–11 contains such a hymn,[9] and that Paul employed such pre-existent material to powerfully punctuate his message.

Not only do we find evidence that Paul preached the same Jesus as the primitive church, but he himself speaks of that tradition and claims that

---

[7] 1 Corinthians 1:13, 23, 2:2; Galatians 2:20, 3:1, 6:14.

[8] The Gospel had already begun to spread. Paul himself was *en route* to Damascus to track down the Christian mission there when he was confronted by Christ on the road (Acts 9:1–3).

[9] See Raymond E. Brown, *An Introduction to the New Testament* (New York: Doubleday, 1997), 489–493.

he is "handing down" what he had "received" himself. This is true for the Lord's Supper (1 Cor. 11:2, 23), the understanding of Christ's crucifixion and resurrection as historical events (1 Cor. 15:1–3), general teachings about Christ (2 Thess. 2:15, 3:6; Phil. 4:9), and the Gospel proper (Rom. 6:17; Gal. 1:9, 12). The phrases that Paul uses draw from technical terminology that he would have learned in the rabbinical schools—language that pertains to the passing on and receiving of a tradition.[10] He certainly saw himself in that tradition of apostolic witness.

In addition to his consciousness of the apostolic tradition, Paul shows in several places that he had knowledge of Christ's very words. I have already noted this in regard to the Lord's Supper (1 Cor. 11:23–5). It is equally true for the Lord's instruction on marriage (1 Cor. 7:10), payment of ministers (1 Cor. 9:14), his phrase about faith that could "move mountains" (1 Cor. 13:2), the sermon on the mount (Rom. 12:14; 1 Cor. 4:12–13; cf. Matt. 5:44), and Jesus' summary of the law in love (Rom. 13:9; Gal. 5:14; cf. Matt. 22:37–40).[11] Also, according to Luke's record in Acts, Paul speaks to the Ephesian elders using the very "words of the Lord Jesus" (Acts 20:35). Keep in mind that Paul wrote most of his letters probably before others wrote the Gospels, and thus his knowledge of Jesus' words at this early period shows a deep intimacy with the apostolic tradition. In fact, the early Church had a tradition which claimed that Luke, being a traveling companion during Paul's missionary journeys, based his Gospel upon the preaching of Paul.[12] The early Church had a high regard for the closeness of Paul's message to that of the historical Jesus. At the very least, these facts illustrate a very early era in which the sayings of Jesus Christ had already established a foundational and authoritative place.

Not only does Paul refer clearly and directly to Christ's words in some cases, but in many others the Savior's words lay just beneath the

---

[10]Joseph A. Fitzmyer. *Pauline Theology: A Brief Sketch* (Englewood Cliffs, NJ: Prentice Hall, 1967), 12.

[11]In this instance Jesus' "summary of the law" was itself taken from the Pentateuch in Leviticus 19:18, and thus one could argue that Paul took his teaching from there; but the peculiar knowledge that Leviticus 19:18 in fact does summarize the law pertains to the teaching of Christ.

[12]Fitzmyer, *Pauline Theology*, 18. See Irenaeus, *Against Heresies*, 3.1.1; Tertullian, *Against Marcion*, 4.5; and Origen as per Eusebius, *Ecclesiastical History*, 6.25.6.

surface of the apostle's. David Wenham, lecturer at Wycliffe Hall, Oxford, has shown countless instances in his extensive works on the subject.[13] A few of his insights will illuminate any Bible study. For example, he sees an interesting parallel between Jesus' words in Matt. 11:25–27/ Luke 10:21–22 and Paul's teachings in 1 Corinthians 1–4. In the Gospel passages Jesus says,

> I thank thee, O Father, Lord of heaven and earth, because thou hast hid these things from the wise and prudent, and hast revealed them unto babes. Even so, Father: for so it seemed good in thy sight. All things are delivered unto me of my Father: and no man knoweth the Son, but the Father; neither knoweth any man the Father, save the Son, and he to whomsoever the Son will reveal him.

Wenham notices the exact same language and ideas scattered throughout the early chapters of First Corinthians. The ideas of God's wisdom being "hidden" (1 Cor. 2:7) from the "wise" (1:19, 27; cp. 2:1, 4) and the "prudent" (1:19), that God "revealed" these things (2:10) to "babes" (3:1), that it pleased God to do this (1:21), that no man knows the Father (1:21), and that one can only know Him by divine revelation (2:11), all together seem to indicate that Paul had some knowledge of the Gospel tradition when he wrote the letter.[14] What could be the common background? Unless there is some freak coincidence, Paul was certainly drawing from the same apostolic tradition which produced the written Gospels.

Paul also exhibits knowledge of Christ's teaching that his followers will identify with His suffering and death, and that they must take up the cross and lose their life for His sake.[15] The Gospel passages (Matt. 10:38; 16:24–26; Mark 8:34–36; Luke 9:23–26) undergird Paul's phrase, "I am crucified with Christ" (Gal. 2:20). Likewise Jesus' teaching that the disciples must be baptized with the same baptism as Him finds a repeti-

---

[13]David Wenham, *Paul: Follower of Jesus or Founder of Christianity?* (Grand Rapids, MI and Cambridge: Eerdmans, 1995). Also see his follow-up, *Paul and Jesus: The True Story* (Grand Rapids, MI and Cambridge: Eerdmans, 2002).

[14]Wenham, *Paul: Follower of Jesus or Founder of Christianity?*, 129–136.

[15]Wenham, *Paul: Follower of Jesus or Founder of Christianity?*, 159–164.

tion in Paul's teaching of participation in Christ's death and His body through the sacraments (Rom. 6:3–6; 8:17; 1 Cor. 10:16–17; 12:13; 2 Cor. 4:10). Jesus' reference is certainly to a challenging "baptism" of suffering and death, and Paul sees the Christian life as one of partaking in Christ's suffering, and he explains baptism in the same manner.

One very interesting example is Paul's teaching about the Lord's return in 1 Thess. 4:13–5:11. Not only does he explicitly refer to "a thief in the night" (1 Thess. 5:2) just as Christ Himself did (Matt. 24:43–44; Luke 12:39–40), but his words recall Jesus' parable of the ten virgins in Matt. 25:1–13. Both passages refer to the Lord being announced by a loud "cry" or "shout" (Matt 25:6; 1 Thess. 4:16). Also, both portray the saints as going out to "meet" Him (Matt. 25:6; 1 Thess. 4:17). The special Greek word used here for "to meet," only appears three times in the New Testament, two of which constitute this parallel.[16] Both contexts likewise speak of those who are asleep rising and of being "with" the Lord. This all indicates that Paul knew Christ's parable.[17] In fact, Paul himself says that the Thessalonians should "know perfectly" (1 Thess. 5:2) what he was teaching, which means that Jesus' parable and teaching about His return was part of the well-known apostolic tradition even before Paul.

Further, Paul's letters show the influence of the Gospel tradition in many other ways. Both speak of the original apostles (Matt. 10:2; 1 Cor. 9:1, 5), with apostolic authority (Matt. 10:1; 1 Cor. 9:4–5), to preach the Gospel (Matt. 10:7; 1 Cor. 9:14–16), to cast out devils and heal the sick (Matt. 10:8; 2 Cor. 12:12), to go especially to Israel (Matt. 10:5; Rom. 1:16; Gal. 2:8–9), to preach without payment (Matt. 10:5; 1 Cor. 9:18; 2 Cor. 11:7), yet the laborer deserves payment (Matt. 10:10; 1 Cor. 9:7–9, 14), to eat and drink (Luke 10:7; 1 Cor. 9:4), moreover to eat and drink whatever is set before them (Luke 10:8; 1 Cor. 10:27), to be "wise" yet "simple" (Matt. 10:16; Rom. 16:19). Furthermore there is a parallel in the teaching that those who reject the apostles thereby reject the One who sent them

---

[16]The third is Acts 28:15 where a group of believers go "to meet" Paul and his traveling companions.

[17]Wenham, *Paul and Jesus*, 96–102.

(Luke 10:16; 1 Thess. 4:8).[18] Yet even these numerous examples barely scratch the surface of the many Wenham has recorded.

Paul's Purpose

We must, however, consider a slightly different question as well. Even though these many instances show that Paul had intimate knowledge of the historical Jesus Christ and His teachings, they constitute a small portion of Paul's actual writing. What are we to make of the fact that Paul does not give a prominent role to the earthly life and ministry of Christ in the way that the Gospels do? Why did Paul not write a Gospel?

The answer is quite simple, and it relates to Paul's purposes in writing to begin with. As we have already seen, Paul often referred in his letters to the traditions his readers had already received. Paul handed down the apostolic tradition concerning Christ which was already being preached. Scholars call this early pre-written message *kerygma*, a word that comes from the Greek word for "preaching" or "proclamation." Christ Himself started Christian preaching (Mark 1:14–15). In the apostolic era much preaching was done probably before any writing, and most of the early spread of the Gospel should be attributed to this early activity of which we have little record. After his conversion, Paul himself immediately began to preach (Acts 9:19–22), and was himself building on the already-laid foundation of Christ (1 Cor. 3:11).[19] By the time he began to write his letters, preaching had well-established the Gospel as common knowledge among Christians.[20] In his epistles, Paul simply applies and expands upon what Jesus Himself had started. He is much less interested in Christ's day-to-day life than he is in Christ's place as the promised Messiah, the Central Figure of the Kingdom of

---

[18]Wenham, *Paul*, 199. This is a summary of his arguments in *Paul and Jesus*, 190–200.

[19]N. T. Wright, *What St. Paul Really Said: Was Paul of Tarsus the Real Founder of Christianity?* (Grand Rapids, MI: Eerdmans, 1997), 181.

[20]The life and work of Christ always had the priority in the spread of the Gospel. Thus we see Luke, for example, first giving his Gospel to Theophilus (Luke 1:3)—the "former treatise" of (Acts 1:1ff)—and then the history in Acts. See Michael Green, *Evangelism in the Early Church.* Grand Rapids, MI: Eerdmans, 2003 (1970), 439, note 41.

God, and the "real agent of all the tradition developing in the bosom of the apostolic church."[21] Thus we should not expect to see in Paul the kind of narrative of Christ's life that we find in the written Gospels. This was not Paul's purpose.

Nor was it his purpose to merely replicate the message that Christ himself preached. Time had moved on, and Paul now proclaimed the fulfilment of what Christ preached about Himself and the Kingdom of God. The whole point of the early apostolic preaching, including Paul's, centered on the fact that what Christ predicted of Himself was now a fact—He had been raised from the dead by the Father and made Lord and Christ (Acts 2:25–36). Had the apostles come out merely repeating Christ's message—such as the sermon on the mount, the parables, the promises that the kingdom was coming, etc.—they would have been missing the point of it all. N. T. Wright explains,

> [If] Paul had simply trotted out, parrot-fashion, every line of Jesus' teaching—if he had repeated the parables, if he had tried to do again what Jesus did in announcing and inaugurating the kingdom—he would not have been endorsing Jesus, as an appropriate and loyal follower should. He would have been denying him. Someone who copies exactly what a would-be Messiah does is himself trying to be a Messiah; which means denying the earlier claim.[22]

The fact that we find Paul and the other apostles preaching Jesus crucified and resurrected, and not merely reruns of Jesus' lessons, means that they saw themselves as faithful *servants* of Christ, not as writers of new literary myths.

Rather, when we come to the letters of Paul we find him engaged in applying his Gospel of the crucified, risen, and ascended Jesus to the concrete situations and problems that the churches faced. In this process, Paul certainly would have been expanding Christian doctrine every day. "What we are looking for is not a parallelism between two

---

[21]Fitzmyer, *Pauline Theology: A Brief Sketch*, 13.
[22]N. T. Wright, *What St. Paul Really Said*, 180–181.

abstract messages. It is the *appropriate continuity* between two people living, and conscious of living, at different points in the eschatological time table."[23] Paul was simply championing the Kingdom of God on the resurrected heels of its King. He pushed to drive the Gospel into new territory regularly while constantly writing back to his previous converts in order to encourage further growth of the victory over their hearts. And yet while he is so engaged in cutting-edge Christianity, his teaching perfectly joins up with that of Jesus Christ. Wright again:

> [It] should be comparatively easy to work through the actions and message of Jesus, and the agenda and letters of Paul, and to show that there is between them, not (of course) a one-for-one correspondence, but a coherence, an appropriate correlation, an integration that allows fully for the radically different perspective of each. Jesus was bringing Israel's history to its climax; Paul was living in the light of that climax.[24]

It should not surprise us, then, to see the great climactic events of Jesus' life dominating Paul's letters. Paul lays the foundation first and then the several stones upon Him. Besides, the vast majority of pastoral problems find their resolution in the grander themes of the Gospel: humility, self-sacrifice, perseverance, faith, hope, love, etc. Paul simply asked his readers to live in the light of the fact that the historical Jesus Christ is the resurrected and ascended Lord and Savior.

Conclusion

This chapter has addressed the first of the two main accusations against the biblical writings of the apostle Paul, that Paul had only a mythical Christ in mind when he wrote. On the contrary, Paul quite clearly has a view of Christ that is consistent with the historical Gospel accounts. He sees Jesus as a real human person; divine, to be sure, but divine and yet fully entered into history, and "manifested in the flesh" (1 Tim. 3:16). The pagan critics greatly weaken their case when they make the extrava-

---

[23]N. T. Wright, *What St. Paul Really Said,* 181.
[24]N. T. Wright, *What St. Paul Really Said,* 182.

gant claim that Paul did not know a historical Jesus. The Bible speaks too clearly to the contrary. With their wild accusation the critics prove that they have not read Paul closely, and have not challenged their own presuppositions.

We have also seen that Paul's main purpose in writing was to further the Kingdom by faithfully applying the truths about Jesus the Messiah to the world. He had no idea of writing a narrative of Jesus' life, but to preach the truth of that life and establish churches where the Savior would reach and rule the lives of His people.

We must still, then, answer the second objection, that Paul was primarily a pagan thinker, combating Jewishness of all forms. The next chapter will show that such a view fails on as many counts as the first objection has.

Was Paul a Pagan Thinker?

Paul was fighting to free the Jesus mysteries from unnecessary ties to Judaism and to make them attractive to more Hellenized Jews like himself . . . a highly Hellenized Jew traveling from one Pagan city to another.[1]

The events with which the Gospel is concerned took place upon a stage largely prepared by the history which is recorded in the Old Testament. . . . The questions to which the New Testament gives the answer are the questions asked by the Old Testament. The hopes and aspirations which are the burden of the prophets are those whose fulfilment is declared by apostles and evangelists. We have described the New Testament as the record of a divine revelation in history. More properly, it is the New Testament read in relation to the Old that constitutes such a record.[2]

IN THE LIGHT of what Paul himself tells us about his view of Jesus Christ as an historical figure, the mystery-religion theory falls under even more shame. Its failure can be demonstrated further. Paul, the critics hold, is primarily a Greek thinker influenced by the schools of philosophy and mystery religions at his home town of Tarsus. When he came to

---

[1]Timothy Freke and Peter Gandy, *The Jesus Mysteries: Was the "Original Jesus" a Pagan God?* (New York: Three Rivers Press, 1999), 203.

[2]C. H. Dodd, "The New Testament." in *The Study of Theology*, ed. Kenneth E. Kirk, 217–246 (New York and London: Harper and Brothers, 1939), 233.

the Gospel as it was being preached, he infused it with all kinds of pagan concepts drawn from his early years. Since the Gospels had probably not yet been written, Paul's strongly Hellenized version of Jesus spread and formed the basis of later writing and thought. This belief is foundational to the mystery-religion theory. But does Paul really exhibit such Greek influence in his writings? What do we know about the background influences on the apostle Paul?

Paul versus Pagan Idolatry

To begin with Paul must have been a very well cultured and educated man. His ability to travel the entire Roman Empire preaching the Gospel, planting churches, training leaders, interacting with all types of people, arguing in courts and before philosophers, operating in prison and from house arrest, writing letters, settling disputes, etc., shows him to be a multi-talented, versatile genius of thought and social skill. Few people could compile such a resume without a great amount of character.

Not only this but Paul exhibits specific knowledge of local cultures in many of his letters and in the accounts about him. For example, when confronting the Stoic and Epicurean philosophers on Mars' Hill, Paul quotes their own poets—Epimenides and Aratus—to them (Acts 17:28), and thus appears to be versed in more than one pagan writer.[3] He shows familiarity with Stoic vocabulary, style, and thought in Romans 1–2[4] and again quotes Epimenides in Titus 1:12. From such usage it appears that Paul must have spent lots of time in the Greek literature of his day.

Getting below the surface, however, provides a somewhat different picture. The context of Paul's confrontation in Acts 17 begins with him being moved at the great *idolatry* of the city of Athens: "While Paul waited for [Silas and Timotheus] at Athens, his spirit was stirred in him, when he saw the city wholly given to idolatry" (Acts 17:16). Paul was not merely playing philosopher as an intellectual game, but he "disputed" first with

---

[3]See Greg Bahnsen, *Always Ready: Directions for Defending the Faith,* ed. Robert R. Booth (Texarkana, AR: Covenant Media Foundation, 1996), 260–262.

[4]Richard J Gibson, "Paul and the Evangelization of the Stoics" in *The Gospel to the Nations: Perspectives on Paul's Mission,* eds. Mark Thompson and Peter Bolt (Downers Grove, IL: InterVarsity Press, 2000), 316, 323.

the Jews and then with anyone in the market who would listen (Acts 17:17). The subjects were idolatry, false worship, and superstition. Once he drew the attention of the philosophers, he confronted them also on the same charge. But he was able to quote from their own poets to drive the point home.

Why was Paul the Jew so quickly able to recite pagan poetry? Aratus' poem enjoyed wide circulation, since he wrote one of the most popular textbooks on astronomy for his day.[5] Every student in Greek and later in Latin would have read his verses. The book was read as widely as Homer in the schools. If Paul was schooled during his early years in Tarsus then he, too, might well have memorized it. It would naturally have come to mind when trying to relate to the Greek thinkers. In their culture, "Everyone would have known Aratus's poem."[6] This understanding makes Paul's argument all the more powerful: he undermined the proud professional philosophers of his day with what every school-child would have known! Paul simply used well-known Greek poetry to challenge the misguided thinking of the Athenians.

Furthermore, Paul gave his challenge in an unmistakably Jewish-Christian manner. So much attention has been given to the fact that he actually quoted Greek literature that scholars have often missed the larger picture of Paul's speech. "What a Stoic audience might not realize is the extent to which Paul draws on Old Testament creation and temple theology (Gen. 1:1–25; Exod. 20:11, 1 Kgs. 8:27; Is. 42:5; 57:15–16; Amos 5:12–23)."[7] The entire meeting at Mars' Hill represents a typically Jewish attitude against pagan idolatry. Paul simply commandeered their own language to preach the Gospel to them.[8] Far from showing Greek influence in Paul's thought, the scene depicts Greek thought under the judgment of the conquering King Jesus Christ (Acts 17:30–1).

---

[5]Everett Ferguson. *Background of Early Christianity*, 3rd ed. (Grand Rapids, MI: Eerdmans, 2003), 356.

[6]Ferguson, *Background of Early Christianity*, 356.

[7]Gibson, "Paul and the Evangelization of the Stoics," 320.

[8]Gibson, "Paul and the Evangelization of the Stoics," 323.

Paul and Old Testament Theology

We have to immediately suspect, then, those arguments that would force Paul into a Greek mold over against a Jewish background. This is not to say that Paul was not familiar with Hellenistic culture—he certainly shows that he was. Arguments, however, that force Paul to be primarily a Hellenistic thinker have to ignore or radically redefine too much of what he said. Thankfully, recent times have seen a blossoming of thought regarding the Jewish origin and background of everything about the Apostle Paul. This new and welcome emphasis in Pauline studies complies more with the apostle's own words. He said, "I am verily a man which am a Jew, born in Tarsus . . . yet brought up in this city at the feet of Gamaliel, and taught according to the perfect manner of the law of the fathers" (Acts 22:3). He also emphasized his Jewish background to the Philippians. He wrote that he was, "Circumcised the eighth day, of the stock of Israel, of the tribe of Benjamin, an Hebrew of the Hebrews; as touching the law, a Pharisee" (Phil. 3:5). Paul's ready identification of his roots directs us to the source of his world-view, and it is not pagan.

In this respect, the most recent New Testament studies have provided the Christian world with some of the finest scholarship in decades. N. T. Wright[9] follows a precedent set by W. D. Davies in his 1948 *Paul and Rabbinic Judaism,* which sees Paul primarily as "a Jewish rabbi who believed that Jesus of Nazareth was the Jewish Messiah,"[10] and, "Rejects outright the attempt to derive Paul's thought from Hellenism."[11] Working from this viewpoint—which has been greatly developed since Davies—Wright proceeds to exegete sections of Paul's letters that leap out with a fresh clarity.[12]

---

[9]Wright has drawn some criticism, especially from parts of the Fundamentalist, Lutheran, and Reformed worlds, over the issue of justification. Whether the critics have a correct perception of him on the matter has not been hammered out. This particular debate aside, Wright's New Testament scholarship is currently some of the best in the business and should be valued as such. He is beating the liberal critics at their own game.

[10]N. T. Wright. *What St. Paul Really Said: Was Paul of Tarsus the Real Founder of Christianity?* (Grand Rapids, MI: Eerdmans, 1997), 16.

[11]N. T. Wright. *What St. Paul Really Said,* 16.

[12]The following section is taken from Wright's *What St. Paul Really Said,* 63–75.

In many places we can see Paul referring to the classic Jewish tradition of monotheism. This tradition includes all the obvious features of the Old Testament doctrine of God: it confronts any idea of God that does not include him as the good Creator of the physical universe, and thus it contradicts the dualists, Platonists, and gnostics. It confronts any earthly ruler who would make a claim to sovereignty or divinity, and thus it rejects Caesar as lord. Likewise, it rejects the whole spectrum of pagan gods and myths both as nonsense and as idolatry. This teaching is summarized in that foundational confession of Judaism, the *shema*: "Hear, O Israel: The LORD our God, the LORD *is* one! You shall love the LORD your God with all your heart" (Deut. 6:4–5 NKJV).

It is just this verse that Paul draws upon when he confronts idolatry in Corinth, but he adds a new twist: he elevates Jesus to the status of one Lord as well.[13] He begins in 1 Cor. 8:1–3 by teaching that the worship of God is not a matter of mere knowledge, but of love ("Love the LORD your God. . ."). He then reveals a typically Old Testament attitude toward pagan idolatry: "We know that an idol is nothing in the world, and that there is none other God but one" (1 Cor. 8:4). Then he drops the bomb on every theory that tries to paint him or early Christianity as Hellenistic: against the so-called "gods many, and lords many" of the pagans, Paul quotes the *Shema*: "But to us *there is but* one God, the Father, of whom *are* all things, and we in him; and one Lord Jesus Christ, by whom *are* all things, and we in him" (1 Cor. 8:6). In order to see how Paul places Jesus within the monotheism of the Jewish tradition, Wright places the verses side-by-side:[14]

The Lord our God	One God . . . the Father . . .
The Lord is One	One Lord . . . Jesus Christ . . .
(Deuteronomy 6:4)	(1 Corinthians 8:6)

Now we have a true parallel! Paul's mission to the Corinthians was one of a Jew, convinced that Jesus was the Messiah, prosecuting that mes-

---

[13]N. T. Wright. *What St. Paul Really Said*, 65–67.
[14]N. T. Wright. *What St. Paul Really Said*, 66.

sage against the idolatry of the pagan world. Right when we would expect Paul to try to find some common point of departure with his pagan audience (as sometimes he does), he falls back upon the most basic of Jewish Scriptures and places Jesus squarely in the middle of it.[15] Wright adds, "This verse is one of the most genuinely revolutionary bits of theology ever written."[16] Paul at once surpasses Judaism with Christianity, and rejects pagan polytheism and idolatrous practices.

A second example[17] also finds Paul placing Jesus as the object of prominent Old Testament Scripture. To the Philippians Paul writes, "That at the name of Jesus every knee should bow, of *things* in heaven, and *things* in earth, and *things* under the earth: And *that* every tongue should confess that Jesus Christ *is* Lord, to the glory of God the Father" (Phil. 2:10–11). This verse directly references Isaiah 45:23, which in context proclaims Old Testament monotheism against all other claims of divinity—"I am God, and there is none else" (Is. 45:22). Paul had this stark declaration in mind when he set Jesus Christ before the Philippians. He saw Jesus as the fulfilment of this Old Testament claim, and thus set Jesus equal to that singular God.

The theology involved with this Philippians passage also corresponds to the larger vision of Isaiah 40–55. In Phil. 2:5–9, Paul portrays Jesus as leaving behind the glories of heaven and pure godhood in order to become an incarnate servant and to suffer death upon the cross. This teaching parallels the suffering servant of Isaiah 52:13–53:12. Paul likewise presents Jesus parallel to the "Holy One of Israel" who is exalted over all the earth, including the gentiles (Is. 54:3–5; 55:5). The Old Testament background is so clear that it seems as if Paul had Isaiah opened next to him while he wrote the Philippian epistle.

Wright adds to these two Pauline passages Colossians 1:15–20, in which Paul presents Christ as the Creator of the world, Sustainer of the world, Firstborn from the dead, Redeemer of "all things," and Head of the Church. This resume concurs with that of the Yaweh of the Old Tes-

---

[15]N. T. Wright. *What St. Paul Really Said*, 67.
[16]N. T. Wright. *What St. Paul Really Said*, 67.
[17]N. T. Wright. *What St. Paul Really Said*, 67–69.

tament which the Jews had held against paganism for centuries. Add to this a passage such as 2 Cor. 4:6—"For God, who commanded the light to shine out of darkness, hath shined in our hearts, to *give* the light of the knowledge of the glory of God in the face of Jesus Christ"—in which Paul recalls Genesis 1:3–4 in a New Testament context. Paul's Christianity arises from the Old Testament foundation and not from any hint of Greek philosophy or mystery religions. In fact, the whole mystery religion idea looks pretty silly when compared to the rich background Paul had in the Old Covenant.

"Son of God" and "Lord"

When we begin to see the Old Testament force behind Paul's theology, then many other aspects of his writing begin naturally to fall into place. Whereas so many liberal critics have argued that Paul took such phrases such as "Son of God" and "Lord" from well-known pagan backgrounds, we can now see that those titles have a more likely home in the Old Testament Scriptures. They were common discussion among the Jews of first-century Palestine;[18] but more importantly they have very clear Scriptural antecedents.

For example, the title "Son of God" grows directly out of the Old Testament. Even though it had been used by pagans to describe Pharaohs, Eastern monarchs, Caesars, great men, and mythical heroes (all for slightly different reasons),[19] Paul had no need (nor desire) to follow those idolatrous traditions. Rather he would have naturally learned the phrase from the Jewish Scriptures. It appears in various contexts throughout the Old Testament (Gen. 6:2; Job 1:6; 2:1; 38:7; Ps. 29:1; Dn. 3:25). Among the more outstanding examples stands Exodus 4:22, where Moses is instructed to speak, "Thus saith the LORD, Israel *is* my son, *even* my firstborn." Sound familiar? Compare Romans 8:29 where Paul refers to God's son as the "firstborn." Also among Old Testament passages "Son of God" describes the King of Israel (2 Sam. 7:14, Ps. 2:7–12; 89:26–7), and we can see how easily this fits with Paul's knowledge of

---

[18]Fitzmyer, *Pauline Theology: A Brief Sketch*, 7–8.
[19]Fitzmyer, *Pauline Theology: A Brief Sketch*, 31–22.

Jesus Christ as both Son of God and King. It should not surprise us at all then, to see Paul calling Jesus Christ the Son of God and the seed of David in the flesh (Rom 1:3–4).[20] This same incarnate Son of God came to die for sinners and lead them to become adopted sons of God themselves (Rom. 8:3, 14–19).

The second title, "Lord," has been even more highly impugned even though its uniqueness as a Christian claim stands out even more clearly. While it is often stated that Caesar worship held a monopoly on the title in New Testament times, that was far from the case. Hans Lietzmann, who more than once urges mystery-religion influence on Christian doctrine, sees something genuinely exclusive in the early Christian claim, "Jesus is Lord." Whereas it had been part of Emperor worship to claim "Caesar is Lord," the Christians often refused and turned their praise to Christ. Lietzmann sees in Paul a very early form of that simple creed: "Paul expressed the Christian antithesis to the pagan polytheistic faith in the sentence 'Yet to us there is one God . . .and one Lord, Jesus Christ.'"[21] In typical Pauline fashion this teaching challenged both Jews (by stretching monotheism to include Jesus) and pagans (by rejecting the polytheism, mystery worship and state worship all for one God, and only the one Jesus Christ). That Lietzmann, a liberal, would see at least part of this is telling,[22] but much more to the story remains.

The reason the term "Lord" so readily applied to Christ is that it had a definite Old Testament precedent, especially in the Greek language. In the Greek translation of the Old Testament—known as the Septuagint, or LXX, and which was begun in the third century before Christ—the Greek word for "Lord" (*kyrios*) is the normal replacement for both the name of God (Yaweh) and His title (Adonai). Thus the Greek version of

---

[20]All of this is also noted in Fitzmyer, *Pauline Theology: A Brief Sketch*, 32–33.

[21]Hans Lietzmann, *Volume II. The Founding of the Universal Church.* In *A History of the Early Church* (vol. 1), trans. Bertram Lee Woolf (Cleveland and New York: World Publishing Company, 1967), 105–106. The reference to Paul is from 1 Corinthians 8:6. See Lietzmann, *A History of the Early Church*, 105, note 8.

[22]Lietzmann does try to imply that the Christian confession arose from copying the pagans, "by the congregation all speaking in unison when they were seized by ecstacy." (Lietzmann, *A History of the Early Church*, 105), but he provides no support for this supposition. Paul did confront such pagan worship in Acts 19:34.

the Old Testament which Paul so often quotes uses the very term for "Lord" that Paul passes on to Christ. This not only proves that Paul did not need the pagan traditions to derive the title from, but it again exalts the person of Christ to the status of the Old Testament Yaweh. "The use of *Kyrios* for Jesus in the early Church bestowed on him the ineffable name of Yaweh in its LXX form."[23]

The Growing Scholarly Consensus

Once all has been taken into account, Paul's Jewish background stands out so clearly that it takes a Ph.D. in Higher Criticism to miss it. Against such folly N. T. Wright concludes,

> It is easier by far, historically, exegetically and theologically, to suppose that Paul the Jew reflected Jewishly, in the light of the Jewish scriptures on the one hand and the resurrection of Jesus on the other, on the claim that Jesus was indeed the Jewish Messiah, in whom the promises had been fulfilled.[24]

This view has also been the summary of some of the best historians who have tackled the early Church in our time. Once Oxford professor Henry Chadwick writes, "From the first the Church was deeply conscious of its solidarity with Israel, and of the continuity of God's action in the past with his present activity in Jesus of Nazareth and his followers."[25] W. H. C. Frend wonders how Paul ever succeeded in the gentile world because,

> People more Jewish-looking than Paul and his companions were evidently difficult to imagine . . . his recorded thoughts in his letters and his actions in Acts show little evidence of insight into the workings of the non-Jewish mind that he needed in order to succeed.[26]

---

[23]Fitzmyer, 37; N. T. Wright. *What St. Paul Really Said,* 71.

[24]N. T. Wright, *What St. Paul Really Said,* 175.

[25]Henry Chadwick, *The Early Church* in *The Pelican History of the Church* (Harmondsworth, Middlesex, England: Penguin Books, 1977 (1967), 1:12.

[26]W. H. C. Frend, *The Rise of Christianity* (Philadelphia: Fortress Press, 1984), 98.

A few scholars have responded to this more Jewish understanding of Paul's theology as well as the growing amount of archaeological data since WWII, and many more have begun to follow. The consensus is growing that Paul was primarily an Old Testament thinker living in the light of Christ's resurrection. He went on a mission to preach "to the Jew first, and also to the Greek" that which the "Jews had always believed: that 'the gods of the nations are idols, but our God made the heavens' (Psalms 96:5)."[27]

Wright reminds us of the early Church heretic Marcion, who rejected the Old Testament and hated its Creator God. He rejected as well any part of the New Testament that relied too closely to Old Testament thought, and he only retained selections from Paul and Luke which he could harmonize with Plato's philosophy. It should not surprise us that someone who follows the Platonic rejection of matter and history would chop up the Bible in this way. For anyone who followed this particular Greek understanding, "To reject the Old Testament and its doctrine of creation led inevitably in a gnostic direction."[28] The liberals and radicals, however, argue that only Marcion truly understood Paul, who belonged to the Greek world over against the Jewish. Wright counters, "This is a dangerous half-truth, and the wrong half at that."[29] Like their forerunner Marcion, the critics of today must ignore all that we have seen of Paul's indebtedness to the Old Testament in order to make their case. With the unfathomable riches of the Old Testament beneath all that Paul did, "[T]heories about Mithras and Herakles are rendered as unnecessary as they were in any case unlikely."[30]

The views that portray Paul as dabbling in mystery religions and which rely upon the work of the old German history-of-religions school have been left behind academically. The theory has been barren for decades. Wright critiques journalist A. N. Wilson for following such outdated fancies in his popular book on Paul: "It is not so much that Wilson is try-

---

[27]Wright, *What St. Paul Really Said*, 75.

[28]Michael Green. *Evangelism in the Early Church* (Grand Rapids, MI: Eerdmans, [1970] 2003), 196.

[29]Wright, *What St. Paul Really Said*, 171.

[30]Wright, *What St. Paul Really Said*, 172.

ing to lock the door after the horse has bolted. He is trying to ride across open country on a hobby-horse."[31] The point stands for all the mystery-religion followers. The more historical and archaeological evidence that turns up, the more the original formulators of the theories are proven wrong, and the more a Jewish background accounts for the ideas of early Christians.[32] The critics may claim to stand on the shoulders of giants, but they refuse to see that those giants long ago sank in the quicksand of their own making. The critics are now in up to their necks.

Paul's Theology in Action

A few theological themes in Paul's work surface from their Old Testament background into particular instances that contrast against the pagan world. In Acts 17:18, the Athenians question Paul for preaching "strange gods"[33] called "Jesus" and "resurrection." The philosophers misunderstood that Paul's terms to both refer to deities, and in doing so called them "strange" or "foreign." This shows that these Greeks had no understanding of "resurrection" either as a doctrine or as a deity, before Paul preached to them. This subtle fact makes it highly unlikely that Paul drew *his* doctrine from *their* culture.

Rather, he could easily draw it from Old Testament precedents. "Paul's beliefs concerning the resurrection were Pharisaic, traceable back to Daniel 12:2 if not beyond."[34] Daniel 12:2 definitely foreshadows the early Church doctrine. It says, "And many of them that sleep in the dust shall awake, some to everlasting life, and some to shame *and* everlasting contempt." Jesus himself alludes to this verse when he speaks of the future resurrection of the dead (John 5:28–9). Other Old Testament examples stand out as well. In Isaiah 53 the account of the suffering

---

[31]Wright, *What St. Paul Really Said*, 172.

[32]Frend, *The Rise of Christianity*, 2–3.

[33]Wright, *What St. Paul Really Said,* 176. The Greek word here which is translated "gods" could better be translated "demons." The word is *daimonion* (not *theos*) and is nowhere else in Scripture translated as "gods," though such might make sense from the pagan's perspective.

[34]Frend, *The Rise of Christianity*, 98. Also see N. T. Wright, *The Resurrection of the Son of God* (Minneapolis: Fortress Press, 2003), 109ff.

servant implies his death and resurrection. Isaiah 53:7–9 speaks of the servant's death and burial, and Isaiah 53:10–12 relates his triumph and blessing after his death and burial.[35] Apparently something happens to render the dead and buried servant able to triumph and "prolong his days." Likewise, Hosea prophesies of God's raising His people up in the third day (Hosea 6:2) and of God rescuing them from the grave and redeeming them from death (13:14). Paul quotes this part of Hosea in 1 Corinthians 15:55. Finally, what Sunday school child could not remember Ezekiel's vision of the valley of dry bones (Ezek. 37)? God asked the prophet, "Can these bones live?" (37:3), and then proves that He can resurrect them. God then promises, "O my people, I will open your graves, and cause you to come up out of your graves, and bring you into the land of Israel" (37:12). While the immediate context of Ezekiel is an allegory of God restoring his people from captivity, the idea of physical bodily resurrection stands out clearly.

So Paul could honestly write to the Corinthians, "For I delivered unto you first of all that which I also received, how that Christ died for our sins *according to the scriptures*; And that he was buried, and that he rose again the third day *according to the scriptures*." (1 Cor. 15:3–4).[36] The Scriptures provided all that Paul needed to back his teaching of Christ's resurrection.

Positing a mystery-religion origin for Paul's theology misses the entire thrust of his claims about Jesus. The mystery religions had vague, really no ideas of a god returning bodily from death. What ideas they had were ethereal and mythological, and above all, they were syncretistic. They built upon other myths from other regions, renaming deities and retelling the old lore to suit new circumstances. But for Paul, the resurrection was historical, final, and consummate. The Old Testament parallels are all tied to physical people, physical land, and real history. The resurrection of Jesus has no other parallel and could not be set along side any pagan superstition. It is not surprising that "superstition"

---

[35] Wright, *The Resurrection of the Son of God*, 116.

[36] Wright begins his chapter on death and resurrection in the Old Testament. See Wright, *The Resurrection of the Son of God*, 85.

drove Paul to encounter the Athenians (Acts 17:30–1): for Paul, "Jesus the Jewish Messiah was the reality of which all other pagan idols were the parody."[37]

Paul taught the resurrection of Christ as the climax of traditional Jewish eschatology. The word "eschatology," here, is not meant merely the doctrine of the "end times," but the totality of God's redemptive work as it breaks into and drives all of history. Both the scholars and the popular writers have missed the point and have contradicted themselves by claiming that Paul was a connoisseur of the pagan mysteries on the one hand, while yet holding a decisive Old Testament eschatology on the other. Paul viewed the death and resurrection of Christ as God's predestined redemptive events breaking into history as promised by the Scriptures, and this view completely contradicts the *mythological* perspective of the mysteries. Again, we have history verse myth. Liberal scholars and atheists have either labored to square a circle by stuffing Paul's Old Testament eschatology into a pagan Greek mold of their own theorizing, or have happily ignored it altogether. Even the liberal Albert Schweitzer defended Paul against them:

> Since all [of Paul's] conceptions and thoughts are rooted in eschatology, those who labour to explain him on the basis of Hellenism, are like a man who should bring water from a long distance in leaky watering-cans in order to water a garden lying beside a stream.[38]

The method of the apostle Paul, the rest of the apostles, and the early Church for that matter, sees Jesus Christ as the historical fulfilment of all the Old Testament promises. The doctrine of Paul is nothing less than the New Covenant in Christ Jesus as the fulfilment of God's salvation history.

An endless stream of unbelieving critics try hard to deny this with various approaches, all with no lasting success. Today, the scholarly world is returning to this original and fruitful approach to the New Tes-

---

[37]Wright, *What St. Paul Really Said*, 176.
[38]Quoted in Wright, *What St. Paul Really Said*, 175.

tament as the history of salvation. F. F. Bruce engaged in just this sort of biblical study in his *New Testament Development of Old Testament Themes*. After reminding us that one of the best liberal scholars in the twentieth century, Rudolf Bultmann, totally rejected any historical continuity between the Testaments, as well as any need for an historical basis for the New Testament, Bruce proceeds:

> This is not how I read the New Testament. As I read it, it not merely presupposes but positively and repeatedly emphasizes the continuity which Professor Bultmann cannot admit, a continuity which is expressed preeminently in the history of salvation.[39]

Such a reading is welcome today: it returns us to the type of biblical work that the apostles and early Church fathers did, and it redirects our efforts to studying what the Bible itself says rather than vacuous theories *about* the Bible.

Looking to the Old Testament first provides the background for nearly every Christian doctrine, and retires every claim of mystery-religion borrowing. Instead of digging up obscure myths of which we have only tiny fragments and glimpses, in order to understand Christian resurrection, we look to such biblical passages as we have just seen. The Lord's Supper likewise grows directly out of the Jewish Passover. Paul notes that Christ is our Passover, sacrificed for us (1 Cor. 5:7), and the references to eating Christ's flesh in John 6 make sense in relation to the Jews eating the Passover lamb. Moreover, the very wording of the New Testament formula for the Supper parallels Moses in Exodus 16:15, "This is the bread which the LORD hath given you to eat"; and also in Exodus 24:8, "Behold the blood of the covenant, which the LORD hath made with you concerning all these words."[40] Baptism also replaces a former Old Testament sacrament. Paul links baptism and circumcision (Col. 2:11–12) and the rite remains sacramentally similar. Both symbolize the removal of uncleanness: circumcision by cutting it away, baptism

---

[39]F. F. Bruce, *New Testament Development of Old Testament Themes* (Grand Rapids, MI: Eerdmans, [1968] 1977), 21. Wright, *What St. Paul Really Said*, 36ff.

[40]Arthur Darby Nock, *Early Gentile Christianity and Its Hellenistic Background* (New York: Harper Torchbooks, 1964), 125.

by washing. The change between the Testaments shows God's mercy: replacing the bloody rite with an easy one.[41]

In some cases, when they follow what the Bible says, even the famous liberal scholars have arrived at a proper conclusion. "History-of-religions school" leader Adolph Harnack saw the Old Testament connection in relation to the Lord's Supper. He wrote,

> As an act of sacrifice, all the [official terms] which the Old Testament applied to sacrifice could be applied to it, and all the wealth of ideas which the Old Testament connects with sacrifice could be transferred to it. One cannot say that anything absolutely foreign was therewith introduced into the ordinance.[42]

Would that more critics began with Moses and worked forward, instead of assuming the importance of mystery religions first.

Once the proper view of New Testament theology is set then we can see how Paul actually approached pagan religions: as idolaters who needed to repent. But he did so in such a way as to use what he could to relate to their understanding, and transfer as much of the true history of salvation—beginning in the Old Testament—to his hearers. Along these lines, a fabulous piece of scholarship has been produced via a doctoral dissertation by Susan Elliott entitled *Cutting Too Close for Comfort: Paul's Letter to the Galatians in its Anatolian Context*. While I do not agree with everything she says, or does not say, her method and general conclusions are well worth noting. She first asks what the religious mind of Paul's pagan hearers would likely be. What baggage did they have when the Gospel reached them? Galatia was a rural, mountainous region im-

---

[41]I realize that there is much more to sacramentology than I have stated. Baptism symbolizes more than just cleansing from sin. The point here is to show Old Testament precedent, not to produce a treatise on the sacraments. Nevertheless, writers are often hastily judged on what they do not say, so I have included this qualifier to put my selectiveness into perspective.

[42]Adolph Harnack, *History of Dogma*, seven volumes bound as four, trans. Neil Buchanan (New York: Dover Publications, [1900] 1961), 1:211. Harnack goes on to doubt whether the founder of Christianity intended the sacrament to be understood as a sacrifice or a memorial, but he indeed notes the Old Testament precedent clearly. I have translated the latin phrase *termini technici* as "official terms."

mersed in paganism and the worship of Cybele "the Great Mother of the Mountains." In that region "every city had its temple to the Mother."[43] A central aspect of Cybele worship was castration and its caste of eunuch priests. What would have been running through converts' minds when certain Judaizing brethren came to their local church urging circumcision? The question is well worth asking whether Paul was cutting down two fallacious views at once—Jewish and pagan—when he uses half the letter to argue against circumcision. In fact, when Paul says, "I would they were even *cut off* which trouble you" (Gal. 5:12), he uses a stronger Greek word for "cut off" than is normally used in the New Testament for "circumcision." Was he alluding to anything in particular? Likewise, since the cultists worshipped the "Mother of the Mountains," Paul's reference to two mothers, Sarah and Agar, may have double impact. Sarah and Agar, both mothers representing two covenants. Paul ties Agar to a mountain—Sinai—and links her to the bondage of the old covenant. Sarah, in contrast, represents the covenant of freedom. This would have obvious impact with a Jewish audience, but the pagans, converts from Cybele, would have immediately heard Paul replacing the old Mother of the Mountain with a "Jerusalem which is above" (see Gal. 4:22–31).

Elliott's work has much to commend it despite its overly academic style (dissertations just do not convert well into popular books). She asks the kinds of questions that New Testament scholars need to ask. What were local receptions of the Gospel really like? By comparing biblical theology with what we know from historical studies we can learn a lot about the early Church's mission. We need "an examination of early Christianity at particular points of contact with other particular cults."[44] None of the proponents of mystery-religion theories has even thought about doing this, let alone produced any historical or biblical studies along these lines. They content themselves with misrepresenting Paul to the point of slander, missing the force of the Old Testament, and over-

---

[43]Susan Elliott, *Cutting Too Close for Comfort: Paul's Letter to the Galatians in its Anatolian Cultic Context. Journal for the New Testament Supplement Series*, No. 248. ed. Stanley E. Porter (London and New York: T& T Clark International, 2003), 109.

[44]Elliott, *Cutting Too Close for Comfort*, 12.

generalizing the mystery religions themselves. I suppose Paul would hope that they were cut off.

Conclusion

This chapter has labored the idea that Paul was primarily a Jewish thinker, working from the Old Testament promises and seeing Jesus Christ as their fulfilment. He had no need to pilfer pagan mysteries or any other pagan contribution. As an Old Testament thinker he saw them as idols that needed to be confronted and torn down. The vast storehouse of ideas found in the Old Covenant Scriptures provided all that Paul and the other apostles needed to found the Christian faith as we know it.

The wealth of Scriptural evidence we have seen in this chapter and the previous one, supports the two ideas that 1) Paul knew a historical Jesus, and 2) he knew Him within God's salvation history founded in the Old Testament. The two themes can stand to be labored, for they cut the heart out of the mystery-religion theory. If Paul is no longer wrongly seen as hocking history in favor of a spacey mythological hero, and as a paramour of pagan mystery religions, then the air has escaped from the critics' case. Their fortress deflates and the glorious body of Christ which they have tried to obscure stands as it always has: traditional, miraculous, and eternal.

It remains, then, only to see the various machinations by which the frauds have kept their case afloat so long. The next chapter will outline the fallacies in the reasoning of mystery-religion theory, as well as summarize and illustrate the case against it.

6

Whom Can You Trust?

It is the winners who write history—their way. No wonder, then, that the traditional accounts of the origins of Christianity first defined the terms (naming themselves "orthodox" and their opponents "heretics")[1]

History will be kind to me, for I intend to write it.
— *attr. Winston Churchill*

Thou shalt not bear false witness against thy neighbor (Exodus 20:16).

THE CLAIM THAT only winners write the history books holds some truth and has been touted to a large extent by critics in reference to the early church. The argument emphasizes the power of who tells the story. Whoever writes it can edit and mold it in such a way that makes them look good and their enemies bad. Of course, this presupposes some desire to fudge the facts just a bit, but most scholars are willing to accept that even Christians (dare we admit) have been guilty of such. One problem, however, is that the complaint of winners writing history silently implies that the truth is *necessarily* lost or suppressed in

---

[1]Elaine Pagels, *The Gnostic Gospels*. Quoted in Timothy Freke and Peter Gandy, *The Jesus Mysteries: Was the "Original Jesus" a Pagan God?* (New York: Three Rivers Press, 1999), 11.

the process. While there may be examples in history of this happening, it is by no means automatic that all historical writing suffers from some fatal defect of overwhelming prejudice.[2] The issue, in the big picture, is not whether the winners write the history or not, but whether they write it *correctly*.

A greater problem yet attends this one: the ability to trust *any* historical writer. How can we know for sure that what any random "scholar" says is believable? As an illustration, take the quotation from Churchill that begins this chapter. How do we know that Churchill actually said this? Well, it sounds like something Churchill would say, and it displays his famous wit. A quick internet search turns up dozens of sites that say Churchill said it. It seems obvious. But a little questioning drives the point home. Not one of those dozens of sites gives a *source* for the quotation; and nowhere on the internet have I seen one provided. In fact, I further searched ten different dictionaries of quotations, including Oxford's and Bartlett's, and *not one* of those scholarly sources even lists the quotation. So, did Churchill really say it?

You may ask, "So what?" Why the big stink about one insignificant quotation? Surely the quotation is not that important, but the point is, when writers make bold historical claims, they had better get them right, and they had better be able to back them up with sound, traceable scholarship. Interestingly, President George W. Bush, in a speech given at the Library of Congress on the occasion of a Winston Churchill exhibit, employed the very quotation in question, attributing it to Churchill.[3]

---

[2] If it were the opposite, then the critics would need to count their own fabrications as products of their own historical and personal defects, and therefore just as fatally biased. Of course they do not. They want us to believe that their accounts are honest and purely factual.

As for the possibility that the winners in history were right, and that the history they have written is laudable, we may take a moment to enjoy F. F. Bruce's justifiably famous quip, "[T]he gnostic schools lost because they deserved to lose." (See Bruce, F. F., *The Canon of Scripture* [Downers Grove, IL: InterVarsity Press, 1988], 277). I will conclude that the same can be said on behalf of the mystery religions.

[3] "President Bush Discusses the Importance of Democracy in the Middle East," Remarks by the President on Winston Churchill and the War on Terror, Library of Congress, Washington, D.C.: http://www.whitehouse.gov/news/releases/2004/02/20040204-4.html, as of June 17, 2006; The speech was given on February 4, 2004 at 2:31 p.m. I suspect his speech-writer merely grabbed the quotation from the internet.

Suppose the quotation had been important and had some lasting consequence in history. Then its use by a major influential figure would take on an even greater ethical importance. "So what?" is answered by, "Because ideas have consequences." Political and religious influence are areas that require the greatest caution and certainty possible.

The issue is one of discernment and judgment. If we need such caution when handling events that occurred within a century of us, how much more when dealing with those from two millennia past? The way modern writers and critics have often carelessly treated early church history betrays either an agenda or ineptitude. We cannot leave the work of religion and history to radicals and their special interests—they simply do not have the proper methodology. What do I mean by this?

Methodology is a big word for *how* scholarship is done. There are different methodologies for different areas of scholarship and varying approaches to different disciplines (and even sometimes within a single discipline). For example, an historian must collect artifacts and accumulated knowledge of people, places, and events from a distant era. In his reconstruction of what happened, he must sort a mountain of data—or sometimes little at all—and rely on educated interpolations here and there. The homiletician (one who studies preaching and communication) attends less to historical dating and archaeology; he wants to learn what makes his audience tick, how to bridge culture gaps between audiences, how to relate imagery and ideas, etc., in order to persuade and influence his hearers. At some point, though, every discipline overlaps and relies on others. The historian must learn how to communicate to an audience, and the homiletician must study history lest he spout falsehoods. In any event, whatever discipline you labor in and however you approach it, the underlying rule beneath all scholarship is the ninth commandment: *Thou shalt not bear false witness against thy neighbor* (Ex. 20:16). The endeavor is an ethical one, not merely intellectual or persuasive. Our methodology must be one of faithfulness, integrity, patience, and a desire to get to the bottom of the facts. This rules out all propaganda and spin which aims to promote one group or idea over another. It also should make us suspicious of those who at the start deny the God of that commandment, for they have no necessary interest in keeping it.

But the critics begin with the personal attack of claiming bias and suppression. They say that a certain faction of "literalists" and "polemicists" gained control of the churches, imposed their views, excluded the gnostics, overran the mysteries, lied about the history, censored early writings and ruled religion like despots. This theory, considered purely as a hypothesis, might have deserved at least some study had it rested on some incontrovertible evidence; but as it stands, none has been produced. Orthodox scholars for centuries have examined the exact same evidence as the critics and have arrived at traditional conclusions. Why the great disparity over the same evidence? Because the liberals and neognostics *begin* with the belief that the orthodox representatives of the early Church suppressed the truth for their own gain. Then they progress through evidence, interpreting it according to their prior belief, and arrive at the very "conclusion" they started with. Funny how that works. The whole project is a circular argument. Alexander Pope nailed this type of critical error in 1711: "All looks yellow to the jaundic'd eye."[4]

Against such unprincipled posturing, good scholarship requires two important things. First, it must take into account *all* known data, not leaving out that which might challenge our view or better explain some phenomenon, nor suppressing that which we do not like. It must explain the hard data as well and not just present those pieces which can be molded to support a pet theory. This means lots of consideration, contemplation and caution for the scholar. Secondly, good scholarship requires a person acting out of *moral character* who will not budge from presenting even the ugly side of the facts, and who will not fear to see a pet theory challenged. Facts never speak for themselves, but are always interpreted. So when scholars encounter evidence—be it an artifact, manuscript, or another scholar's work—they are pressed by an obligation to report what they have seen truthfully and faithfully. Any writer

---

[4]Alexander Pope, "An Essay on Criticism" in *The Complete Poetical Works of Alexander Pope: Cambridge Edition*, ed. Henry W. Boynton (Boston and New York: Houghton Mifflin, 1903), part 2, line 559, page 74.

can sound persuasive, and anyone can compile mounds of footnotes from other sources to look scholarly; but the real question is whether they are faithful to the whole truth or not.

With these two basic requirements—comprehensive data and faithfulness to that data—scholarship is set to begin, and biases of all sorts are set to be leveled. Such a method simply constitutes good judgment. Let us look at an example of how mystery-theory writers fail in this regard.

An Epiphany

One case in which the ancient mystery religions appear to parallel Christian doctrine comes from the Greek playwright Euripides. This figure stands out because he lived and wrote in the fifth century before Christ, and thus if we do find a clear parallel to Christian religion in his writings, we must it take seriously as a possible influence.

In *The Jesus Mysteries,* authors Freke and Gandy purport to do just that. They claim that Euripides' play *The Bacchanals* presents its lead character—the mystery-religion god Dionysos—as the Son of God just like Christ. They argue that Jesus cannot be the "only begotten Son of God," because Dionysus (and a host of others that they imply) predated Christ in that role.[5] They proceed to present very clear sounding parallels:

1. Just as Christ is the "only begotten Son of God," so Dionysos is "Son of Zeus, in his full nature God."

2. Just as Christ is "Very God of Very God," so Dionysus is "Lord God of God born!"

3. Just as Christ is "the Word made Flesh," so Dionysus is the "Godhead in mortal shape . . . manifest to mortal men." In Dionysos' words, "I have changed my immortal form and taken the likeness of man."[6]

Freke and Gandy seem to have uncovered a real pagan gem in Euripides! How can Christians deny the obvious fact that the Greek writer antici-

---

[5]Timothy Freke and Peter Gandy, *The Jesus Mysteries: Was the "Original Jesus" a Pagan God?* (New York: Three Rivers Press, 1999), 28–29.
[6]Freke and Gandy, *The Jesus Mysteries,* 28–9.

pated such a central Christian doctrine? And by 500 years! It seems as if the authors have done a great deal of homework and detective work to find this out. How can the bedazzled Christian scholar respond?

What is at stake here is nothing less than the Christian doctrine of the Incarnation of the Son of God. Euripides at first pass seems to present Dionysus in the same manner, but a closer look reveals that Dionysos only changes his *appearance* to that of a man. The Greeks, remember, do not like the flesh, and so it does not surprise us to find Euripides having a God masquerade as a man but only in appearance and likeness. Christ, on the other hand, permanently joined his divinity with human flesh. With Him we have a true Incarnation, not just another pagan myth of gods changing shape to impress men.

How, then, can Freke and Gandy present Dionysus as a God made flesh like Jesus was? Let us apply the two criteria. Have Freke and Gandy presented all the possible evidence, and have they presented that which might contradict their case? The simple answer to both questions is no. To begin with, they have used—probably unknowingly—a very poor translation of Euripides' play. They may not have known that more accurate translations exist, but they clearly do. For example, they appear to lift the phrase, "Lord God of God born!" from an excerpt quoted in Jane Ellen Harrison's book *Prolegomena to the Study of Greek Religion*.[7] The problem is, Harrison herself employed a popular but poor translation of the section. The original Greek text simply refers to a group of people crying out with one voice to, "Zeus' seed."[8] How the earlier translator got "Lord God" I do not know, for the Greek word for "Lord" appears nowhere in the text.

This tiny instance, however, is not nearly as important as the other quotations. This one only speaks of Dionysus as Zeus' son, and the fact that Greek gods had sons in their mythology is no surprise, for they did

---

[7]Freke and Gandy, *The Jesus Mysteries*, 261, note 9; Jane Ellen Harrison, *Prolegomena to the Study of Greek Religion* (Princeton, NJ: Princeton University Press, [1903] 1991), 445.

[8]Euripides, "The Bacchanals." In *Euripides III. The Loeb Classical Library*, eds. T. E. Page and W. H. D. Rouse, trans. Arthur S. Way (New York: MacMillan, 1912), 60–61, Lines 725–726. This could as well be translated as "god's seed."

it all the time (usually through fornication in the form of an animal with a human female). The quotations that appear shocking deal with Dionysus manifesting in the flesh, for these appear on the surface to sound like the Christian doctrine of Incarnation. This, however, does not hold true. Again, we have translation issues to consider. When Euripides has Dionysos say that he is a god, "manifest to mortal men," the Greek word for "manifest" (*emphanes*) simply means "visible" or "revealed." The same claim is used more than once by Dionysos.[9]

Since this is all that is being claimed by Dionysus, the alleged parallel loses all its power. Such appearances of God were made all throughout the Old Testament,[10] so the Christian religion would not have needed Euripides even in this regard. The word for "manifesting" is important to the Christian world, too, because we get our word "Epiphany" from the same Greek root.[11] The season of Epiphany is traditionally when Christians celebrate the manifestation of the Christ Child to the gentile world. This season emphasizes God's grace to the world, that Christ is the light of the world, and the account of the visiting magi is read from Matthew 2. Thus this manifestation is very different from the shapeshifting of the pagan myths. The Christian Gospel has behind it the Incarnation of the Son of God.

This is because Christianity does not stop with appearances: Christ did not merely appear as a man, but was *made flesh, and dwelt among us* (John 1:14). Not only does St. John's Gospel present a clear contrast, but the language he uses is very special. The Greek word for "dwelt" is a rarely used verb that refers specially to dwelling in a tent. It most likely refers to the Old Testament tabernacle, which was a tent of skins in which the presence of God dwelt with the Israelites in the Old Testament. The tabernacle housed the ark of the covenant, and was therefore were the Law and Word of God met the seat of God's mercy and atonement. By describing the Incarnation of Jesus in this way, John is saying

---

[9]Euripides, "The Bacchanals," 6–7, Line 22; Euripides, "The Bacchanals," 8–9, Line 42.
[10]Genesis 3:8; 11:4–9; 12:7; Joshua 5:13–15, to name a few.
[11]*Epiphanes* and *emphanes* both are derived from the root *phaneros*—"known, evident, plain, visible."

that Christ is now the abiding presence of God among men. He replaces the Old Covenant. He now *is* the tabernacle: the living ark of the Covenant; the living Word; the place where man meets God, where God and man are reconciled by God's mercy. Unlike Dionysos, who simply took the appearance of a man, Christ *became flesh.* He entered our condition, and, "was in all points tempted like as we are, yet without sin" (Hebrews 4:15).

Despite all of this, Freke and Gandy casually present Euripides as a precursor to Christianity. But we can clearly see that such a parallel is the result of poor scholarly judgment. The two authors have not presented all of the possible data in this case nor have they presented anything that might challenge their thesis. They have left important translations of the text of Euripides either untouched or unaccounted for, and they have not presented the doctrine of Christ's Incarnation in its fullness or its Old Testament background. The parallel is false. Like the god they are promoting, their argument has nothing but an appearance of reality.

Conclusion

This chapter has discussed the power of who tells the story. Behind this power, I have argued that there lies a serious obligation on the part of the scholar—a judicial and ethical responsibility. Any endeavor done in the flesh will have such a judicial responsibility. God gave us commandments to live by, and all of life—including scholarship—must be governed by this code of ethics. Who can you trust? Too often that question is answered in service to a personal agenda, or by the desire of the fallen heart to escape the sovereignty of God in history. In the end, however, we can only trust that scholarship which aims to stay true to the facts, to parse those facts honestly, and to tell the story according to all the facts available.

Along these ethical lines, this chapter also lays down a very basic model for historical research: considering all the data, including all of the perspectives and implications of the data, and then interpreting that data in such as way as to present the most honest report possible. This may—and often should—result in the historian saying, "I don't know," but such an admission is rare among mystery-religion theorists. Rather we more often than not see sweeping inaccuracies and impossible connections bound together in a smooth narrative painted with a very broad brush indeed. The whole endeavor seems to be one gigantic incident of what David Hackett Fischer in *Historians' Fallacies* calls the "fallacy of the possible proof."[12] This error of judgment attempts to prove a theory true based on arguments for its mere possibility in history. The mystery-religion theory is certainly *possible* theoretically speaking—the mysteries did exist, they did have myths, some of them did promise some form of rewards in the afterlife, they were contemporary with Christianity in some respects—but this possibility by no means leads to proof. Anything is possible. It is *possible* that a civilization currently exists on Mars, but we have no real evidence to make it appear probable. In order to begin to establish proof, the historian must draw the evidence together and begin to ask the right critical questions—questions which could prove or disprove the theory. The procedure must be designed to sift the data and elicit factual information.[13]

The mere question "Is *X* possible?" when applied to early Christian doctrine and when used to present half-truths as history, resembles its very near cousin, "Hath God said?" (Gen. 3:1). Unfounded doubt is the door to deception. We have seen one detailed case of how pagan mythology can be presented to look like a parallel to Christian doctrine, even though the contrast between the two religions dwarfs any supposed similarity. The next chapter will continue this dismantling of the mystery-theory charade of scholarship by applying sound judgment to many more cases.

---

[12]See David Hackett Fischer, *Historians' Fallacies* (New York and Evanston: Harper Torchbooks, 1970), 53f. Fischer lists dozens of fallacies commonly found in historical works, even that of great scholars. One could make a book by applying all the different fallacies that apply to mystery religion scholarship and liberal Christian histories.

[13]Fischer, *Historians' Fallacies,* 55.

7

Mystery Religions and Mysterious Methods

As would be expected in view of the fragmentary and occasionally ambiguous evidence, different investigators have arrived quite at divergent results . . . Such widely divergent opinions are due, at least in part, to differences in methodology in dealing with the evidence.[1]

Something more is necessary than learning and perception to draw the right conclusions from the facts: sound common sense and well-balanced judgment.[2]

---

[1] Bruce M. Metzger, "Methodology in the Study of Mystery Religions and Early Christianity," *Historical and Literary Studies: Pagan, Jewish, and Christian,* ed. Bruce M. Metzger (Leiden: E. J. Brill, 1968), 2, 4. Among articles dealing with mystery religion scholarship, Metzger's work stands out due to its sheer precision and depth of research. In twenty-four pages, Metzger clears away a century of academic refuse about the mysteries and Christianity. The essay can also be found in *The Harvard Theological Review,* XLVIII (1955), 1–20, where it was first published and also on the web at: http://www. frontline-apologetics.com/mystery_religions_early_christianity.htm. This chapter is an attempt to put the ideas of his article into more popular language. I here rely upon Metzger's work even where I do not explicitly reference it.

[2] Philip Schaff, *History of the Christian Church,* 8 vols. (Peabody, MA: Hendrickson Publishers, 1996), 1:208.

ANY STUDENT OR scholar who enters very far into the mystery-religion debate soon realizes that what weighs most heavily in the many reconstructions of the history is the interpretation placed upon it by the scholar. The writer's disposition, beliefs, methods and quality of critical thinking primarily determine the picture. The amount of error allowed to get through—either consciously or unconsciously—will contort the story that is told. Much has slipped through in the past century. What follows is a summary of some of those errors.

Who Borrowed and When?

The first such error deals with the chronology of the evidence and of the idea of "borrowing." We have seen that Christians did in fact adopt certain pagan ceremonies and symbols—although this "borrowing" should more properly be understood as confiscating, because Christians converted the pagans and then used their own symbols, re-infused with new meaning, to teach them the Christian faith. In some cases it might be argued that the Church went too far in its tolerance of such practices, and there were debates among the early Church fathers as to where to draw the line. But the very fact that such debates existed shows that there already existed a body of truth—a "faith which was once delivered unto the saints" (Jude 3)—which the fathers sought to protect against pagan corruption.

Furthermore, such Christian and pagan interaction does not really heat up until the fourth century. Most of the evidence dates to this time and not to the early decades of the Church. Scholars who cover the period of the great pagan conversions treat it from the fourth century on, not as a phenomenon of the early church.[3] So we must distinguish between the faith and practice of the early Church and that of subsequent centuries.[4] Ronald Nash nails it best when arguing that Mithraism flow-

---

[3]Ramsay MacMullen, *Christianity and Paganism in the Fourth to Eighth Centuries* (New Haven and London: Yale University Press, 1997).

[4]Metzger, "Methodology in the Study of Mystery Religions and Early Christianity," 4.

ered way too late to affect the development of Christian doctrine: simply put, "The timing is all wrong."[5]

The Nature and Amount of Evidence[6]

For any theory, a massive hurdle exists in the fact that we have few written records of the mystery cults. While archeologists have discovered several meeting places, excavations have yielded scant textual material. Take the case of mithraism for example. The scarcity of textual evidence puts us in a situation where "the religion is known almost exclusively from the numerous Mithraic sanctuaries and their art that has been discovered."[7] The earliest textual evidence for that cult comes from Plutarch (d. A.D. 126) whose *Life of Pompey* gives us an early literary reference to Mithraist pirates being captured and taken to Rome. His 67 B.C. date, however, strains credulity with many historians,[8] and he makes no actual mention of mithraism being established at that time.[9] We are left with statues and monuments which have been dated from the late first to early second century, well after the Gospels were written and Christian doctrine established.[10]

The same problem of inadequate evidence is noted by the liberal historian Hans Lietzmann in relation to the mysteries in general. He writes,

> A confused variety of records, both inscriptions and documents, have survived, but, as yet, it is impossible to analyze them satisfactorily. They belong to eight different centuries, and to all the lands of the Roman empire, and it is only by combining data of the most different origin that we are able to gain any compre-

---

[5]Ronald H. Nash *Christianity and the Hellenistic World* (Grand Rapids, MI: Zondervan/Probe, 1984), 147.

[6]Metzger, "Methodology in the Study of Mystery Religions and Early Christianity," 6.

[7]Everett Ferguson, *Background of Early Christianity*, 3rd ed. (Grand Rapids, MI: Eerdmans, 2003), 287.

[8]M. J. Vermaseren, *Mithras, the Secret God* (London: Chatto & Windus, 1963), 27–29; C. M. Daniels, "The Role of the Roman Army in the Spread of Mithraism," *Mithraic Studies*, ed. John R. Hinnels (Rowman and Littlefield: Manchester University Press, 1975), 2:250.

[9]Nash, *Christianity and the Hellenistic World*, 147–8.

[10]Vermaseren, *Mithras, the Secret God*, 29–30; Ferguson, *Background of Early Christianity*, 290–1.

hensible idea of the nature of these mysteries. So far, it is impossible to sketch the evolution of a mystery religion, its different forms in various places, or its active and passive relationships with other mysteries.[11]

But though he gives this damaging admission, he, like so many writers, fills in the gaps by using distinct Christian language, referring to the "death and resurrection of Osiris,"[12] and of many of the other mystery cults likewise. How can such a learned scholar see and clearly explain the obvious hodge-podge of evidence and then pretend he has a clear enough picture to make such claims? Who would try to build a house from materials found in a trash heap? The critics' endeavor is like erecting a cardboard box, painting it the same color as the chapel down the street, and then claiming the chapel ripped off your design. It just will not work. Anyone with a clear look at the evidence sees the fraud for what it is. The critic might as well make stained-glass with magic-marker, copy *The Last Supper* with crayon, and play Bach on a kazoo.

Taking into account the pure lack of detailed records and the late date of what we do have, scholars must consider the likelihood that the cults varied in their practices over time and from region to region. We cannot assume that what one third-century account describes, for example, applies to every local meeting of the same mystery over all the previous decades; nor can we necessarily assume that the cult previously existed at all. Differences have been documented in more than one case of the mystery cults who claimed to worship the same deity,[13] so any assumption of uniformity should fall under severe scrutiny. For a scholar to pretend that the cults clearly existed before Christianity and that they were in a position to influence the Church says more about

---

[11]Hans Lietzmann, *A History of the Early Church*, trans. Bertram Lee Woolf, 2 vols. (Cleveland and New York: World Publishing Company, 1967), 1:169.

[12]Lietzmann, *A History of the Early Church*, 2:42. See 2:42–44.

[13]Metzger, "Methodology in the Study of Mystery Religions and Early Christianity," 6–7; Susan Elliott, *Cutting Too Close for Comfort: Paul's Letter to the Galatians in its Anatolian Cultic Context. Journal for the New Testament Supplement Series* 248. ed. Stanley E. Porter (London and New York: T& T Clark International, 2003), 96.

that scholar's personal beliefs than any hard data. The evidence itself will not lead you to that conclusion.

The Jewish Rejection of Paganism

We have explored the Jewishness of Paul's mind-set in the previous chapter and found that the apostle had a profound and pervasive dependence upon the Old Testament. This very background would have been even more pronounced in the earliest church in Palestine. Their monotheism and exclusivity would have placed adopting any pagan doctrines out of the question. Had Paul been a proponent of the mysteries, these Jewish Christians would have rejected him outrightly and completely. The Jew and Gentile churches clashed hard enough as is was. Can we imagine that the radical Judaizers, who attacked Paul over the fundamental Old Testament issue of circumcision, would have said nothing about his dragging Mithra or Cybele alongside the One God and Lord? Would they have strained the gnat of circumcision and swallowed the camel of rank idolatry?[14]

Archaeological evidence supports this view of Palestine as it was in the early Church era. While hundreds of mystery-religion artifacts have been found scattered all over the former Roman Empire, only one has turned up in Palestine. This sole piece of evidence seems to be nothing more than a coin—which could have been carried by any traveler through the region—and even it is dated after A.D. 135.[15] In addition, a second-century manuscript that includes a list of places in which Isis was worshiped indicates that the cult got no closer to Jerusalem than the farthest reaches of the Palestinian coast.[16] Even the attempts of the invading ruler Hadrian to impose paganism on the region ultimately failed.[17]

---

[14]Metzger, "Methodology in the Study of Mystery Religions and Early Christianity," 7.

[15]Metzger, "Methodology in the Study of Mystery Religions and Early Christianity," 8, note 1.

[16]Metzger, "Methodology in the Study of Mystery Religions and Early Christianity," 8, note 1.

[17]Metzger, "Methodology in the Study of Mystery Religions and Early Christianity," 8, note 1.

So as far as we can determine from historical evidence, the church of Palestine prevailed in the Old Testament mandate against idolatry. While other regions reveled in the practices of paganism, the gates of Palestine shut them out. To assume otherwise is to leave the historical data and cleave unto a wish—a wish derived from not allowing the theology of the historical individuals involved to speak for itself, but rather forcing the modern critic's own philosophy in place of the facts.

Parallels: Real and Imaginary

We have looked in a previous chapter at the treatment of similarities as the early Church fathers themselves dealt with them. Not only do the alleged parallels look much different outside of some modern critics' claims, but the fathers provided a much more profound and reasoned response than the critics have given them credit for. The disparity between the portrait that liberal scholars paint and the stories we have read of the myths stands out as an example of modern imagination at work. Scholars have simply taken various pieces of information from disparate sources and fused them together artificially.[18] But just because you pour eggs, flour, sugar, cocoa, baking soda, etc., into the same cake-pan does not mean you have a chocolate cake, especially if you have the wrong amounts of each ingredient, or indeed the wrong ingredients to begin with. The mystery religion theory is a pseudo-myth, it is pseudo-history, and it is pseudo-truth, which is to say, it is a lie. Early Church scholar F. C. Conybeare—by no means partial to the orthodox—yet decried "the untrained explorers [who] discover on almost every page connections in their subject matter where there are and can be none, and as regularly miss connections where they exist."[19] Edwin R. Bevan provides the classic critique of the charade:

> Of course if one writes an imaginary description of the Orphic mysteries, as [Alfred] Loisy, for instance, does, filling in the large

---

[18]Metzger, "Methodology in the Study of Mystery Religions and Early Christianity," 9.
[19]Quoted in Metzger, "Methodology in the Study of Mystery Religions and Early Christianity," 9, note 1.

gaps in the picture left by our data from the Christian eucharist, one produces something very impressive. On this plan, you first put in the Christian elements, and then are staggered to find them there.[20]

Such imaginary parallels continue to circulate only when the storyteller is not forced to read from the original evidence. Once Christians begin to counter the haphazard claims of pagan priority with the simple demand for dated, confirmed, and relevant *textual evidence,* then we can expose the assumptions of careless critics in their want of pre-Christian sources.

In cases in which parallels may appear, we should first inquire as to the extent and nature of the similarity. We must keep a stark distinction between that type of parallel which has arisen through direct influence in history and that which is a mere analogy, which is a perception of some apparent similarity which could exist due to any number causes. The first is a matter of *A* causing *B*. In the second, *A* only resembles *B*, but the two arise independently and neither requires the other for its existence.

By way of illustration, we may note a similarity between the types of canoes used by Amazonian natives and those employed in the past by natives of the South Pacific. Both amount to little more than hollowed-out logs. But no historian would judge from this similarity that one group had somehow influenced the development of the other. Rather, each case most likely arose through similar subjects (human beings) having similar needs and similar raw materials. By the same token, we can see stark differences between, say, a modern battleship and an eighteenth century "ship of the line" such as the *HMS Victory* which Lord Nelson maneuvered in the Battle of Trafalgar. Although both are sea vessels designed for warfare, they are made of different materials, carry vastly different weaponry and guidance systems, and rely on different sources of power. Yet the modern ship stands directly in a genealogical line of develop-

---

[20]Quoted in Metzger, "Methodology in the Study of Mystery Religions and Early Christianity," 9.

ment from the earlier vessel.[21] Any argument that relied only on surface appearance in either case would sink under its own weight.

This is because historical judgments based merely on visible parallels can be very deceptive. In one particular case, historian Marc Bloch notes two major figures of the Roman church who were each converted while reading the Lives of the Saints, founded religious orders dedicated to the same patron, saw their orders suppressed by popes bearing the same name, and then died on the same day of the year, each in Italy.[22] He presents other instances of uncanny similarities in history that appear to have no necessary genealogical connection to the other. Bloch concludes, "[C]oincidence is one of those freaks which cannot be eliminated from history."[23] Of course we cannot automatically assume that every similarity in history is a mere coincidence, but, "Before we assert literary or traditional connection between similar events in story or myth, we must satisfy ourselves that such communication was possible."[24]

Furthermore, not only must direct influence have been possible, but we must ask how likely it would have been between any two given groups. Possibility is one thing; *probability* quite another. Into this sphere of argument enters the Old Testament ethics of the early Church versus an invasion of paganism. This we have already seen is highly unlikely, both theologically and archaeologically. Rather the probability is higher that the mystery religions would have adopted bits of Christian language and ceremony. Once Christianity began to spread and to make converts from the mystery cults, the cults logically would have reacted by changing their face to match the competition. It was a desperate attempt by the pagan priests who were watching their mystery-cult king-

---

[21] A naval historian may see fit to correct me on a fine point or two, but the overall illustration is, I think, quite sea worthy.

[22] Marc Bloch, *The Historian's Craft*, trans. Peter Putnam (New York: Vintage Books, 1953), 123. St. John Colombini founded the Order of the Jesuates (shut down by Clement IX) and died on July 31, 1367, in Siena. St. Ignatius of Loyola founded the Order of the Jesuits (banned by Clement XIV) and died on July 31, 1556, in Rome. Noted in Metzger, "Methodology in the Study of Mystery Religions and Early Christianity," 10–11, note 4.

[23] Bloch, *The Historian's Craft*, 124.

[24] Conybeare as quoted in Metzger, "Methodology in the Study of Mystery Religions and Early Christianity," 10.

doms crumble down around them. One interesting change shows up in the cult of Cybele where the bath in bull-blood, which promised initiates eternal life effective for twenty years, for some reason is changed in one manuscript to a once-for-all efficacy. Likewise the Emperor Julian is said to have mimicked Christian patterns during his failed pagan revolt in the fourth century.[25] All this implies that we can better interpret some parallels as being adoptions by the pagans and not the early Christians.

With that said, an even better explanation of similarities between any religions deals with the most ancient of prophecies being passed down and corrupted through millennia—as discussed in an earlier chapter—as well as the constant nature of fallen man. All people, believers or not, bear the Image of God and are therefore inescapably religious. The difference for the Christian tradition lies in also having a repository of special revelation passed along by which to preserve and interpret the common. This one true tradition continued through the law and promises of the Israelites (Rom. 9:4–5). Meanwhile, pagan cultures continued with permutations of the same corrupt religion combining ancient ideas with fallen human experience. We should be more surprised, therefore, if we found *no* similarities among religions rather than the general (though vague) unity that we do observe. Much like the two unconnected tribes of natives building similar canoes, pagan religions simply represent similar fallen humans reacting to similar situations. Some resemblance to true religion should not surprise us. Even a canoe and a battleship have basic similarities.

Once we have gotten a grip on scrutinizing parallels and questioning whether an alleged similarity is based on historical connectedness or only upon superficial analogies created by the writer, we begin to understand that the mystery-religion theory has very little to commend it. As far as unquestionable historical, genealogical evidence goes, none exists.

---

[25]Metzger, "Methodology in the Study of Mystery Religions and Early Christianity," 11, note 2.

Emphasizing the Differences

Instead we see profound differences. From the very vocabulary that she employed to the most fundamental aspects of her doctrine, the early Church proves to be unique and untainted by the pagan mysteries. This remains true from many perspectives.

For example, many technical terms used by the pagan mysteries do not appear in the early writings of early Christians. If these authors had been borrowing their faith from the mysteries, as is claimed, we would expect to see at least a moderate amount of the technical verbiage that those cults used. Instead we observe almost a total absence. In the few cases that the same terms do appear, they obviously differ in meaning. One case in point deals with the use of the very word "mystery" itself. Whereas outside the New Testament the term often refers to the mystery religions and their secret rites in themselves, Paul consistently uses the term in a more common way—to refer to a previous secret that God has now revealed.[26] His usage does not come from the mystery cults, but directly from the Greek version of the Old Testament which used the term in the same way, and had been around for 300 years before Paul came along.[27]

Other obvious contrasts arise. Christianity is an historic religion, founded upon historical events, set in a verifiable historic setting. This is one reason the New Testament emphasizes eye-witness accounts so often (Luke 1:1–3; John 19:35–6; 21:24; 1 Cor. 15:5–8; 2 Pet. 1:16–18; 1 John 1:1–3). We have seen how frequently Paul refers to Christ as an earthly, fleshly, historical person. Against this the mythological nature of the mysteries suffers. The cult stories would lose nothing of substance if they included, "Once upon a time . . ." and, "Happily ever after." As it was, no cult member ever expected their hero figure to step out of fantasy and into the real world. To do so may very well have constituted as blasphemy against the Greek view of matter versus idea. A truly incarnate God would have been unacceptable, a crucified God a laughingstock (1 Cor. 1:23). Instead, the mysteries were a means of emotional

---

[26]Nash, *Christianity and the Hellenistic World*, 185–187.
[27]See the quotation from Mircea Eliade to this effect in Nash, *Christianity and the Hellenistic World*, 187.

escape for the initiate. Through their myths, adherents believed they could transcend matter into the realm of secret knowledge.

Such lust for hidden knowledge was sated by the secrecy of the cults. Meetings were held at night and in caves in order to make the secrecy emphatic. Initiates took oaths and guarded their prized knowledge closely. In contrast, Christianity preached from the highways and roof tops. The only barrier to understanding the mystery of the Gospel was—and is—the condition of the heart. Early Christians made their documents available to all and taught openly.[28] The only exception comes in the early Christian Eucharist: unbelievers were asked to leave. But this was because the Eucharist was for the baptized only, not because the Church sought to hide their teaching behind a veil of secrecy.

Christian sacramental theology also differs widely from the few pagan parallels that critics have exaggerated. To begin with, the very nature of the cases contrast. The early Church saw their sacraments as gifts given out of grace to the undeserving and gave thanks for them.[29] The ceremonies were gifts from God who sealed in them promises which were received in faith. In contrast, the pagans took their rites for granted as automatically conferring effects upon the person due to the act itself. Tertullian ridiculed the pagans for this magical belief:

> Therefore, if the mere nature of water, in that it is the appropriate material for washing away, leads men to flatter themselves with a belief in omens of purification, how much more truly will waters render that service through the authority of God, by whom all their nature has been constituted! If men think that water is endued with a medicinal virtue by religion, what religion is more effectual than that of the living God?[30]

---

[28]Metzger, "Methodology in the Study of Mystery Religions and Early Christianity," 13 and notes 1 and 2. See also Michael Green, *Evangelism in the Early Church* (Grand Rapids, MI: Eerdmans, [1970] 2003), 218.

[29]Metzger, "Methodology in the Study of Mystery Religions and Early Christianity," 14; Arthur Darby Nock, *Early Gentile Christianity and Its Hellenistic Background* (New York: Harper Torchbooks, 1964), 132. Nock refers to Justin Martyr, *Apol.* I. 65. See also Green, *Evangelism in the Early Church*, 217–218.

[30]Tertullian, *Of Baptism*, chap. 5. In *Ante-Nicene Fathers*, eds. James Donaldson and Alexander Roberts (Albany, OR: AGES Software, 1997), 3:1215.

Tertullian could declare the superiority of the Christian sacraments because they represented the promises of the eternal God who stood behind them. None of the cults had anything comparable, either in the full form of the ceremonies themselves, or in the significance of those practices. While some had washings, and some had meals, none can be said to truly parallel the Christian rites either in detail or meaning.[31] Scholars who try to portray pagan rites as forerunners to Christian doctrine rarely if ever present the reader with quotations from the original sources or dates of any sources they site. The reason for this is that once they lay paganism and Christianity side-by-side, the contrast leaps off the page.

The same fallacious exaggerations characterize the claims about "dying and rising gods" who supposedly preceded Christ. Contrasts abound. In pagan myths, the gods in question never die in voluntary sacrifice like Christ did, but only by compulsion—jealous murder, conspiracy, hunting "accidents." Moreover, Christianity is unique in its foresight of triumph at Christ's death. Whereas the pagan "mourns" upon the death of his idol,[32] the Christian knows that Christ's death is a triumph. The crucifixion is where, "The forces of evil have played their trump card and lost."[33] The battle is over before it begins.

Where the mysteries have been said to have their hero revivified on the "third day" must be tested closely in every case. In the case of Attis, we have no evidence of a three-day period being observed before the late second-century A.D. In fact, no evidence even shows him to be the dying sidekick of Cybele before A.D. 138, let alone resurrected.[34] Adonis, too, is a latecomer in this regard. The nature of Osiris' reanimation is odd in that he remained in the afterlife while his physical body stayed in the grave (which was the common view of the Egyptians concerning

---

[31]See Metzger, "Methodology in the Study of Mystery Religions and Early Christianity," 14–17, for further elaboration.

[32]Compare once again the Old Testament "abomination" of "women weeping for Tammuz" (Ezek. 8:13–15).

[33]Nock, *Early Gentile Christianity and Its Hellenistic Background*, 106. The article from which this quotation is derived was originally published in 1928. Also Metzger, "Methodology in the Study of Mystery Religions and Early Christianity," 18.

[34]Metzger, "Methodology in the Study of Mystery Religions and Early Christianity," 20.

death, and is why they mummified their VIPs). We could hardly call this a resurrection; and that he was brought-to on the third day appears in only one of several differing accounts of the myth.

Even if there did exist a clear "third-day" example before Christ, it would have to fall subject to the same improbabilities as any other pagan parallel. In the light of so many accounts and instances of "three days" and "third day" appearing in the Old Testament, the need for Christianity to borrow such obscure details from the mysteries is extremely slim. Christ in the Gospels referred to the example of Jonah (Matt. 12:39–40; Luke 11:29–32; Jonah 1:17 is in view). While at first glance this may seem to be a stretch in exegesis, Jonah explicitly refers to the fish's belly as "the belly of hell" (Jonah 2:2).[35] The reference to death and the grave is clear.

In all of these crucial particulars—terminology, historicity, openness and clarity, sacramental details and meaning, and resurrection—Christianity stands unique in contrast to the mysteries. Ironically it is in most of these very cases that claims of parallels and borrowing are made. Nothing could be less evident once the facts are gathered in one place and the test of honesty applied to their interpretation.

Philosophy of History

A final but vital area relates to the differing philosophies of history upon which Christianity and the mysteries are respectively built. The contrast both illustrates the difference in ancient times and accounts for the current excitement surrounding the mystery religions. The pagan myths rely on a Greek view of the universe: creation and matter are corrupt and evil, and time and history are cyclical. As with all such dualist systems, the mystery initiate has as their goal to gain enough secret knowledge to escape the cyclical process of earthly time and transcend into the wafts of eternity. This view essentially denies the meaningfulness of history and historical events. Since many of the promoters of the mystery cult theory today see themselves as modern gnostics, their assumed view of history implies that they might have no problem writing "history" ac-

---

[35]I am hopelessly addicted to the King James Version for many reasons; but here, "hell" comes from the Hebrew *Sheol* and could better be translated "grave."

cording to their purposes, for to them, the myth they pass down is more important than what actually happened in history anyway.

This type of Greek thought, characteristic of the mystery religions and of gnosticism, has as its key goal to perpetuate a secret reality known only to initiates. For these individuals—today ranging from rationalist academics to deranged occultists—factual history is replaced by "the secrets," or "holy history," or some other form of mythology.[36] The most popular tactic of this ilk is to offer a secret or "real" meaning of history, especially of the Bible or early Church history.[37] This process of hijacking history involves the complete re-writing of it, and there has been no shortage of this endeavor. The greatest problem, though, is that to do this kind of work the gnostic must deny that history already has a meaning and direction determined by God. The mystery proponent sets himself in the place of God as the autonomous interpreter of history. It is no wonder that so many conflicting, diverse, and ridiculous views have evolved since the first efforts of higher criticism in the nineteenth century. When man places himself in charge, the results are chaos, confusion, and finally collapse. In this situation any true historical scholarship becomes impossible, for, "To accept myth is to reject history."[38] The peddlers of myths today have done just that.

Against all of this the biblical view which the early Church shared sees history beginning with creation. History is linear: it had a definite point of beginning defined by the Creator's fiat, and it will have a very specific end at the hand of the same Sovereign God. At this definite end awaits final judgment by God, and it is this that the unbeliever tries to escape above all. Along the time-line between these two extremities exist many unique and very meaningful events, all decreed and guided by the Triune God of Scripture. Creation is good, time is important, and historical facts have crucial and lasting meaning for the future. Into this scenario God the Son entered and died as an historical person, signify-

---

[36]Rousas J. Rushdoony, *Man as God: A Study of Modern Thought Since the Marquis de Sade* (Vallecito, CA: Ross House Books, 2003), 153–154.

[37]Rushdoony, *Man as God*, 154.

[38]Rushdoony, Rousas J., *The Biblical Philosophy of History* (Vallecito, CA: Ross House Books, 2000), 87.

ing both the penalty for the sin of mankind and the love of God towards us. The Son beat death and arose from the grave, still in that same historical time-line, to proclaim God's victory over sin and death and to promise the same to all believers.

Conclusion

This chapter has continued the previous one by enumerating many more instances in which the basic ethical criteria for scholarship have been ignored, for whatever reason, allowing the claims of parallels and Christian thievery to continue to spread. The critics have ignored the basic chronology of the evidence, the nature and amount of the evidence, and the attitude of early Christians against idolatry. They have failed to produce any genuine parallel of a genealogical sort and only a few analogies; they have glossed over many striking differences on almost every important point of comparison between Christianity and the myths; and they have replaced true Christian history with a myth of their own making. These many cases of error and fallacy illustrate that the mystery religion theory is completely implausible. Not only this, but its propagators continue to present remote possibilities as facts and then proceed to the next paragraph as if the former were an indisputable conclusion—building error upon error. This practice by its very nature rejects the necessary method of historical research. It is essentially an argument for gnosticism which *denies history* in favor of mythology. In reading the various works of their foremost authors, the construction of a new mythology of religious history is the most outstanding feature.

Our culture has made much more of these mystery cults than need be. We could blame this on a lust to degrade the Christian religion. But we need only to poke their theory with a pin to watch the whole thing collapse. Christians need to take the offensive against the poor judgment and shoddy compilations of pagan mystery enthusiasts. It is only in the honest pursuit of truth that progress in knowledge is made, and the Law of God provides the necessary tools for the kind of critical judgment that is required. Once Christians reset the standard, it will be left to the critics either to edit themselves or wear the banner of quackery. The choice is either Christ, the anchor of our souls, or paganism, a plank, bobbing with each wave, leaving its hanger-on to gulp the sea; and the sharks are circling.

8

Why the Word Made Flesh?

Forasmuch then as the children are partakers of flesh and blood,
he also himself likewise took part of the same; that through death
he might destroy him that had the power of death, that is, the
devil; And deliver them who through fear of death were all their
life time subject to bondage. (Hebrews 2:14–15)

For of His becoming Incarnate we were the object, and for our sal-
vation He dealt so lovingly as to appear and be born even in a
human body.[1]

The storm-centre of controversy in the attack and defense of the
faith has been and will always be the Incarnation.[2]

THE INCARNATION OF Jesus Christ is the most important event of history. It is the point on which the calendar of human events hinges, turning from B.C. (Before Christ) to A.D. (*Anno domini*—year of the Lord), and thus it is the focal point of all of human history. Its importance theologically is surpassed only, perhaps, by the subsequent death and resurrection of Jesus. The Word made flesh brings mankind to the apex of *theology*, for it is this Incarnate Word who fully and truly de-

---

[1]Athanasius, *On the Incarnation of the Word*, 4.3. In *The Nicene and Post-Nicene Fathers*, ed. Philip Schaff (Albany, OR: AGES Software, 1997), 4:277.

[2]Oliver Chase Quick, *Essays on Orthodoxy* (London: MacMillan and Co., Ltd., 1916), Chapter 7. http://www.anglicanlibrary.org/quick/essays/07.htm, as of August 8, 2006.

clares to us the very God (John 1:18) Who created us, and that we have so blindly groped at by our own efforts (Acts 17:27; 2 Cor. 4:3–4). As well, the Incarnate Word elevates man to the pinnacle of *humanity*, for He is the perfect man, sinless man, and the One Who fully and truly represents man unto God, in His life and death, in a way that fallen man could never do himself.

Since the thrust of this book is a refutation of an erroneous view of Jesus, much of the time has been spent addressing errors and repairing falsehoods. This chapter seeks to make good on the old saying, "You can't beat something with nothing." In other words, the positive truth must be set in place of that which we refute. A lot of this has been done already, especially in the chapters dealing with Paul's theology, but the subject which this book defends—that Jesus Christ was *Manifested in the Flesh*—deserves its own place before we conclude.

What is the Incarnation?

The definitive statement of the nature of our Savior is the Creed of Chalcedon, formulated in A.D. 451. It affirms the truth of Scripture and the earlier creeds (including the Apostles' Creed and the Nicene Creed), that Christ is both *fully God* and *fully man*. In the language of the Creed, our Lord Jesus Christ is, "at once complete in Godhead and complete in manhood, truly God and truly man . . . of one substance with the Father as regards his Godhead, and at the same time of one substance with us as regards his manhood; like us in all respects, apart from sin."

The classic statements of the doctrine by theologians have followed the formula of Chalcedon. These include Athanasius' *On the Incarnation* (A.D. 318–323) and Anselm's *Cur Deus Homo?* (or *Why the God-Man?*, A.D. 1098 A.D.), as well as the relevant chapters of John Calvin's *The Institutes of the Christian Religion.*[3] These agree in affirming that Christ is both fully God and fully man: the two natures abide (quoting

---

[3] John Calvin, *Institutes of the Christian Religion*, ed. John T. McNeill, 2 vols. (Philadelphia, PA: Westminster Press, 1960). See Book II, Chapters XII–XIV. In more recent times, see the exhaustive work by Millard Erickson, *The Word Became Flesh* (Grand Rapids, MI: Baker Books, 1991).

the Creed again), "Without confusion, without change, without division, without separation," yet, "being in no way annulled by the union."

To the human mind this may sound like a contradiction. How can something be both non-human and human at the same time and in the same Person?

The understanding of the Church has been that the doctrine is a true *mystery*. Not a mystery in the sense of the pagan mystery religions, but rather a doctrine that is clearly taught in Scripture, but beyond human ability to comprehend. Other Christian doctrines fall in this category, such as the Trinity—that God is Three Persons and One Essence at the same time. By believing that Christ is One Person with two natures, Christians are not running into a contradiction, but simply affirming that God surpasses our understanding. It is impossible for man to understand but not impossible for God to *do*.

Christians readily and easily accept the doctrine of the Incarnation with all of its mystery. The pagan scoffs. He believes that all events must have a naturalistic explanation. He does not mention that this atheistic belief involves him up front in a few restrictive assumptions. First, it implies that the full extent of reality is such that it can be comprehended by the mind of man, which is quite a condescension under which to place reality. It involves the assertion, with no proof, that nothing exists which cannot be fully measured and accounted for by human brain-power. A transcendent God, of course, would not pass such a test. He is, therefore, tossed out of the pagan's mental world and with Him the doctrine of the Incarnation. Pagan skepticism is proof that if you set your bar low enough, you can achieve any goal.

Secondly, at the same time it bans God from the universe, it elevates man's mind to the level of divine judge. It proceeds as if the human body and mind are capable of infinite measuring and calculating. It attributes to the human mind the ability to judge correctly the truth or falsity of something that by definition exceeds its capacity. Scrutinizing a divine mystery by the standard of mere human reason denies the mystery from the start. The pagan would have the creature judge his Creator by the creature's standards. Might as well ask your spare tire to expound the existence of Charles Goodyear.

Thirdly, it assumes that man *deserves* to know everything, which is quite an unwarranted elevation of the status of humanity. The idea of human rights in the pagan worldview grows in cancerous fashion, and man ultimately bars nothing from himself. But only by presuming that no ethical limitation exists beyond his own gut would he so tread his dirty shoes upon holy ground. God has created us with certain limitations and has only revealed to us that portion of truth that He wanted to (Deut. 29:29). While the pagan cannot stand this fact, because he cannot stand God Himself, Christians have no problem submitting to the idea that we cannot understand some things and do not need to know others.

All the objections that paganism raises against the idea of the Incarnation find their end, if pagans would only open their eyes, in the very Incarnation they deny. John's Gospel teaches that God truly became flesh and dwelt among us (John 1:14), and that this enfleshed Word actually shows us God *so that humans can understand Him*: "No man hath seen God at any time: the only begotten Son, which is in the bosom of the Father, he hath declared him" (John 1:18). To the pagan who objects that he will have nothing but his own senses, God explicitly manifested Himself to human senses. Not only did He do this, but God's coming as a man was a *perfect* representation of God in the form of man. Christ is, "the express image of his person" (Heb. 1:3). St. Paul accords, "For in him dwelleth all the fullness of the Godhead bodily" (Col. 2:9), "Who is the image of the invisible God" (Col. 1:15).

The Perfect Man

Not only does the Word made flesh perfectly show us the Father, but He is the Perfect Man in our stead as well. The human side of the Incarnation is every bit as important as Christ's divinity, though it suffers in societies like ours where liberals overemphasize it to the point of denying the divine. Conservative Christians often react by stressing Christ's divinity to a point that draws Christianity away from humanitarian efforts, social causes, law, economics and politics. In this knee-jerk reaction, we become no better than the mystery-religionists and gnostics who relegate Christ's manhood to mythology, and make religion a thing of individual whim. On the contrary, we must consider Christ as the perfect man to the same extent we preach Him as God.

The quest for the perfect man is an obsession of pagan man. Mystery religions and gnosticism both revolve around the idea of gaining secret knowledge and receiving enlightenment, but in each case these are merely means to an end—the end of becoming divine. Their ultimate goal is to compile the knowledge necessary to transcend the material universe into some form or status of divinity. This quest is inherent in the heart of fallen man: "How art thou fallen, O Lucifer, son of the morning! . . . For thou hast said in thine heart, I will ascend into heaven" (Isa. 14:12–3). This belief has manifested in various forms throughout history. The German philosopher Friedrich Nietzsche is famous for expounding his philosophy of the "superman." He believed that if man only followed his natural lust for power and denied the oppressive force of Christian morality, an ensuing struggle in society would lead to the triumph of a higher man. The highest aspiration of man, for Nietzsche, is to be such a superman—man at his pinnacle, transcending all of the follies of hisself and of previous races.

I refer to Nietzsche's view of man and man's future for two reasons. First, because the central aim of modern humanism follows his path. The constant attack on Christian morality, the ridicule of Christian piety and chastity, the sexual revolution, political radicalism, relativism, meaninglessness, and even terrorism all trace back to man's attempt to chart his own course of law and creativity, which, like a tireless evangelist, Nietzsche so whole-heartedly preached. His view of man is the ultimate expression of fallen human pride and arrogance, and modern man has carried his gospel of the higher man to the farthest reaches of Western Civilization.

Secondly, and more importantly for this study, is the origin of Nietzsche's philosophy: he drew it directly from the Greek mystery religion of Dionysos. Nietzsche himself gave the pagan god credit: he writes, "I

am actually the very opposite of the type of man who so far has been re-
vered as virtuous. Between ourselves, it seems to me that precisely this
is part of my pride. I am a disciple of the philosopher Dionysus; I should
prefer to be a satyr to a saint."[4] The admission is not necessary, however,
as the philosopher spends lots of time praising Dionysos as a model of
life over against Christ.[5] He writes a section explicitly on "Dionysus versus the 'Crucified,'"[6] and concludes that only the pagan god knows the
way to true human happiness.

But in the end this "higher man" proves to be no improvement at all.
Dionysos, being the god of wine and revelry, cannot regenerate man,
cannot enter into man's condition and represent him before God, and
cannot, therefore, save man. He can only numb and stupefy. Nietzsche
finds delight in Dionysos because with him, "the sexual act arouses pro-
fundity, mystery, reverence."[7] Here the higher man finds his pleasures;
and here he reveals his true nature: a slave of drunkenness and orgy.
What a man our philosopher has given us! What exactly has his higher
man "transcended" but decency and morality? He could better be called
an under-achiever than a superman. The early Church father Athanasius (A.D. 295–373) ridiculed such a backward view of the drunken Greek
god: "Dionysus is worshipped among them because he has taught man
drunkenness; but the true Savior and Lord of all, for teaching temper-
ance, is mocked by these people."[8]

The push of paganism, in all of its forms, to find the perfect man,
always ends in despair. The very fact that such "higher man" philosophies and religions exist shows that the pagans themselves know that
man as he currently is, needs a change. The American journalist, H. L.
Mencken, himself a fan of Nietzsche, had no illusion in this regard:

---

[4]Friedrich Nietzsche, *Ecce Homo*, Preface 2, in *On the Genealogy of Morals and Ecce
Homo*, ed. and trans. Walter Kauffman (New York: Vintage Books, 1989), 217.

[5]Friedrich Nietzsche, *The Will to Power*, trans. Walter Kaufmann and R. J. Holling-
dale (New York: Vintage Books, 1968), (sec. 1003–1052) 520–543.

[6]Friedrich Nietzsche, *The Will to Power*, (sec. 1052) 542.

[7]Friedrich Nietzsche, *The Will to Power*, (sec. 1052) 542.

[8]Athanasius, *On the Incarnation of the Word* 49.3 in T*he Nicene and Post-Nicene
Fathers*, Vol. IV. ed. Philip Schaff (Albany, OR: AGES Software, 1997), 4:335.

Man, at his best, remains a sort of one-lunged animal, never completely rounded and perfect, as a cockroach, say, is perfect. If he shows one valuable quality, it is almost unheard of for him to show any other. Give him a head, and he lacks a heart. Give him a heart of a gallon capacity, and his head holds scarcely a pint. The artist, nine times out of ten, is a dead-beat and given to the debauching of virgins, so-called. The patriot is a bigot, and, more often than not, a bounder and a poltroon. The man of physical bravery is often on a level, intellectually, with a Baptist clergyman. The intellectual giant has bad kidneys and cannot thread a needle. In all my years of search in this world, from the Golden Gate in the West to the Vistula in the East, and from the Orkney Islands in the North to the Spanish Main in the South, I have never met a thoroughly moral man who was honorable.[9]

Not much has changed since Mencken wrote in 1923—save, perhaps, a little more education on the part of Baptist clergymen—because human nature has not changed. We are dealing with no new material, despite Nietzsche's prediction of a higher man. There has been plenty of war and bloodshed since cultures began to adopt his ideals, but there has been no progress in the nature of man. Only a divine savior, coming to us in the form of the perfect man, begotten in a unique way by God, could save humanity from its desperate condition. Had Mencken taken his Bible as seriously as he took his Nietzsche, he might well have understood the reason for man's twisted condition and looked to the solution that God provided in the perfect man, Jesus Christ.

Christians know that human evolution will not produce a higher man, because man is fallen from his original created state. He is a corrupt and depraved being. His highest aspirations in this condition can amount only to the glorification of himself and creation. No perfect man will emerge from this fallen mass. The follower of Dionysos may call himself superman, and may call his drunken orgy "a form of thanksgiving and affirmation of life,"[10] but his religion betrays him. The fol-

---

[9]"The Good Man" in *A Mencken Chrestomathy*, ed. H. L. Mencken (New York: Vintage Books, [1949] 1982), 19.

[10]Nietzsche's phrase in *A Mencken Chrestomathy*, 19.

lower is not changed or saved, for his god is his own lust. The follower of Dionysos gets drunk, and wakes up with a headache. He repeats his folly. The follower of Christ dies and wakes up glorified—once and for all. The Dionysiac cannot climb out of bed the next morning. The Christian climbs out of his grave.

The Creator Rescuing Fallen Creation

Man does play a crucial role in the doctrine of the Incarnation: his sin made it necessary. Even pagan religions continually exhibit this fact. They continually strive after something new. Yet all of their promises of enlightenment, all of their skepticism and efforts of scholarship, all of their claims of secret knowledge, all of their elaborate mystery ceremonies, and all of their intellectual sewing of fig leaves, cannot arrive at the simplicity of God entering history to save mankind. But their efforts, which seem to have no end, do illustrate one very important thing. They show the underlying belief that if man is to be saved from his wretched condition, then *something extraordinary must happen.* They cannot figure out exactly what this may be, and they run from the truth, but they know it to be true. Something is wrong with man, his condition is not normal; in fact, it is so abnormal that it requires something drastic to fix it.

All of man's efforts at alleviating his fallen condition fail. This is because man's sin enslaved him to a debt that he would never be able to pay. Only one higher than man could pay that price; salvation had to come from above. God knew that the condition of the human race was hopeless unless He took the initiative. This He did, for Christ,

> being in the form of God, thought it not robbery to be equal with God: But made himself of no reputation, and took upon him the form of a servant, and was made in the likeness of men: And being found in fashion as a man, he humbled himself, and became obedient unto death, even the death of the cross. (Philippians 2:6–8)

The Incarnation of Jesus Christ was, therefore, the ultimate act of condescension to the human race, done to redeem His people from their spiritual bankruptcy by the power of God.

The classic works on the subject agree in this reason behind the Word being made flesh. Anselm eloquently responds to pagan skepticism,

> For did they but carefully consider how fitly in this way human redemption is secured, they would not ridicule our simplicity, but would rather join us in praising the wise beneficence of God. For, as death came upon the human race by the disobedience of man, it was fitting that by man's obedience life should be restored. And, as sin, the cause of our condemnation, had its origin from a woman, so ought the author of our righteousness and salvation to be born of a woman. And so also was it proper that the devil, who, being man's tempter, had conquered him in eating of the tree, should be vanquished by man in the suffering of the tree which man bore.[11]

So that he cannot be accused of "painting upon a cloud"[12] with using such beautiful language, Anselm lays out his case more straightly:

> Does not the reason why God ought to do the things we speak of seem absolute enough when we consider that the human race, that work of his so very precious, was wholly ruined, and that it was not seemly that the purpose which God has made concerning man should fall to the ground; and that moreover, that this purpose could not be carried into effect unless the human race were delivered by their Creator himself?[13]

The reference to the active Agent in salvation as "Creator" brings us back to God's original creation and purpose for man. The fall of the first man, Adam, necessitated the Incarnation of a new man, Jesus Christ, as the force behind a new humanity and a new creation. In his line of reasoning Anselm draws upon St. Paul's letter to the Romans, where the apostle makes clear that Christ's coming as man was done to reverse the curse that the original Adam had brought upon the human race. Paul writes,

---

[11]Anselm, *Cur Deus Homo,* 1.3 in *St. Anselm: Basic Writings.* trans. S. N. Deane (La-Salle, IL: Open Court Publishing Co., 1962), 197.

[12]Anselam, *Cur Deus Homo,* 1.4 in *St. Anselm,* 198.

[13]Anselm, *Cur Deus Homo,* 1.4 in *St. Anselm,* 198.

> Wherefore, as by one man sin entered into the world, and death by sin; and so death passed upon all men, for that all have sinned: (For until the law sin was in the world: but sin is not imputed when there is no law. Nevertheless death reigned from Adam to Moses, even over them that had not sinned after the similitude of Adam's transgression, who is the figure of him that was to come. But not as the offence, so also *is* the free gift. For if through the offence of one many be dead, much more the grace of God, and the gift by grace, *which is* by one man, Jesus Christ, hath abounded unto many. And not as *it was* by one that sinned, *so is* the gift: for the judgment *was* by one to condemnation, but the free gift *is* of many offences unto justification. For if by one man's offence death reigned by one; much more they which receive abundance of grace and of the gift of righteousness shall reign in life by one, Jesus Christ.) Therefore as by the offence of one *judgment came* upon all men to condemnation; even so by the righteousness of one *the free gift came* upon all men unto justification of life. For as by one man's disobedience many were made sinners, so by the obedience of one shall many be made righteous. (Rom. 5:12–19)

Without this substitution for the first man, now fallen, of the new man, Jesus Christ, there would be no way out for mankind. Only the Creator of that original man could save that man, and He did so by entering humanity itself and renewing it. Believers in Christ partake of that new humanity which Christ redeemed and renewed. This is what Paul means when he writes, "Therefore if any man *be* in Christ, *he is* a new creature" (2 Cor. 5:17). Not only are we inwardly renewed through spiritual rebirth, but we are counted as righteous, reconciled to God, as part of Christ's own perfect humanity.

Christ is, therefore, effecting the re-creation of man. God created the world by His Word, and by the same Word Incarnate He saved it. Christ truly is the Alpha and the Omega: He is the original Creator (Col. 1:15–16), and He is the final depository of knowledge (Col. 2:3), Divinity (Col. 2:9), and life (Rev. 1:18).

Conclusion

The Incarnation of the Son of God provides for the needs of mankind in every imaginable way. The debt of sin is paid in the death of Christ; the power of life is restored in His resurrection. The Incarnation redirects the attempts by pagan man to evolve a perfect man from a fallen mass. Order does not arise from chaos: God must enter the fallen world and redeem it from its fallen state. Men come to see God for the first time in the person of Jesus Christ, and God is reconciled to men in the substitution of the Perfect Man in our behalf.

9

Implications of the Incarnation

The natural does not ascend to the divine or the supernatural. The bridge is gulfed only by revelation and by the incarnation of Jesus Christ. Salvation therefore is not by man nor by means of man's politics, or by any other effort of man.[1]

. . . even now those barbarians who have an innate savagery of manners, while they still sacrifice to the idols of their country, are mad against one another, and cannot endure to be a single hour without weapons: but when they hear the teaching of Christ, straightway instead of fighting they turn to husbandry, and instead of arming their hands with weapons they raise them in prayer.[2]

And Jesus came and spake unto them, saying, All power is given unto me in heaven and in earth. (Matthew 28:18)

THE FACT THAT the Son of God was manifested in the flesh has far reaching implications. The basic formula of Christ as *fully God and fully man* extends to the way we understand religion and salvation personally and collectively. God speaks to us through the Mediator, the

---

[1]Rousas John Rushdoony, *The Foundations of Social Order: Studies in the Creeds and Councils of the Early Church* (Farifax, VA: Thoburn Press, [1968] 1978), 67.

[2]Athanasius, *On the Incarnation of the Word*, 52.2–3 in *The Nicene and Post-Nicene Fathers*, Philip Schaff (Albany, OR: AGES Software, 1997), 4:338–339.

man Jesus Christ (1 Tim. 2:5–6, Heb. 1:1–2), the Word made flesh, and through the written Word of the Scriptures. Any attempt by any individual or group of individuals to present some other path, revelation, method of relating to God, or means of salvation, necessarily rejects the truth of God and replaces it with the religion of fallen man—a false incarnation.

The End of Mysticism

Since Christ is both fully man and fully God, a correct understanding of His Incarnation corrects errors on two fronts: those who would diminish His deity and those who would deny his true humanity. The former run into the error of seeing Christ as only a man: a special man, perhaps, but only a man, nonetheless, and therefore, unable to save man. The opposite error is the subject of this book: the denial of Christ's humanity. This scenario reduces Christ to a phantom of human imagination. He may be a "god," but since this god has no historical manifestation, then he suffers the fate of all the gods of human history: he is relegated to mythology. More importantly, since this alleged god cannot reveal himself in history, then it is left to man—each individual man—to define this god as they like.

This "personal Jesus" view is simply another version of what has always been known as "mysticism." Mysticism is the belief that one only needs to know God through their own inward witness and not through an objective revelation such as the Scriptures and the Incarnation of Christ. The problem with mysticism is that once the Scriptures and Christ's perfect humanity have been set aside, the resulting images of God begin to look more and more like the people who make them. Talk of Christ as an historical reality ceases, and talk of "What Christ means *to me*" grows more popular. Mysticism reduces God to a spirit only, and denies that He has ever entered history in a defining way. Thus the defining is left to the individual; and, as a result, every man creates his own god and his own rules.

Late Oxford professor O. C. Quick explains the dangers of such unguided mysticism. He begins,

We need a guide along the path who is familiar also with the surrounding country. We are on the edge of an abyss, the moment we emphasize the reality of the inner communion with God in such a way that God Himself begins to be represented simply as an inward presence pervading human life or the life of the world as a whole.[3]

He continues, exposing the relativistic nature of mysticism:

It is well to assert that the Word of God is very nigh to us, in our mouth and in our hearts, and that He Himself is closer to us than our own bodies. Yet it is fatally easy to pass from that assertion to the thought that we are ourselves divine, that to vex ourselves over sins and limitations is a waste of energy, that all we have to do is realize how great and good we may be—and forthwith the mists of our doubts and the shadows of our failures will vanish in the new light shed by the revelation of our own higher and diviner self.[4]

Notice that the elements which mysticism partakes of parallel those of the mystery religions: exclusive knowledge (of self), enlightenment, and man as divine. All of this becomes a logical option to man the minute we forget that Christ came as the full and perfect revelation of both God and man. The lust to touch God purely through inward reflection denies that God has already descended to man, and died in his place.

Mysticism aims to preserve the all-important spiritual side of religion, that God can and does reveal Himself in a very real way through individual experience. But as far as it pursues a direct line to God to the exclusion of Christ's very real historical manifestation in the flesh, mysticism denies the truth rather than preserves it. In such a case,

we cannot escape the practical result, that the centre of gravity in our religion shifts from our Lord to our own souls . . . It will be to

---

[3]Oliver Chase Quick, *Essays on Orthodoxy* (London: MacMillan and Co., Ltd., 1916), chapter 2: http://www.anglicanlibrary.org/quick/essays/02.htm.

[4]Quick, *Essays on Orthodoxy*, chapter 2: http://www.anglicanlibrary.org/quick/essays/02.htm.

our own experiences, our own feelings, our own achievements, that we shall turn in our search for communion with God. We shall judge Christ by them, instead of judging them by Christ. The last stage will be reached when we regard the Godhead Itself as no more than an experience of our own; and just when we think we have scaled heaven itself, we shall in reality have done no more than drag down with us into the pit where we have fallen a god of our own imagination. For our religion will be self-centered, and nothing can draw us, out of the morass save the divine compassion of the Savior we have misunderstood.[5]

This "practical result" is the great sin of our era—relativism—and it lays behind the re-emergence of mystery religions that promise that the way to God is found through personal knowledge or personal experience.

The Incarnation of Christ signals the end of all pretended mysticism. In order that man has a truer understanding of the nature of God than that available through his own feelings, the Son of God descended and manifested Himself in the flesh. He thereby revealed God perfectly to men, revealed man perfectly to man, and represented man perfectly to God. No individual or organized group of individuals can pretend to have any greater personal experience of God than the simple Person of Jesus Christ, as revealed in history and, especially now, in the Scriptures. The minutest deviation from the definitive revelation of Jesus Christ is an error of the human heart, and a false path to God.

Liberty

A recurring theme of modern man is emancipation, or liberty. In many of the wars and revolutions of the modern period, the rallying cry involved some notion of freedom. Yet we still have a world of oppression, war, and debt. This is because all modern revolutions have been *political* at heart, and not ethical. They have aimed to rearrange the conditions of society, rather than to renew the hearts of men. Where man seeks to achieve any level of goodness apart from the true revelation of

---

[5]Quick, *Essays on Orthodoxy*, chapter 2: http://www.anglicanlibrary.org/quick/essays/02.htm, as of August 14, 2006.

God and man in Jesus Christ, the effort will devolve into some form of coercion or chaos.

Nietzsche's attempt at replacing Christ with a "higher man" provided following generations with plenty of intellectual ammunition with which to assault Christian liberty. Under the plan of elevating man to a status where he could truly enjoy life, Nietzsche set in motion the wheels of the war machines of human avarice. He, in a sense, saw this coming. He knew that the overthrow of traditional values, which he saw as lies (funny that someone engaging in a war on morality would worry about lies), would mean the end of human peace. He writes,

> For when truth enters into a fight with the lies of millennia, we shall have upheavals, a convulsion of earthquakes, a moving of mountains and valleys, the like of which has never been dreamed of. The concept of politics will have merged entirely with a war of spirits; all power structures of the old society will have been exploded—all of them are based on lies: there will be wars the like of which have never yet been seen on earth.[6]

This being first published in 1908, the astute observer will note that history has proven Nietzsche correct in this regard. The war against Christianity has indeed been disastrous on all fronts. This is the inevitable result when man—collective man, governmental man, tyrannous man, machine-gun, tank, helicopter, nuclear missile-armed man—is not ruled by a higher, divine law but sets his own law and agenda.

Against all the failures of man, Christ has revealed the true path to human liberty: "If ye continue in my word, *then* are ye my disciples indeed; and ye shall know the truth, and the truth shall make you free" (John 8:31–2). The foundation of human liberty is found in following Christ, the living Word of God. Thus, a proper understanding of Christ becomes all too important for social order.[7] By understanding Christ alone as truly divine and yet fully man, entered into history, we deny

---

[6]Friedrich Nietzsche, *Ecce Homo*, "Why I am a Destiny," 1 in *On the Genealogy of Morals and Ecce Homo*, ed. and trans. Walter Kauffman (New York: Vintage Books, 1989), 327.

[7]See Rushdoony, *The Foundation of Social Order*, 63–82.

that either divinity or true humanity can be found in mere human institutions. No individual and no institution—State, school, or church—can claim ultimate authority in the earth. Christ rules all of heaven *and* earth (Matt. 28:18), and His Incarnation makes this possible. Where mysticism leaves open the question of God to each individual, of who shall be God incarnate, or who represents God, Christianity claims that Christ is God Incarnate, and He represents God. If man answers the question for himself, then some collective agent of man will eventually triumph. It will be either the power of the mob, or the power of a tyrannical state. There will be a higher man, but he will be either in a black suit with a tax bill, or in a blue suit with handcuffs and a gun. The State becomes the ultimate representative of man, the highest appeal in the earth, and therefore an incarnate deity. It then takes on a messianic role, claiming to provide for the welfare of its people. Men then become subjects to the care of the State, rather than free men under God. God provided a way out of human tyranny in the Incarnation of Christ: no State has a legitimate claim to ultimate authority, because Christ is the true King of kings in the earth.

True freedom can only be found in the shadow of God's wings. Likewise, true safety, welfare, and salvation. All of the things that modern man desires, but denies in principle through his self-centered humanism and mysticism, God has provided through Jesus. Only when the State bows beneath the rule of the King of kings will men begin again to experience a free society; for only when the power of both individual and collective man is checked by the ethical rule of law will men be free from the haunt of his tyrannous fellows. The Incarnation lays the foundation of this liberty, for only there is man seen as a new creature, able to follow God's ethics, and only there is God manifest in history so that no other ruler has ultimate authority in the earth.

Conclusion

We must not follow a man-made god, but rather the One true God-made-man. We must not allow human imagination to intrude upon the "express image" of God in Jesus Christ. The Incarnation of the Son of

God meets the needs of human salvation and godliness at all levels (2 Pet. 1:3). It exposes the easiness of a mere "inner" spirituality as spiritual laziness and self-centeredness, in that Christ truly manifested in the flesh in history. Thus the mystic must deal with the historical revelation of God before and ever above his own feelings. As well, the Incarnation denies tyranny and demands that all rulers reign justly beneath the Prince of the kings of the earth (Ps. 2:10–12; Matt. 28:18; Rev. 1:5–6). The law of God is revealed as the path of order and righteousness in the earth, and the lust to rule on the part of mere men is checked by the rule of Christ on earth. If we truly mean it when we pray, "Thy will be done *in earth*, as it is in heaven" (Matt. 6:10), then we must take the true understanding of Christ as fully God and fully man, and apply that truth to all of life.

10

Isis Unveiled. . . and She's Ugly

*And upon her forehead was a name written, MYSTERY BABYLON
THE GREAT, THE MOTHER OF HARLOTS AND ABOMINATIONS
OF THE EARTH. . . . Babylon the great is fallen, is fallen, and is
become the habitation of devils, and the hold of every foul spirit,
and a cage of every unclean and hateful bird* (Rev. 17:5; 18:2).

*With her much fair speech she causeth him to yield, with the flat-
tering of her lips she forced him. He goeth after her straightway, as
an ox goeth to the slaughter, or as a fool to the correction of the
stocks; Till a dart strike through his liver; as a bird hasteth to the
snare, and knoweth not that it is for his life. Let not thine heart
decline to her ways, go not astray in her paths. For she hath cast
down many wounded: yea, many strong men have been slain by
her. Her house is the way to hell, going down to the chambers of
death* (Prov. 7:21–7).

WE HAVE NOW seen, from several angles, the mystery-religion theory
of Jesus for the charade that it is. No pagan god wearing any mask
approaches anywhere near the profound depths of the Incarnate Son of
God, Jesus Christ. Osiris, Dionysos, Mithras, Attis, Isis—we have un-
masked the whole lot of them, only to find the empty skull of fallen human imagination behind the facade. They have tried to disguise them-

selves and mimic Christ, but their act is just not convincing. Just as the early Church fathers exposed the pagans in their day, so is their folly manifest unto all men today.

We have seen that the pursuit of truth hinges on personal ethics. One's report of reality depends upon their ultimate allegiance—whether it be to a selfish agenda, or to the Creator. When the scholar leaves the narrow walk of the truth—and let us face it, truth *is* a very narrow thing—he betrays his true love. This is why Scripture often portrays false doctrine as harlotry. The image comes to its most eloquent form in the book of Proverbs, which compares false knowledge to the "strange woman" (Prov. 2:16; 7:5), and true wisdom to a virtuous woman (Prov. 1:20–3; 8–9; Also cf. Prov. 3:15 with 31:10.) The false woman operates by flattery and leads her deceived simpleton to death. "False rumors are like mistresses: more exciting initially than wives, but more deadly."[1]

In 1877, one such false rumor was codified in the blathering of a very influential mystic named Madame Helena Petrov Blavatsky. Her two-volume work was entitled *Isis Unveiled: A Master Key to the Mysteries of Ancient and Modern Science and Theology*.[2] In 1350 pages of a dexterous ball-under-the-shell-game, with a covering of bitterness and arrogance, she trots out every possible quote from unbelieving scholars, does a hatchet-job on the church fathers, and ignores the orthodox scholars of her day. Her driving belief is that,

> . . . except a handful of self-styled Christians who subsequently won the day, all the civilized portion of the Pagans who knew Jesus honored him as a philosopher, an *adept* whom they placed on the same level as Pythagoras and Apollonius.
> . . . .Had not the Christians burdened themselves with the *Revelations* of a little nation, and accepted the Jehovah of Moses, the Gnostic ideas would never have been termed *heresies;* once relieved of their dogmatic exaggerations the world would have

---

[1] Gary North, *The Sinai Strategy: Economics and the Ten Commandments* (Tyler, TX: Institute for Christian Economics, 1986), 188.

[2] Madame Helena Petrov Blavatsky, *Isis Unveiled: A Master Key to the Mysteries of Ancient and Modern Science and Theology,* 2 vols. (Pasadena, CA: Theosophical University Press, [1877] 1988).

had a religious system based on pure Platonic philosophy, and surely something would then have been gained.[3]

This treacherous book enjoyed several printings, although it never exploded in the way that some have today. One reason for this is the incoherence of both her logic and rhetoric. The average reader would do well to finish a page without exhaustion, let alone a thousand.[4] Unfortunately, the time was ripe, as I recounted in Chapter One, for such a mystical, universal, and anti-Christian theory, and so Blavatsky did not entirely disappear. *Isis Unveiled* continues to be an underground source for mystery-cult buffs precisely because of the immense nature of the work, its coarse sacrilegious tone, and its extensive use of contemporary unbelieving sources.

But now Isis has truly been unveiled, and she is not a pretty sight. She is nothing less than that great whore, Babylon the great, continually trying to divert God's people through her deceptive batting of the eyes. The whole mystery-religion theory collapses when we critically confront just a few of the main ideas, and its downfall parallels the demise of every other false doctrine in history—the fall of that great harlot and her patrons. We have seen that they fail on every major point of scholarship—history, theology, and critical judgment. In surveying these areas we have seen that:

> 1. The modern mystery-religion theory exactly parallels the serpent's deceptions in Genesis 3, beginning with a rejection of God's Word, then offering a promise of enlightenment, and then a promise of becoming divine.
> 2. All forms of attacks on the Christian faith stem from the deeper issue of finding a covering for sin.

---

[3]Blavatsky, *Isis Unveiled*, 2:150, 155.

[4]She admitted such when she later reviewed her own work, saying, "*Isis* was full of misprints and misquotations; that it contained useless repetitions, most irritating digressions . . . had some very gross mistakes . . . has no system to it; and that it looks in truth, as remarked by a friend, as if a mass of independent paragraphs having no connection with each other, had been well shaken up in a waste-basket, and then taken out at random and—published." See Blavatsky, "Appendix: My Books" in *Isis Unveiled*, 45.

3. The fad of a mystical understanding of Jesus Christ is no new discovery, but a very old pagan trend that has resurfaced in history many times.

4. The mystery-religion theory arose in our time directly from forcing the doctrine of naturalistic evolution onto historical study.

5. The popularity of mystery religions today signals a breakdown of philosophical and political systems, just as it did during the declining Roman era.

6. The pagan myths themselves do not say exactly what the critics portray them as saying.

7. None of the few records that may resemble Christian doctrines can be dated prior to the second century, well after Christian doctrine had developed.

8. None of the alleged similarities of paganism to Christianity truly parallel Christian doctrine in substance, only in appearance.

9. The early Church fathers, so often maligned as ignorant and caught off-guard by the mysteries, actually forged and wielded a well-reasoned defense grounded in the Old Testament Scriptures.

10. The Old Testament itself accounts for the fundamental ideas in pagan rites, corrupted though they be.

11. Paul saw Jesus as an earthly, historical figure, divine, who was born of a woman, of the seed of David, and who had died a real death and was truly raised from the dead, according to the Scriptures.

12. Paul said that he had received his doctrines as part of already-existing Christian tradition.

13. Paul himself had his vital foundation in the promises and teachings of the Old Testament, from which he drew extensively in writing his letters.

14. Claims about mystery religions influencing Christianity rely on poor scholarly judgment, forcing decisions where none should be reached and missing evidences that would overturn their theory.

That some writers have presented these facts otherwise and have thereby arrived at wilder conclusions, can only betray either profound ignorance or crusading malice. We shall not assume the latter. In either case, those who persist in denying a competent understanding of the facts will prove either that they have no desire to seek out the truth or, like Pilate, cannot see it when it is right before their eyes.

From Here On Out

Meanwhile, until the day comes that the most radical and counterfactual fabrications no longer pass for scholarship, receive book awards, or become best-sellers, Christian scholars and pastors have a lot of work to do. In today's "information society,"[5] Christians need to quickly grow aware that factual truth is not free, but comes at the price of diligence, self-correction, and faithfulness.[6] We must clear away the abuse of historical fact and restore truth to our generation. This is the burden of Christian scholars and teachers today. Of course, it has been since the atheistic and radical skeptics ran roughshod through biblical studies in the nineteenth century.

Toward this goal, Christians—especially those that labor in teaching or apologetics—should often remind themselves of a few fundamental realities. First, the battle of human autonomy (the serpent's lie) versus God's law has raged throughout history, and every historical period has seen major representatives on each side. In the early Church the apologists such as Irenaeus, Aristides, Justin Martyr, Tertullian, Origen, and later Augustine, Chrysostom, and Eusebius, among others, all confronted the multi-faced paganism of their day. The same held true for the early middle ages and the Reformation. In the modern period, beginning in the mid-nineteenth century, the radical unbelieving side laid the groundwork for both the atheistic takeover of academics as well as the onslaught against the faith by mystics and occultists. Interestingly enough, the most radical of the radicals, such as Blavatsky, thoroughly employed atheistic and skeptical scholarship such as Ernest Renan's work and the anonymous *Supernatural Religion* that appeared in England in 1874. Without such a foundation I wonder how much we would still be hearing out of the mystery-religion propagandists. Today, the continu-

---

[5]See Peter F. Drucker, *The New Realities: In Government and Politics/In Economics and Business/In Society and World View* (New York: Harper and Row, 1989), 173ff.
[6]North, *The Sinai Strategy*, 194.

ing neo-gnostic, mystery-cult movement tends to shy away from citing Blavatsky as a source—probably due to her reputation for quackery[7]— though their platform is exactly the same. And while orthodox scholars such as J. B. Lightfoot and B. F. Wescott beat the liberals squarely on their own turf in the nineteenth century, you do not see too many references to their works among the mystery-cult scholars. The atheists and mystics show no sign of having given serious consideration to orthodox scholarship anywhere along the line. I am constantly reminded of Origen's indictment of the unbelieving Celsus, that he despised the Scriptures from the start, "as not containing anything worthy of notice, because you have not ascertained the meaning which they contain, nor tried to enter into the aim of the writers."[8] The mystery-cult proponents do not exhibit the knowledge that one would expect to see if they had attempted to enter into the intent of the Scriptures, the Church fathers, or the works of orthodox scholars from the modern period to date. This type of polarization—that writers show themselves at best ignorant of their opponents' strongest arguments and contenting themselves to fight caricatures and straw men—shows that the world of scholarship and publication is still a battleground, not merely a marketplace.

Secondly, we must remember that the New Testament was produced within the Church and for the Church, and therefore it can only be properly understood by those who appreciate and love the Word of God. While it is not impossible for unbelievers to collect true facts about history, exegesis, or to think critically, the message and teachings of the Bible can only be a blessing to those who believe the Gospel. To the unbeliever, it will always and only present, ultimately, a condemnation. The life of the Church today grows out of and depends upon

---

[7]As early as 1931 the famous American journalist H. L. Mecken said of her, "She was a fraud pure and unadulterated—a fraud deliberate, unconscionable and unmitigated. She started out in life as a professional spiritualist, and the banal tricks of that amusing trade were always her chief reliances." See "Hooey from the Orient" in *A Mencken Chrestomathy*, ed. H. L. Mencken (New York: Vintage Books, [1949] 1982), 355–357. While placing Blavatsky among his articles on "quackery," he nevertheless agrees with her conclusions about the mysteries in Christianity!

[8]Origen, *Against Celsus*, 3.74 in *Ante-Nicene Fathers*, eds. James Donaldson, Alexander Roberts, and A. Cleveland Coxe (Albany, OR: AGES Software, 1997), 4:966.

the very same living Church depicted in the New Testament. "Within the Church, where the Gospel is preached and heard, where the law of Christ is acknowledged, and where we share in an ordered fellowship of prayer, worship and sacrament, the essential clue to the biblical revelation is held."[9] This is a call for pastors to train their teachers and laity in the history of the early Church and the biblical theology which it developed, and to read the early Church fathers as part of their devotions. It is also a call for seminary teachers to impress upon their students the vital connection between the great wars of theology and the divergent histories that rival worldviews necessarily produce.

The continuing Church of Jesus Christ must be impervious enough to repel enemy forces and yet flexible enough to grow, learn, and expand. This is why the apostles stressed that the Church is the living temple of God, made of "lively stones" (Eph. 2:19–22; 1 Pet. 2:5ff).[10] These living stones comprise an immovable building of the finest architecture, built upon an Immovable Foundation. God-haters try to destroy her in every way imaginable, but every new attempt fails. They put her to the fire of criticism, but stone will not burn; they swing the wrecking-ball of slander, but her walls are too thick. No pick, no hammer, no drill prevails. The only tactic they have left is to build up around her to obscure her from the world's view. They try to buy up the real-estate of culture and then erect their ghettos against the face of Christ. But even this effort is doomed to failure, for God's kingdom—these "living stones"—are organic. They live and grow and spread, and in their ever-steady expansion they consume and conquer all around them until the glorious face of Jesus Christ shines to all the world.

The game is won: history is merely the gradual realization of this truth. Atheism is the sore loser: it has been blind-sided by the truth and has gotten up crying foul. But the play was legal: Christ conquered death forever. The Kingdom then started small and undetected and grew into

---

[9] C. H. Dodd, "The New Testament," *The Study of Theology*, ed. Kenneth E. Kirk, (New York and London: Harper and Brothers, 1939), 243.

[10] It must pain the mystery-cult theorists, who believe so strongly in a final division between the Jewish and Gentile church factions, that Peter and Paul agree on something so fundamental, which is at once Jewish and Spiritualized! Of course, this assumes that mystery-cult theorists can indeed feel pain.

the most imposing force in world history. It has rounded the corner and smacked the atheist in his chin-strap. But the atheist cannot accept defeat. He keeps watching the replay in slow motion looking for reasons to complain, "Look! There! See that!" But it is too late. The game is over, the devil lost; and the rest of history is Christ's victory parade (Col. 2:15).

* * * *

Great indeed, we confess, is the mystery of godliness: He was manifest in the flesh, vindicated by the Spirit, seen by angels, proclaimed among the nations, believed on in the world, taken up into glory . . .

O Timothy, guard the deposit entrusted to you. Avoid the irreverent babble and contradictions of what is falsely called "knowledge," for by professing it some have swerved from the faith.

—(1 Tim. 3:16; 6:21–22, ESV)

Appendix I
Presuppositions and New Testament Studies

LIBERAL AND RADICAL scholars always hide behind the mask of science claiming that they have produced works of reason and science over against the fanciful wishes of orthodox believers. They claim to simply report the facts without relying on supernatural interventions like believers do. This is the popular image they promote anyway. At least, in order to keep their university peers happy, they had better put up the front. Claims about faith are bad for business in the scholarly world, you see. The public must be led to believe that the scholars are hard-bent over "evidence" and the latest archaeology. The truth, however, is far from this public face. Dig even just a bit below the surface—like a few taps from the archaeologist's hammer and trowel—and the whole facade crumbles to dust, and the skeleton of a dead specimen is exposed. The monster of liberal scholarship can be seen in all of its carnivorous glory.

Liberals have displayed a ferocious anti-Christian agenda from their beginning. In the early to mid-1800s, German scholarship began to brood under the nurturing wings of tax funded universities. The flurry of scholarship employed new humanistic methods of interpreting history which denied the possibility of divine revelation and miracles, and therefore of nearly every basic tenant of the Christian religion. Not surprisingly some historians immediately lowered their sights on the early Church in order to determine how Christianity "really" developed. The new methods contrasted with established conservative scholarship, and two schools emerged around the study of early Church history.

Church historian Philip Schaff, writing at the end of the nineteenth century, notes how this divide has affected historical studies. He writes,

Never before in the history of the church has the origin of Christianity, with its original documents, been so thoroughly examined from standpoints entirely opposite as in the present generation . . .

The two theories of apostolic history, introduced by Neander and Baur, are antagonistic in principle and aim, and united only by the moral bond of an honest search for truth. The one [Neander] is conservative and reconstructive, the other [Baur] radical and destructive . . . The one proceeds on the basis of faith in God and Christ, which implies faith in the supernatural and miraculous wherever it is well attested; the other proceeds from disbelief in the supernatural and miraculous as a philosophical impossibility, and tries to explain the gospel history and the apostolic history from purely natural causes like every other history.[1]

Schaff clearly saw the presuppositions of both sides. He knew that the two interpretations of history were primarily matters of competing faiths—belief versus unbelief—not brute scholarship *per se*. The sides argue over the same facts, read the same sources; but draw from two very different wells of interpretation: faith in God versus faith in matter. Schaff knew that these presuppositions determined what the scholars wrote and how they told the story. He said, "The controversy turns on the question whether there is a God in History or not."[2]

The controversy does indeed hinge upon such a belief, but unfortunately it has always been the Christians who have been ridiculed for having "faith," whereas the liberal critics are thought of as "scientific." The truth is that the liberals fall back just as much on faith, though their credo simply begins with anti-theism. Apologist Cornelius Van Til, who expounded the problems of presuppositions throughout his career, explains how differing views of God profoundly affect how one approaches the sciences, and by extension the historical sciences as well. I quote him at length:

---

[1] Phillip Schaff, *History of the Christian Church*, 8 vols. (Peabody, MA: Hendrickson, 1996), 1:205, 208.

[2] Schaff, *History of the Christian Church*, 1:208.

[T]he difference between the prevalent method of science and the method of Christianity is not that the former is interested in finding the facts and is ready to follow the facts wherever they may lead, while the latter is not ready to follow the facts. The difference is rather that the former wants to study the facts *without God*, while the latter wants to study the facts in the light of the revelation God gives of himself in Christ. Thus the antithesis is once more that between those for whom the final center of reference in knowledge lies in man, and those for whom the final center of reference for knowledge lies in God, as this God speaks in Scripture.[3]

The conflict, therefore, is never one of science versus religion, or facts versus faith. To set the argument up in that way is to assume an atheistic answer from the start. The question is whether the God of the Bible rules history or not; and how you answer that question will determine how you interpret the facts which come along. The facts cannot speak first, but are interpreted via the handler's worldview. The Christian sees the facts through Christian ethics; the atheist sees facts through the distortion of atheistic reasoning and materialism. Thus it is not the facts only which need checking but the coherence of the worldviews. In the end, one view must be proven heretical.

This fact drove home to Schaff the point that the radical scholars of his day paralleled the heretics that the early Church in question had to deal with. He explained, "This modern criticism is a remarkable renewal of the views held by heretical schools in the second century."[4] The reason the nineteenth-century liberals worked so hard to defend the Gnostics and to liberate them from the label "heretics," was because they loved and identified with that theology. The same can be said for nearly every radical scholar: the various presentations of the "historical Jesus" or the "real Jesus" all oddly seem to look a lot like their authors. Lutheran scholar John Warwick Montgomery comments on this continuing trend: "Yet in the twentieth century there has been a powerful

---

[3]Cornelius Van Til, *A Survey of Christian Epistemology* (Phillipsburg, NJ: Presbyterian and Reformed, 1932), 9.
[4]Schaff, *History of the Christian Church*, 1:210.

tendency to create Jesus in the image of the time rather than to find out what the documents say about Him."[5]

The various attempts all revolve around the lust for human autonomy and consequently the methodology has become increasingly *Arian*. Arius, you will remember, is the arch-heretic of the early Church who essentially argued that Jesus was not divine but only a finite creature. This belief appeals to unbelieving hearts (in all ages) which also see Christ as merely human, and so the pseudo-scholarly mills begin to churn, trying to produce a justification of Arian historiography—history written on the assumption that miracles do not happen and that Christ was not divine.

Theology always rules every idea below it and every undertaking of man will show the effect of his theological beliefs at some level. When we read the nineteenth-century critics, this is exactly the picture we get: the ultimate commitments of materialism and historical determinism rule the facts. One of the most important popularizers and scholars of the era, Ernest Renan, illustrates this for us: he writes, "That the Gospels are in part legendary, is evident, since they are full of miracles and of the supernatural."[6] Did you get that? "Since," or "because" the Gospels include accounts of miracles, then they must of necessity be legends and myths. No *real* or *true* account would included such uncivilized barbarism as . . . *miracles*. The trap door of the naturalistic mind snaps shut and the case is closed! In their presupposed system, miracle equals forgery; the possibility is denied up front.

The Gospel of John as a Test Case

Many scholars have noted the presuppositional nature of New Testament studies. Leon Morris in his studies on the Gospel of John notes that conservative scholars have been accused of holding "dogmatic presuppositions."[7] Liberals do not like our belief in a God Who rules his-

---

[5]John Warwick Montgomery, *Where is History Going? Essays in Support of the Historical Truth of the Christian Revelation* (Minneapolis, MN: Bethany Fellowship, [1969] 1972), 54.

[6]Ernest Renan, *The Life of Jesus* (New York: The Modern Library, [1863] 1927), 33.

[7]Leon Morris, *Studies in the Fourth Gospel* (Grand Rapids, MI: Eerdmans, 1969), 216–217.

tory, you see. But Morris counters with five presuppositions, compiled by J. A. T. Robinson, which have clearly driven liberal scholarship.[8] He concludes, "[I]t is these presuppositions rather than a careful weighing of the evidence that has usually been decisive."[9]

Such bias has had damaging effects on the course of biblical scholarship. For starters, it has led to the careless treatment of evidences. Morris explains, "An interesting aspect of much recent Johannine study is the refusal to take seriously the evidence that the apostle John was the author. Very few recent scholars make a sustained attempt to grapple with the evidence."[10] Of course, evidence is not that important when the scholar has already made up his mind that the Gospel is inauthentic and that there is no God who judges history. Evidence can, in this case, actually become a hindrance: not only is combing through facts and evidences boring work, but think what consternation comes from evidence that continually confirms your enemy's case. The way around such problems is to ignore them, or present elaborate theories of early Church history which essentially act as a smoke-screen behind which to ignore the problem. When one's assumptions rule the procedure, all kinds of problems can be explained away and then tossed down the memory hole. Morris complains, "For long enough it has not been the evidence but the presuppositions that have decided the matter."[11] He laments that modern methods have provided a framework with which to ignore the classic works of historical evidence, such as the work of B. F. Westcott: "Westcott these days is not so much controverted as bypassed."[12] Likewise, New Testament scholar Donald Guthrie decries the dismissal of original sources themselves. He writes,

> The evidence of Irenaeus has been subjected to searching criticism and many scholars have not been disposed to grant its va-

---

[8]Morris, *Studies in the Fourth Gospel*, 217.
[9]Morris, *Studies in the Fourth Gospel*, 217.
[10]Morris, *Studies in the Fourth Gospel*, 216.
[11]Morris, *Studies in the Fourth Gospel*, 218.
[12]Morris, *Studies in the Fourth Gospel*, 265.

lidity. Their reluctance to do so springs mainly from the fact that Irenaeus' evidence conflicts with their critical conclusions.[13]

Guthrie understands the situation: "It is difficult to approach the problem without preconceptions."[14] In noting the path of Johannine studies since Westcott's days F. F. Bruce comments that Westcott's argument was, "cogent enough to those who shared his presuppositions;"[15] but others soon arose with "other presuppositions" claiming variously: 1) the author created a "fictitious narrative under the guise of an apostolic eyewitness," 2) the Beloved Disciple was a idealized character, not a real person, or 3) Mark preceded John and therefore any material in John which does not fit the narrative of Mark cannot be historical.[16] To Bruce these various permutations of theories are, "more ingenious than convincing."[17]

Liberal scholars have often been as candid, or at least obvious, with their presuppositions. J. Louis Martyn believes that if we can even slightly detect in the Fourth Gospel, "the voice of a Christian theologian who writes *in response to contemporary events and issues*,"[18] then, "it becomes imperative that we make every effort to take up temporary residence in the Johannine community."[19] In other words, he thinks that if we can perceive a possible theological influence upon the Gospel which we decide is not original with Jesus himself, then that outside influence must become the ruling framework for understanding the origin of the Gospel as a whole. This approach, however, *begins* by assuming that the Gospel is the work of mere men and purely historical forces, and not the word of God. Ruling God out in this way is a dishonest approach which frankly begs the question; and yet the liberal scholars praise each others' works as if each page were a revelation from God. Of course,

---

[13]Guthrie, *New Testament Introduction* (Downers Grove, IL: InterVarsity Press, 1973), 258–259.

[14]Guthrie, *New Testament Introduction*, 241.

[15]F. F. Bruce, "Johannine Studies Since Westcott's Days" in B. F. Westcott, *The Epistles of St. John* (Grand Rapids, MI: Eerdmans, 1966), lxi.

[16]Bruce, "Johannine Studies Since Westcott's Days," lxi.

[17]Bruce, "Johannine Studies Since Westcott's Days," lxiii.

[18]J. Louis Martyn, *History and Theology in the Fourth Gospel* (Nashville: Abingdon, 1979), 18.

[19]Martyn, *History and Theology in the Fourth Gospel*, 18.

when you do not believe in supernatural revelation, you have to get it somewhere.

In the case of the Fourth Gospel, however, we would do well to consider the statement of Guthrie that, "It would seem at least a reasonable conclusion to maintain that there are no irrefutable historical grounds for rejecting the identification of the beloved disciple as John the son of Zebedee."[20] If we can honestly make this claim—and the work of Bruce, Carson, Guthrie, Morris, Westcott, etc., gives us good warrant—then we should not be too bothered by spectacular theories which derive from diminishing or destroying the role of God's apostle, or which require outrageously intricate webs of historical patchwork to make their case. Further, we should immediately understand that those theories can only arise where the theorist has little or no theological need for infallible revelation: for example, liberals like Martyn, or Roman Catholics such as Raymond Brown. In the traditional approach, as D. A. Carson notes, "We are freed from the suffocating burden of trying to reconstruct the Johannine community out of merely possible inferences . . . and are driven to listen more acutely to what the Evangelist says about Jesus."[21]

New Testament Studies in General

The phenomenon of presuppositional bias lay at the root of all biblical studies, and affects every area of the discipline. The liberal scholar and mouthpiece Rudolf Bultmann certainly did not hide his radical motivation: "The cosmology of the New Testament is essentially mythical in character . . . Can Christian preaching expect modern man *to accept the mythical view of the world as true?* To do so would be both senseless and impossible."[22] This was his selling point to the modern mind and his starting point theologically: "Miracles are mythical and do not happen in the real world, now let's understand the Bible this way!" Similarly he rants,

---

[20]Guthrie, *New Testament Introduction*, 249.

[21]D. A. Carson, *The Gospel According to John* (Grand Rapids, MI: Eerdmans, 1991), 81.

[22]Rudolf Bultmann, "New Testament and Mythology" in *Kerygma and Myth: A Theological Debate*, ed. Hans Werner Bartsch, trans. Reginald H. Fuller (New York: Harper Torchbooks, 1961), 1, 3.

It is impossible to use electric light and the wireless and to avail ourselves of modern medical and surgical discoveries, and at the same time to believe in the New Testament world of spirits and miracles . . . to expect others to do so is to make the Christian faith unintelligible and unacceptable to the modern world.[23]

Of course this understanding fails at the outset: it is only *because* men have obeyed God's ethical laws in history that many technological advances have come about. Historical and biblical studies are no different, even if liberal scholars see no need for God's "mythical" revelation today. Evangelical scholar George Eldon Ladd finds the same candor in Bultmann:

Bultmann frankly admits his presuppositions . . . As a historian, Bultmann candidly rejects the biblical worldview, which he insists is intolerable in the twentieth century . . . Neither can the modern historian believe in a God who acts directly in history.[24]

Ladd mentions this in the greater context of New Testament criticism as a whole. He critiques the naturalism inherent in much of the field, saying that often,

A scholar is not considered to be truly "critical" unless he accepts the basic naturalist presuppositions of the modern historical-critical method, rejects every trace of the supernatural, and interprets the Bible exclusively in strict historical terms as the word of men.[25]

The situation leaves no room for progress between believers and unbelievers in the realm of New Testament studies. There is no neutrality. You must either adopt naturalistic standards, or allow for the supernatural—either assume that no god acts in history, or believe that God can, and has, inspired his holy apostles. Ladd spies well the division between the competing methods: "Between scholars who hold this view of criti-

---

[23]Bultmann, "New Testament and Mythology," 5.
[24]George Eldon Ladd, *The New Testament and Criticism* (Grand Rapids, MI: Eerdmans, 1984), 47.
[25]Ladd, *The New Testament and Criticism*, 39.

cism and evangelical scholars, there is little if any common ground for mutual interaction or scholarly debate."[26]

The presuppositional nature of New Testament studies reminds us once again that the real problem with historical questions and the Gospels is not ultimately intellectual, but ethical. Gary North presents this point clearly: "The real motive of higher criticism is ethical . . . man's problem is not a lack of knowledge about God, but a *lack of obedience to God*. The higher critics seek to confuse men by blurring the universal ethical requirements of God's holy word."[27] We are reminded that historical judgment, and in fact all judgment, can never be value-free. It will never take place in a truly neutral setting, but will conform to the ethical rules of the scholar's underlying commitments. New Testament scholar C. H. Dodd noted as much in 1939: he writes,

> In any passage of history where the spiritual interests of mankind are deeply involved, the historian, if he is to be more than a mere chronicler, is forced to make judgments of value, explicit or implicit, upon the subject-matter with which he deals, and these judgments will affect his presentation. In the case of the New Testament such judgments cannot be avoided. The report given of the *data* will show that the reporter *either affirms or denies the main assumptions which the New Testament makes.*[28]

Dodd proceeds to make it clear that the worldview of the Bible indeed conflicts directly with that of the unbelieving world around it. This battle climaxed in the cross of Jesus Christ, and afterward in the preaching of that cross. Against those who argue that Paul and the other New Testament writers were at home in the pagan world and propagated pagan myths, Dodd responds,

---

[26]Ladd, *The New Testament and Criticism*, 40.

[27]Gary North, *The Hoax of Higher Criticism* (Tyler, TX: Institute for Christian Economics, 1989), 37–38.

[28]C. H. Dodd, "The New Testament" in *The Study of Theology*, ed. Kenneth E. Kirk, 217–246 (New York and London: Harper and Brothers, 1939), 242. I have added the last string of italics.

> We have the testimony of the Apostle Paul that after his best endeavors, his Greek hearers still felt the Gospel to be 'foolishness.' It is possible, by sympathetically studying, say, the Hermetic writings, to put oneself temporarily in the position of those Greeks, and to feel just how foolish this 'word of the cross' must have sounded.[29]

The foolishness of the cross (1 Cor. 1:18–31) cuts through all sophistication and gets right to the corrupt heart of the issue. It pulls back the shade from the hidden secrets of the heart and exposes our trifling excuses—so often falsely labeled as "science" or "reason"—for the cowardice and spiritual sloth that they are. A message so simple and so "foolish" as the Gospel, forces the hand of mankind: it makes him choose either God or self. Dodd concludes that the Gospel "might be stated in Hellenistic terms, but it shattered the presuppositions of Hellenistic religion."[30]

Such a foundation as the Gospel forces us to adhere to unmovable standards for what we accept as scholarly progress or not. These standards in turn assure that our biblical and historical studies remain true to God's demands and remain honest about the limitations of bare scientific historical investigation. A method which accounts for the authors' presuppositions must analyze rival theological commitments in addition to considering evidences; and then compare the theories based on their inherent plausibility along with their interpretations of the data. We will logically have to ask which theological framework is in itself superior before we pursue which one accounts for the evidence best.

On the other hand, if overly critical and skeptical methods have free reign, and sound traditional views are ignored, a chaotic situation ensues in which the only obvious results are confusion and the abandonment of the authority of the text. D. A. Carson explains that the web of presuppositions and beliefs created by some scholars, "rests on merely possible inferences, not particularly plausible ones, the resulting matrix being used as a grid to eliminate the most natural inferences from both

---

[29]Dodd, "The New Testament," 238.
[30]Dodd, "The New Testament," 238.

internal and external evidence."[31] Thus the main result of beginning with humanistic assumptions, he argues, is that the histories and conclusions turn out just as arbitrary and chaotic as the human will itself. The liberal says, "I'll have the *Gospel du jour!*," or rather, "I'll *cook* the pot myself!"

Conclusion

While we should be vigorous in seeking progress, we should likewise be wary of naturalistic methods which force us to deny the truth of God and the requirements of His world-order. On humanistic grounds Christian scholars gain nothing unless they are replacing it. This means that New Testament scholarship is as much a war as a dialogue. Bultmann himself knew this. He envisioned his theological *coup d'ètat* of New Testament studies as a monumental task: "It will tax the time and strength of a whole theological generation."[32] Conservative scholars would do well to have a long-term vision of comparable weight.

A positive and optimistic view of biblical studies will place the scholar or student in the midst of the Bible itself while they study the higher critical claims. Only from within that biblical framework and upon its One Foundation is the kingdom of God built. For too long students have been made to slave over the works of higher critics in order to taste the dregs of unbelieving skepticism (the liberal sacrament!); and the liberals have filled the ullage of Christian ignorance with vinegar instead of pure wine. The endeavor sends students home from seminary having studied a whole lot *about* the Bible, without having studied the Bible much at all. Then they go fill pulpits and feed congregations . . . ? I propose a return to dependence upon the law and language of God. It is not Baur and Bultmann, but every Word from the mouth of God that feeds us. In the meantime, let the higher critics "drown in their own footnotes, the way that Arius died by falling head-first into a privy. Let the dead bury their dead, preferably face-down in a scholarly journal."[33] Arian

---

[31]Carson, *The Gospel According to John*, 80.

[32]Bultmann, "New Testament and Mythology," 15.

[33]North, *The Hoax of Higher Criticism,* 52. I have edited the name Arius in this quotation.

theology (denying that Christ is God) leads to Arian scholarship, Arian history books, Arian classrooms, Arian pulpits, Arian governments, and Arian culture. It also leads to the judgment from God that Arianism deserves, in both history and eternity. Our presentation of the New Testament and of early Church history, and our communication of the same to posterity are matters of eternal import. Lest we be found unfaithful teachers, we must tear up faulty scholarship from its corrupt root, and replant the seeds of godliness in its place.

Appendix II
Mithraism and Franz Cumont: A Case of Academic Tyranny

NOTHING SHOWS THE failure of the mystery religion theory better than a case of good-old academic back-stabbing. The career of Franz Cumont, distinguished as it was, illustrates one such case where academic rivalry led to advances based on personality, and the scholarly world was left to suffer under seventy years of suppression.

David Ulansey points out that modern scholarship of Mithraism has taken a path almost as strange as the cult itself.[1] Cumont, by placing his interpretive volume beside his comprehensive 1896 collection of known Mithraic archaeological material, gained worldwide authority on the subject. Furthermore, he labored to propagandize his work while suppressing others.[2] "The result was seventy years of scholarship in which the interpretation of Mithraism by Cumont and his followers went almost completely unchallenged."[3]

Part of Cumont's legacy includes his insistence that mystery religions such as Mithraism affected the development of early Christianity doctrine. This belief pervades the claims of his followers to a ridiculous extent. For example, Vermaseren strains to parallel an obscure medieval text of Persian sayings with the Christian Eucharist.[4] In 1925, Samuel

---

[1] David Ulansey, *The Origins of the Mithraic Mysteries: Cosmology and Salvation in the Ancient World.* (New York and Oxford: Oxford University Press, 1989), 6ff.

[2] Manfred Clauss, *The Roman Cult of Mithras: The God and His Mysteries* (New York: Routledge, 2001), xix.

[3] Ulansey, *The Origins of the Mithraic Mysteries*, 8.

[4] M. J. Vermaseren, *Mithras, the Secret God* (London: Chatto & Windus, 1963), 103–104.

Angus based an entire volume on ungrounded claims. Of the mysteries he wrote,

> As an important background to early Christianity and as a chief medium of sacramentalism to the West they cannot be neglected...Above all they emphasized the perfect humanity and passion of the Deity, and suggested a fellowship of suffering...Orphism was steeped in sacramentalism which flooded the later mysteries and flowed into Christianity."[5]

"A chief medium of sacramentalism?" "Flowed into Christianity?" Really? These are not just mere assertions without evidence; Angus has taken unbelievable license with his fabrication. True parallels, as we have seen, do not exist; and yet so many scholars following Cumont's school of thought have made a point to use Christian language in describing them.

The assumption of Christian aping and the use of Christian language in describing the mysteries marks Cumont's followers clearly and can be traced through both academic and popular history. The famous American historian Harry Elmer Barnes made the influence of mystery religions fundamental to what he called "The Evolution of the Christian Religion."[6] His *An Intellectual History of the Western World* appeared in 1937. The very influential and equally atheistic Bertrand Russell, in his 1945 *A History of Western Philosophy*, cites Cumont and follows the mystery-religion thesis.[7] The widely published Will Durant drank deeply from Cumont (among other critics) and concluded, "Christian Fathers were shocked to find so many parallels between their own religion and Mithraism . . . It is difficult to say which faith borrowed from the other."[8] Background research such as this led Durant to begin his

---

[5]S. Angus, *The Mystery Religions and Christianity: A Study in the Religious Background of Early Christianity* (New York: Charles Scribner's Sons, [1925] 1928), viii, x, 154.

[6]Harry Elmer Barnes, *An Intellectual History of the Western World* (New York: Dover Publications, [1937] 1965), 1:268–270, 278–281.

[7]Bertrand Russell, *A History of Western Philosophy* (New York: Simon and Schuster, [1945] 1972), 279–281. He also cites Angus, *The Mystery Religions and Christianity*, on 331.

[8]Will Durant, *Caesar and Christ: A History of Roman Civilization and of Christianity from their Beginnings to A. D. 325* (New York: Simon and Schuster, 1944), 524.

chapter on Jesus asking, "Did Christ exist? Is the story of the founder of Christianity the product of human sorrow, imagination, and hope—a myth comparable to the legends of Krishna, Osiris, Attis, Adonis, Dionysius, and Mithras?"[9] He later says that there is probably some kernel of truth to the historicity of Jesus, but ultimately concludes, "Christianity was the last great creation of the ancient pagan world."[10] Nowhere in his work does he cite or list the great conservative works of the era,[11] but the marks of Cumont and his like abound everywhere.

By 1950, Cumont's view was standard in liberal seminaries. We see a telling example in the most famous American liberal minister of the twentieth century himself: Martin Luther King, Jr. Among his writings collected at Stanford University exist multiple seminary papers arguing the influence of the mystery cults on early Christianity. What was King's take? He wrote, "There can hardly be any gainsaying of the fact that Christianity was greatly influenced by the Mystery religions, both from a ritual and a doctrinal angle."[12] He also parroted other naturalistic explanations handed down by critics. He said, "It seems quite evident that the early followers of Jesus in Palestine were well aware of his genuine humanity . . . And so in order to receive inspiration from Jesus the Greeks had to apotheosize him,"[13] meaning, they had to invent the doctrine of His divinity to suit their philosophical minds.

Even the more conservative historian Kenneth Scott Latourette in his 1953 *A History of Christianity* follows Cumont, calling him "an outstanding authority."[14] The Yale professor thus tells us,

---

[9]Durant, *Caesar and Christ*, 553.

[10]Durant, *Caesar and Christ*, 595.

[11]Neither J. B. Lightfoot nor B. F. Westscott, to name just two, appear in his bibliography.

[12]Martin L. King, Jr. "The Influence of the Mystery Religions on Christianity," *Called to Serve, January 1929–June 1951*, eds. Clayborne Carson, Ralph Luker, and Penny A. Russell, *The Papers of Martin Luther King, Jr.*, 29 November 1949–15 February 1950. Also see King, "A Study of Mithraism" in *Called to Serve, January 1929–June 1951*, 13 September–23 November 1949. Available at http://www.stanford.edu/group/King/mlkpapers/

[13]Martin L. King, Jr. "What Experiences of Christians Living in the Early Christian Century Led to the Christian Doctrines of the Divine Sonship of Jesus, the Virgin Birth, and the Bodily Resurrection." In *Called to Serve, January 1929–June 1951*, 13 September–23 November 1949. Available at http://www.stanford.edu/group/King/mlkpapers/

[14]Kenneth Scott Latourette, *A History of Christianity*, 8 vols. (Peabody, MA: Prince

Mithra, a god of Persian origin, was usually represented as be-
striding a bull and slaying it. From the dying bull issued the seed of
life for the world, and hence the act became the symbol for regeneration. The cult practiced baptism and had a sacramental meal.[15]

The language is misleading. We have no record of Mithraists using the
terms "regeneration," "baptism" or "sacramental" before the late second
century. Cumont himself was even worse: not only did he refer to "baptism" among the Mithraists, but he went so far as to say that they "expected from a Lord's Supper salvation of body and soul."[16] To use such
obviously Christian language is overboard on his part, and I do not see
how he could have escaped the charge of plain dishonesty. Cumont's
and his followers' use of distinctly Christian language to describe phe-
nomena that remotely resembled Christian practices creates the illusion of commonality where none exists. D. E. Aune criticizes Cumont
for the use of such terms as *"églises"* and *"conversion"* saying that, "Cumont has conceptualized Mithraism based on a Christian model."[17] In
other words, like so many radicals continue to do today, Cumont simply
read Christian thought back into the mysteries and then claimed that it
was the Christians who stole. This is simply skewing the evidence.[18] To
his credit, Latourette later makes clear that no evidence exists to link
Christian practice to the mysteries: "There is no proof of either conscious or unconscious copying from the mystery religions by Christians
. . . the similarities are only superficial."[19] He mentions the obvious difference between the mythological nature of the mystery heroes and the
historical nature of Christ as fully man and fully God. He also argues
that the paucity of references to the mysteries by the Church fathers in-

---

Press, 2000), 1:29.

[15]Latourette, *A History of Christianity*, 1:25.

[16]Franz Cumont, *The Mysteries of Mithra*, trans. Thomas J. McCormack (New York:
Dover Publications, [1902] 1956), 190–191.

[17]D. E. Aune. "Expansion and Recruitment among Hellenistic Religions: The Case
of Mithraism," *Recruitment, Conquest, and Conflict: Strategies in Judaism, Early Christianity, and the Greco-Roman World*, eds. Borgen, Robbins, and Gowler (Atlanta, GA:
Scholars Press, 1998), 40.

[18]Aune, "Expansion and Recruitment among Hellenistic Religions," 40.

[19]Latourette, *A History of Christianity*, 1:198.

dicates that the Church had little concourse with the mysteries and was not threatened thereby.[20] The disparity he claims, however, would stand out much clearer and stronger had Cumont's slant not monopolized Mithraic studies and infected Latourette's own prose.

Then the plot really thickens. Problems with Cumont's theory had existed from day one, and viable competitors had also published. But Cumont engaged in tireless self-promotion and authoritative posturing to keep his view in the spotlight. As early as 1869—twenty-seven years prior to Cumont—another German scholar, K. B. Stark, published a theory of Mithraism that tied the cult to the astrology of the period. Cumont, himself a master scholar of ancient astrology, must surely have seen the merit of Stark's work, for he had noted the zodiac and astrological symbols throughout Mithraic art.[21] He nevertheless rejected Stark's ideas. Vermaseren later following Cumont would note astrological ideas but fail to incorporate their force into Mithraic theory.[22] Under the massive weight of Cumont's scorn Stark's hypothesis languished in academic obscurity for over seven decades—a sad testimony to the power of academic naïveté and prejudice.

The situation changed, however, when the many holes in Cumont's thesis became so obvious it could no longer hold water. In 1971, at the First International Congress of Mithraic Studies, scholars presented several papers undermining Cumont's intellectual monopoly. Within a few years an alternative theory was promoted by drawing from Stark's original thesis and taking advantage of the knowledge of Greco-Roman astrology. This effort culminated in David Ulansey's work on the "star map" theory of Mithraism.

What does all this mean for Christianity? As far as the cult itself, not much. The fact that scholars have a better understanding of one mystery group does not necessarily reveal much about any of the cults' relations with Christianity. The whole episode, however, does reveal the

---

[20]An idea shared by Aune, "Expansion and Recruitment among Hellenistic Religions," 42.

[21]Ulansey, *The Origins of the Mithraic Mysteries*, 16.

[22]Vermaseren, *Mithras, the Secret God*, 154–62, esp. 159–160.

rapacity, jealousy, and spiteful ambition at work in the liberal scholarship of that era. Far from being dispassionate and impartial scholars, they often were driven by private agendas and fame to say the least. Who knows how deeply such feelings ran. Meanwhile the resultant body of scholarship always seems to repeat the same refrain: the denial of every meaningful fact of the traditional historical and biblical view of Jesus Christ. The interpretation of the facts, therefore, is as crucial, if not more crucial, than the facts themselves, and the checking of the facts more important yet. These should derive from critical reflection, not from forcing the evidence to fit a preconceived theory, and certainly not from irrational allegiances to the personality of any given scholar. Be careful whom you follow!

Appendix III
"A Very Striking Cover"
Getting Behind the Illusions of
The Jesus Mysteries

THE QUEST TO present Jesus Christ as anything other than what the apostolic tradition has always known Him to be began in the early Church era and has resurfaced many times throughout history. Every generation has had its eloquent unbelievers who lash out at Christ, and ours is no different. It should not surprise us, then, to see a rash of such books break out upon the face of popular religion in our time. The depraved heart cannot stand the idea of a sovereign God who created history, rules it, entered it Himself, conquered it from within, and will *judge* it at His own determined finale. Above all, pagans want to escape the idea of final judgment. So they look for a cover, an excuse, anything to justify their skeptical *jihad*. They need something to cover their sin; but the only cover man could ever muster was a fig leaf, and nothing has changed. So the books of excuses roll forth.

I have in my possession just such a book, this one entitled *The Jesus Mysteries: Was the "Original Jesus" a Pagan God?* by Timothy Freke and Peter Gandy (from here on out *TJM*). From the fraudulent artifact on its cover to its lopsided bibliography, the book is a work of modern mythology. The authors attempt to persuade the reader that Christianity as we know it is nothing but the vestige of ancient pagan mysticism that has been shorn of all its magical value by the fossilizing power of the Roman Catholic Church. They argue (if what they do can be called argument) that Christianity originally developed from the ancient pagan mystery cults and that Jesus Christ probably never existed as an historical per-

son, but as a legend and myth. Later Christians simply believed—igno-
rantly, the authors imply—that the hero figure of their myth actually
did exist, die, and rise again. According to the Freke-Gandy thesis, this
naive group, whom they persistently label "literalists," grew in power
and influence until the true mystical Christians were pushed out and
eventually stamped out by force. These ideas, of course, have been argued in detail since the nineteenth century. Despite the authors' claim
that they stand "boldly" against "taboo" and the "conditioning of our
culture" (*TJM*, 2–3), they offer nothing cutting edge. Even their tilted
rhetoric recalls the hauteur and nose-turning of Madame Blavatsky.
Like all of its predecessors, *TJM* fits the pattern of all fig-leaf excuses:
when it was first sewn together it created a big stir as the latest in atheistic and gnostic fashion; but the first stout wind of critical judgment
exposed the lightweight sham.

One such predecessor appeared anonymously in 1874 with the title
Supernatural Religion: An Enquiry into the Reality of Divine Revelation.
It provoked huge reactions on both sides of the Atlantic. The outpour-
ing of praise from some reviewers grew so overwhelmingly lavish that
Bishop Lightfoot, in his classic response, had to doubt whether he was
reading the same work as they.[1] After he finished exposing the author's
ignorance of Greek, Latin, the Church fathers and other matters, all the
unlearned adulation of the book's alleged "careful and acute scholarship"[2] seemed a bit silly.

Now we have a similar package under a different title: *TJM*. Freke
and Gandy claim to have "focused forensically on the few facts we could
be confident of, as if we were detectives" (*TJM*, 10), and that their book
is "firmly based upon the available historical sources and the latest
scholarly research" (*TJM*, 2). Many reviewers agree: one calls the book
"erudite and well-researched," another "absolutely on target," and still
another sees "thorough documentation." *Daily Telegraph* awarded the

---

[1]J. B. Lightfoot, *Essays on the Work Entitled Supernatural Religion* (New York: Mac-
Millan and Co., 1889), 2–3.

[2]Lightfoot, *Essays on the Work Entitled Supernatural Religion*, 3.

work, "Book of the Year 1999."[3] But upon reading *TJM* with just a little critical judgment I have had to question whether I hold in my hands the same work they have supposedly critically reviewed.

The reason for this may lay in the agenda of mystical paganism that Freke and Gandy and probably many of their sympathetic reviewers seem to adhere to. They have well-fixed theological presuppositions through which they have strained evidence, and by which they determine that which they will even consider as evidence. Although they try to present their thesis as the result of detective work which continually surprised them in its results, they actually betray their agenda when they write on page 3, "We had shared an obsession with mysticism all our lives. . . ." Let me suggest, then, that instead of reading *TJM* as the result of detective work, we read it as "an obsession with mysticism," pure and simple. The work then begins to make perfect sense.

Even with this in the open, the authors contradict themselves in their effort. It strikes me as strange that they introduce their thesis with the "hope" that they are "reclaiming the true mystical Christian inheritance" (*TJM*, 14), yet later they complain that because "literalist" Christians overran the true mystics, "the keys to decode the allegories have been lost and we can only guess at much of the profound metaphor at work in the Jesus story" (*TJM*, 117).[4] Well, if the mystical keys were swallowed by the mythical monster of "literalism," I wonder what exactly the authors intend to "reclaim." Do we stand at the brink of a neo-gnostic revelation? Or shall we wait for Freke and Gandy to "guess at much of the profound metaphor"?

Guesswork would be bad enough, but it appears to me that Freke and Gandy have twisted logic and history into something resembling a pile of religious spaghetti, with a saucy attitude on top. Their fallacies intertwine upon each other like a den of snakes, often within the same sentence. In some cases, the assumptions mounted in one paragraph would take a book to untangle and refute clearly.

---

[3]All of these praises are printed in the unnumbered first leaves of the book itself.

[4]Elsewhere they repeat, "There is now no tradition that can initiate modern Christians into the secret Inner Mysteries encoded in the Jesus story." *TJM*, 255.

This is not only the view of a Christian who sees *TJM* as blasphemy, but even of reputable scholars who have sympathies with paganism. Dr. Graham Harvey of the Open University outside of London, by no means a proponent of traditional orthodoxy, sees the book as a poor effort. He writes,

> Despite copious footnotes and the appearance of careful argu-
> ment, the work remains less convincing than Victorian versions
> of the same kind of narrative. The sense of breathless excitement
> with which banal oversimplifications are asserted is wearying. A
> minor but typical example is the phrase 'as the scholar who un-
> earthed these passages in the Talmud admits'. It is far from true
> that Talmudic polemics about Jesus were unknown until 1975. It
> is ridiculously reminiscent of *Raiders of the Lost Ark* to suggest
> that they required 'unearthing.' And the conspiratorial 'admits'
> is far from impressive. In the end there are more interesting and
> convincing books about ancient Judaism, ancient pagan mys-
> teries, gnosticism, Christianity's polemics and power struggles,
> mysticism, spirituality and ways to improve human life today.[5]

This comes from an avid scholar of pagan religions who has authored or edited several dozen books and articles on the topic. He knows the material. He is also an enthusiast for his field, so you would expect him to readily accept the Freke-Gandy thesis if it held much truth at all; but he appears to expect more solid evidence than the house of cards they provide.

The brief example that Harvey entertains characterizes the whole work. While Freke and Gandy present loads of references, they never challenge themselves with any of the many real scholarly works which would contradict their aim. They never display the kind of learning that results in a balanced, critical weighing of facts, ideas and possibilities, but only selective references to fringe scholars who support their view.

---

[5]Graham Harvey, Review of Timothy Freke and Peter Gandy, *The Jesus Mysteries: Was the Original Jesus a Pagan God?* in *Modern Believing* 41:2 (2000), 50–51.

As easy (and fun) as it be would refute *TJM* point-by-point, the time and energy cannot be justified—especially when just the following few examples can illustrate the characteristic problems.

Example #1—"A Very Striking Cover":

If *TJM* is as shot-through with error and fallacy as I have claimed, how in the world could I ever decide where to begin critiquing the work? Answer: how about the front cover? On the front cover of their work the authors present a rare talisman (now lost, actually), dated to the third century, which depicts the crucifixion; but instead of any recognizable Christian inscription, the piece reads, "Orpheos Bakkikos," a reference to the mystery cult figure Orpheus. The authors found this artifact near the end of their work and called it, "an unexpected confirmation of the Jesus-Mysteries Thesis" (*TJM*, 13). It is too bad that the authors did not themselves confirm this "confirmation," for it turns out that the amulet is a forgery. A now well-circulated fact, reputable experts in the fields of archaeology and Orphic studies have agreed upon the amulet's dubious authenticity. It is not from the third century after all, but probably from the nineteenth.

This knowledge was available at the time Freke and Gandy wrote, and had been around since 1926.[6] When the news finally reached the authors they responded in an internet forum by saying that the amulet was not central to their thesis, but only played a "psychological role." I suppose this is why they used it for the cover of their book. They playfully admitted, "And of course it makes a very striking cover."[7] A very striking cover indeed! But a very deceptive one as well. While they did not intentionally deceive the public—for they apparently did not know before they used it—their willingness to adopt such visual persuasion before

---

[6]See Otto Kern's review of W. K. C. Guthrie's *Orpheus and Greek Religion* in *Gnomon*, 1935, 473–478. Guthrie originally accepted the third-century date for the amulet, but changed his view in a footnote in his 1952 edition. Some of Kern's German article has been translated at: http://sternfels.blogspot.com/2006/03/doubts-about-crucified-orpheus-amulet.html. Kern references the original judgment of forgery made by Reil and Zahn in *Angelos* 2 (1926), 62ff.

[7]Taken from http://www.iidb.org/vbb/showthread.php?p=952718#post952718 .

they had confirmed its veracity shows a certain proneness to use information uncritically when it promotes their cause. That some people claimed that the authors *did* know about the fraud in advance prompted Freke and Gandy to issue a more detailed statement on the matter.[8] But they still had not researched the issue properly, as they demand "references to support the assertion that the object has 'long been suspected of being a fake.' We know of no such suspicions, nor did we come across any in our research. Nor, to the best of our knowledge, has the object ever been proved to be a fake."[9] The references they were stomping for were easily available to anyone with the desire to look. To this date[10] they have not publically commented on the relevant journal articles.

Example #2—Abuse of Sources

Aside from the "striking cover," another telling failure of *TJM* is that the authors constantly insist on name-calling when it comes to orthodox scholars, eary church fathers, or just orthodoxy in general; while at the same time refusing to actually quote or interact with that tradition at the primary level. This constitutes nothing less than pure abuse of scholarly evidence. Their favorite target is the early Church father, and "Father of Church History," Eusebius. They refer to him numerous times in their work, and almost every time his name is mentioned they accompany it with slurs such as "spin doctor," "unreliable source," "propagandist," and "mouthpiece of Catholic propaganda." The authors attribute to him, "fabrications" (*TJM*, 11), "a fake chronology" (*TJM*, 64), "little regard for the truth" (*TJM*, 241), and just plain "lies" (*TJM*, 242). Yet they hardly even quote Eusebius. In fact, though they revile him over and over, they only actually quote *one sentence* from his multiple volumes of works. They never once demonstrate the slightest mistake on Eusebius' part,[11] let alone a deliberate lie. They quote a famous scoff by the eighteenth-century historian, Edward Gibbon, but do not show any knowledge of

---

[8] Posted on Freke's website, www.timothyfreke.com (June 10, 2006).
[9] Posted on Freke's website, www.timothyfreke.com (June 10, 2006).
[10] I write this on July 7, 2006.
[11] Though there are a few to be found.

J. B. Lightfoot's adequate defense against Gibbon's nonsense.[12] I would love to see some real scholarship in relation to their bold claims; and while they nowhere even try to prove anything that they say about Eusebius, they also never consider the fact that their opinions of him might be wrong.

Now, keep in mind that Freke and Gandy boast of "an openness of mind" (*TJM*, 12). These guys, who themselves have objected to a possibly libelous claim (that they knew of the amulet forgery in advance), yet have no trouble slandering Eusebius in the same manner. They claim that the orthodox history of the Christian church "was a gross distortion of the truth," by which, "we had been *deliberately* deceived" (*TJM*, 10).[13] By making such claims without trying to prove them in any rational manner, the authors betray a mind rather set on edge than open.

Example #3—Alexamenos Graffiti:

A third case involves a famous bit of archaeology. In a guard room on Palatine Hill in Rome near the Great Circus where gladiators and wild beasts would murder Christians in sport, a rash of graffiti portrays a figure having an ass's head crucified. Next to this spectacle stands a figure with his hand raised in worship. Below, in very crude scratching, reads, "Alexamenos worships his God." Considering the venue, the era and some contemporary references (we shall see in a minute), Christian and non-Christian scholars generally agree that the graffito is a mock of Christ—showing him as an ass—and of the faith of the character Alexamenos.

In the hands of Freke and Gandy, however, the scene takes on an entirely different meaning. They claim that the picture represents a pagan initiate of the mystery religions at the crucifixion of his lower "ani-

---

[12]J. B. Lightfoot, "Eusebius of Caesarea" in *A Dictionary of Christian Biography and Literature, to the End of the Sixth Century A.D., with an Account of the Principal Sects and Heresies,* eds. Henry Wace and William C. Piercy (Boston: Little, Brown and Co., 1911), 324–326. Please note the date of publication: 1911. Gibbon's "sneer" has been refuted for nearly a hundred years, but Freke and Gandy pay no attention.

[13]Italics added.

mal" nature.[14] This allegedly supports their thesis in that it shows that Romans of the period believed in a crucified god other that Jesus. But where do they get this understanding? I have seen no corroboration from any scholar on such an interpretation.[15] Rather, the figure is almost universally agreed to be a parody of the Christian faith, probably by hateful Roman soldiers. The ass's head does not represent some "lower 'animal' nature," but rather a well-known ridicule of the Christian faith.

We can easily trace this particular attack on Christians through responses of the early Church fathers back to similar charges that Roman historians threw upon the Jews. Josephus, the Jewish historian, dispelled the attack on behalf of the Jews. Against his opponent Apion he wrote,

> for Apion hath the impudence to pretend, that "the Jews placed an ass's head in their holy place;" and he affirms that this was discovered when Antiochus Epiphanes spoiled our temple, and found that ass's head there made of gold, and worth a great deal of money. To this my first answer shall be this, that had there been any such thing among us, an Egyptian ought by no means to have thrown it in our teeth, since an ass is not a more contemptible animal than [...] and goats, and other such creatures, which among them are gods.[16]

---

[14]See Picture 7, found between pages 152 and 153 in *TJM*.

[15]There are a few writers who have tried to find a parallel to the ass-headed god in the Egyptian god Set, but Set is always pictured with either an inexplicable animal head (which scholars call the Set-animal) or a jackal. Nowhere is he depicted with a donkey head. Besides, Set is not crucified in Egyptian mythology, so the image would make no sense if the figure were intended to be him. Furthermore, if it were Set being crucified as a lower animal nature, then why is the "initiate" worshiping him? Do the pagan mystery initiates praise their animal nature? Such an interpretation makes nonsense of the grafitto, despite the desperate claim of *TJM* that the pagan initiate view is "far more likely" (52) and only prevented by "Christian prejudice" (269, note 219).

[16]Josephus, *Against Apoin*, 2.80–81 in *The Works of Josephus: Complete and Unabridged*, trans. William Whitson (Peabody, MA: Hendrickson Publishers, 1995), 798. Josephus continues his defense with no light rhetoric: "Apion ought to have had a regard to these facts, unless he had himself had either an ass's heart or a dog's impudence; of such a dog I mean as they worship; for he had no other external reason for the lies he tells of us. As for us Jews, we ascribe no honor or power to asses, as do the Egyptians to crocodiles and asps, when they esteem such as are seized upon by the former, or bitten by the latter, to be happy persons, and persons worthy of God. Asses are the same with us which they are with other wise men, viz., creatures that bear the burdens that we lay upon them" (2.85–86).

Since the Romans saw Christians as only a small sect of Jews, they apparently leveled the same silly critique against them. Tertullian noted,

> Report has introduced a new calumny respecting our God. Not so long ago, a most abandoned wretch in that city of yours, a man who had deserted indeed his own religion . . . carried about in public a caricature of us with this label: *Onocoetes*. This (figure) had ass's ears, and was dressed in a *toga* with a book, having a hoof on one of his feet. . . . Throughout the city, therefore, Onocoetes is all the talk.[17]

Apparently, the mockery of Christians as worshiping a god with an ass's head gained some popularity during Tertullian's era, roughly the same era as the graffiti at Palatine Hill has been dated. The apologist responds on behalf of Christianity just as Josephus had done for the Jews, that even if the blasphemy were true it should be no big deal to the pagans who themselves worshiped every creeping thing that moved.

> You have amongst you gods with a dog's head, and a lion's head, with the horns of a cow, and a ram, and a goat, goat-shaped or serpent-shaped, and winged in foot, head, and back. Why therefore brand our one God so conspicuously? Many an *Onocoetes* is found amongst yourselves.[18]

Tertullian elsewhere dispels the same libel even more clearly, driving right to the source of the lie:

> For, like some others, you are under the delusion that our god is an ass's head. Cornelius Tacitus first put this notion into people's minds. In the fifth book of his histories, beginning the (narrative of the) Jewish war with an account of the origin of the nation; and theorizing at his pleasure about the origin, as well as the name and the religion of the Jews, he states that having been delivered, or rather, in his opinion, expelled from Egypt, in crossing the vast plains of Arabia, where water is so scanty, they were in extremity

---

[17]Tertullian, *Ad Nationes*, 1.14 in *Ante-Nicene Fathers*, eds. James Donaldson, Alexander Roberts, and A. Cleveland Coxe (Albany, OR: AGES Software, 1997), 3:225.
[18]Tertullian, *Ad Nationes*, 225–226.

from thirst; but taking the guidance of the wild asses, which it was thought might be seeking water after feeding, they discovered a fountain, and thereupon in their gratitude they consecrated a head of this species of animal. And as Christianity is nearly allied to Judaism, from this, I suppose, it was taken for granted that we too are devoted to the worship of the same image.[19]

The early Church father Minucius Felix corroborates Tertullian's accounts, by entertaining the argument that Christians "adore the head of an ass, that basest of creatures, consecrated by I know not what silly persuasion."[20]

So while Freke and Gandy apparently expect the reader to accept their interpretation on their own authority, thorough scholars such as Everett Ferguson present the archaeological evidence, cite the relevant literary evidence in Tacitus, Josephus, Tertullian and Minucius Felix, reference the definitive modern scholarship on the subject, and set the graffiti in its historical context where Christians were persecuted and ridiculed.[21] Which will you believe?

Freke and Gandy either ignore or are not aware of mountains of evidence, though from the numerous times they mention these fathers as well as Josephus, you would expect that they had crossed the relevant facts. Perhaps they have not read the works closely, or have only gathered their references where they are quoted by their own favorite authors, or simply have not pursued the question as diligent researchers should. In any case the obvious deficiency of their scholarship calls into question their endeavor.

This deficiency is not limited to major claims, either. Countless smaller—though by no means insignificant—errors spot the pages of *TJM*. For example, in one place the authors call Justin Martyr a "Roman

---

[19]Tertullian, *Apology,* 16.2.

[20]Minucius Felix, *Octavius,* chap. 9 in *Ante-Nicene Fathers*, eds. James Donaldson, Alexander Roberts, and A. Cleveland Coxe (Albany, OR: AGES Software, 1997), 4:348.

[21]Everett Ferguson, *Background of Early Christianity*, 3rd ed. (Grand Rapids, MI: Eerdmans, 2003), 596. Also see 596, notes 22–23.

Christian,"[22] when he was in fact a Greek philosopher to his bones,[23] and may not even have been versed in Latin literature. Similarly, when they foray into the Greek language, the authors try to argue that modern translations "embellish" Paul's version of the Eucharist. They say the Greek word which is translated "betrayed" (1 Cor. 11:23) can really only mean "delivered up" which contains less emphasis on historicity.[24] My how quickly our mystics become literalists! And bad ones at that. The Greek word *paradidomi* is in no way tied to just this one narrow translation, but is used dozens of times throughout Scripture, with various shades of meaning. Its root meaning is "to give over," and this can express any number of ideas from handing down a tradition to betraying a friend. In fact, the word is used every time the Gospels refer to Judas' betrayal of Christ (Mat. 26:25; Mark 3:19; 14:18; Luke 22:22; John 18:2). So the authors have gone far a-field in their effort, even into linguistic studies, only to fail there as well. After just a few instances like this one, the critical reader, with furrowed brow, feels a certain sense of disgust.

Conclusion

It would not be fruitless to pursue the critique further, though enough has been demonstrated here to illustrate the character of the work. In no instance do the authors demonstrate their thesis beyond a reasonable doubt, and nearly every claim that they make can be challenged by sounder or more modern scholarship. The book is simply one more fig leaf for pagan doubt. It may have a "very striking cover," but it makes a poor covering for the problem of sin.

---

[22] *TJM*, 290, note 6.

[23] See Quasten, Johannes, *The Beginnings of Patristic Literature,* 4 vols. (Westminster, MD: Christian Classics, Inc., 1993), 1:196ff.

[24] *TJM*, 152. Why they give a footnote to Matt. 19:12, I do not know.

Appendix IV
The Apology of Aristides[1]

(Translated from the Syriac)

The following Apology is the earliest defense of the faith that we have outside of the New Testament. It dates probably around A.D. 125, roughly two decades before even Justin Martyr (c. 100–165). Aristides excoriates the Pagan gods of every nationality, ridiculing their debauchery, immorality, base idolatry, and many other sins. Why, he asks, are Christians persecuted for their pure beliefs when pagans follow their gross gods and yet live in peace? There is some evidence that his plea to Hadrian effected the Emperor's decision to relax the discrimination against Christians in his era. This apology has been included because it shows the attitude of the earliest Christian apologists against the pagan mystery religions and pagan gods as pure idolatry to be avoided. It also makes explicit reference to the Incarnation of Christ as an historical event.

Here follows the defense which Aristides the philosopher made before Hadrian the King on behalf of reverence for God:

All-powerful Caesar Titus Hadrianus Antoninus, venerable and merciful, from Marcianus Aristides, an Athenian philosopher.

I. I, O King, by the grace of God came into this world; and when I had considered the heaven and the earth and the seas, and had surveyed the sun and the rest of creation, I marvelled at the beauty of the world. And I perceived that the world and all that is therein are moved by the power of another; and I understood that he who moves them is God, who is hidden in them, and veiled by them. And it is manifest that that which causes motion is more powerful than that which is moved.

---

[1]This version of *The Apology of Aristides* is taken from *The Ante-Nicene Fathers*, vol 10, eds. James Donaldson, Allan Menzies, and Alexander Roberts.

But that I should make search concerning this same mover of all, as to what is his nature (for it seems to me, he is indeed unsearchable in his nature), and that I should argue as to the constancy of his government, so as to grasp it fully,—this is a vain effort for me; for it is not possible that a man should fully comprehend it. I say, however, concerning this mover of the world, that he is God of all, who made all things for the sake of mankind. And it seems to me that this is reasonable, that one should fear God and should not oppress man. I say, then, that God is not born, not made, an ever-abiding nature without beginning and without end, immortal, perfect, and incomprehensible. Now when I say that he is "perfect," this means that there is not in him any defect, and he is not in need of anything but all things are in need of him. And when I say that he is "without beginning," this means that everything which has beginning has also an end, and that which has an end may be brought to an end. He has no name, for everything which has a name is kindred to things created. Form he has none, nor yet any union of members; for whatsoever possesses these is kindred to things fashioned. He is neither male nor female. The heavens do not limit him, but the heavens and all things, visible and invisible, receive their bounds from him. Adversary he has none, for there exists not any stronger than he. Wrath and indignation he possesses not, for there is nothing which is able to stand against him. Ignorance and forgetfulness are not in his nature, for he is altogether wisdom and understanding; and in Him stands fast all that exists. He requires not sacrifice and libation, nor even one of things visible; He requires not aught from any, but all living creatures stand in need of him.

II. Since, then, we have addressed you concerning God, so far as our discourse can bear upon him, let us now come to the race of men, that we may know which of them participate in the truth of which we have spoken, and which of them go astray from it. This is clear to you, O King, that there are four classes of men in this world:—Barbarians and Greeks, Jews and Christians. The Barbarians, indeed, trace the origin of their kind of religion from Kronos and from Rhea and their other gods; the Greeks, however, from Helenos, who is said to be sprung from

Zeus. And by Helenos there were born Aiolos and Xuthos; and there were others descended from Inachos and Phoroneus, and lastly from the Egyptian Danaos and from Kadmos and from Dionysos. The Jews, again, trace the origin of their race from Abraham, who begat Isaac, of whom was born Jacob. And he begat twelve sons who migrated from Syria to Egypt; and there they were called the nation of the Hebrews, by him who made their laws; and at length they were named Jews. The Christians, then, trace the beginning of their religion from Jesus the Messiah; and he is named the Son of God Most High. And it is said that God came down from heaven, and from a Hebrew virgin assumed and clothed himself with flesh; and the Son of God lived in a daughter of man. This is taught in the gospel, as it is called, which a short time ago was preached among them; and you also if you will read therein, may perceive the power which belongs to it. This Jesus, then, was born of the race of the Hebrews; and he had twelve disciples in order that the purpose of his incarnation might in time be accomplished. But he himself was pierced by the Jews, and he died and was buried; and they say that after three days he rose and ascended to heaven. Thereupon these twelve disciples went forth throughout the known parts of the world, and kept showing his greatness with all modesty and uprightness. And hence also those of the present day who believe that preaching are called Christians, and they are become famous. So then there are, as I said above, four classes of men:—Barbarians and Greeks, Jews and Christians. Moreover the wind is obedient to God, and fire to the angels; the waters also to the demons and the earth to the sons of men.

III. Let us begin, then, with the Barbarians, and go on to the rest of the nations one after another, that we may see which of them hold the truth as to God and which of them hold error. The Barbarians, then, as they did not apprehend God, went astray among the elements, and began to worship things created instead of their Creator; and for this end they made images and shut them up in shrines, and lo! they worship them, guarding them the while with much care, lest their gods be stolen by robbers. And the Barbarians did not observe that that which acts as guard is greater than that which is guarded, and that everyone who creates is greater than that which is created. If it be, then, that their gods are too feeble to see to their own safety, how will they take thought for the safety of men? Great then is the error into which the Barbarians wandered in worshipping lifeless images which can do nothing to help them. And I am led to wonder, O King, at their philosophers, how that even they went astray, and gave the name of gods to images which were made in honour of the elements; and that their sages did not perceive that the elements also are dissoluble and perishable. For if a small part of an element is dissolved or destroyed, the whole of it may be dissolved and destroyed. If then the elements themselves are dissolved and destroyed and forced to be subject to another that is more stubborn than they, and if they are not in their nature gods, why, forsooth, do they call the images which are made in their honour, God? Great, then, is the error which the philosophers among them have brought upon their followers.

IV. Let us turn now, O King, to the elements in themselves, that we may make clear in regard to them, that they are not gods, but a created thing, liable to ruin and change, which is of the same nature as man; whereas God is imperishable and unvarying, and invisible, while yet He sees, and overrules, and transforms all things. Those then who believe concerning the earth that it is a god have hitherto deceived themselves, since it is furrowed and set with plants and trenched; and it takes in the filthy refuse of men and beasts and cattle. And at times it becomes unfruitful, for if it be burnt to ashes it becomes devoid of life, for nothing germinates from an earthen jar. And besides if water be collected upon it, it is dissolved together with its products. And it is trodden under foot of men and beast, and receives the bloodstains of the slain; and it is dug open, and filled with the dead, and becomes a tomb for corpses. But it is impossible that a nature, which is holy and worthy and blessed and immortal, should allow of anyone of these things. And hence it appears to us that the earth is not a god but a creation of God.

V. In the same way, again, those erred who believed the waters to be gods. For the waters were created for the use of man, and are put under his rule in many ways. For they suffer change and admit impurity, and are destroyed and lose their nature while they are boiled into many substances. And they take colours which do not belong to them; they are also congealed by frost and are mingled and permeated with the filth of men and beasts, and with the blood of the slain. And being checked by skilled workmen through the restraint of aqueducts, they flow and are diverted against their inclination, and come into gardens and other places in order that they may be collected and issue forth as a means of fertility for man, and that they may cleanse away every impurity and fulfil the service man requires from them. Wherefore it is impossible that the waters should be a god, but they are a work of God and a part of the world. In like manner also they who believed that fire is a god erred to no slight extent. For it, too, was created for the service of men, and is subject to them in many ways:—in the preparation of meat, and as a means of casting metals, and for other ends whereof your Majesty is aware. At the same time it is quenched and extinguished in many ways. Again they also erred who believed the motion of the winds to be a god. For it is well known to us that those winds are under the dominion of another, at times their motion increases, and at times it fails and ceases at the command of him who controls them. For they were created by God for the sake of men, in order to supply the necessity of trees and fruits and seeds; and to bring over the sea ships which convey for men necessaries and goods from places where they are found to places where they are not found; and to govern the quarters of the world. And as for itself, at times it increases and again abates; and in one place brings help and in another causes disaster at the bidding of him who rules it. And mankind too are able by known means to confine and keep it in check in order that it may fulfil for them the service they require from it. And of itself it has not any authority at all. And hence it is impossible that the winds should be called gods, but rather a thing made by God.

VI. So also they erred who believed that the sun is a god. For we see that it is moved by the compulsion of another, and revolves and makes its journey, and proceeds from sign to sign, rising and setting every day, so as to give warmth for the growth of plants and trees, and to bring forth into the air where with it (sunlight) is mingled every growing thing which is upon the earth. And to it there belongs by comparison a part in common with the rest of the stars in its course; and though it is one in its nature it is associated with many parts for the supply of the needs of men; and that not according to its own will but rather according to the will of him who rules it. And hence it is impossible that the sun should be a god, but the work of God; and in like manner also the moon and the stars.

VII. And those who believed of the men of the past, that some of them were gods, they too were much mistaken. For as you yourself allow, O King, man is constituted of the four elements and of a soul and a spirit (and hence he is called a microcosm), and without anyone of these parts he could not consist. He has a beginning and an end, and he is born and dies. But God, as I said, has none of these things in his nature, but is uncreated and imperishable. And hence it is not possible that we should set up man to be of the nature of God:—man, to whom at times when he looks for joy, there comes trouble, and when he looks for laughter there comes to him weeping,—who is wrathful and covetous and envious, with other defects as well. And he is destroyed in many ways by the elements and also by the animals. And hence, O King, we are bound to recognize the error of the Barbarians, that thereby, since they did not find traces of the true God, they fell aside from the truth, and went after the desire of their imagination, serving the perishable elements and lifeless images, and through their error not apprehending what the true God is.

VIII. Let us turn further to the Greeks also, that we may know what opinion they hold as to the true God. The Greeks, then, because they are more subtle than the Barbarians, have gone further astray than the Barbarians; inasmuch as they have introduced many fictitious gods, and have set up some of them as males and some as females; and in that some of their gods were found who were adulterers, and did murder, and were deluded, and envious, and wrathful and passionate, and parricides, and thieves, and robbers. And some of them, they say, were crippled and limped, and some were sorcerers, and some actually went mad, and some played on lyres, and some were given to roaming on the hills, and some even died, and some were struck dead by lightning, and some were made servants even to men, and some escaped by flight, and some were kidnapped by men, and some, indeed, were lamented and deplored by men. And some, they say, went down to Sheol, and some were grievously wounded, and some transformed themselves into the likeness of animals to seduce the race of mortal women, and some polluted themselves by lying with males. And some, they say, were wedded to their mothers and their sisters and their daughters. And they say of their gods that they committed adultery with the daughters of men; and of these there was born a certain race which also was mortal. And they say that some of the females disputed about beauty, and appeared before men for judgment. Thus, O King, have the Greeks put forward foulness, and absurdity, and folly about their gods and about themselves, in that they have called those that are of such a nature gods, who are no gods. And hence mankind have received incitements to commit adultery and fornication, and to steal and to practise all that is offensive and hated and abhorred. For if they who are called their gods practised all these things which are written above, how much more should men practise them—men, who believe that their gods themselves practised them. And owing to the foulness of this error there have happened to mankind harassing wars, and great famines, and bitter captivity, and complete desolation. And lo! it was by reason of this alone that they suffered and that all these things came upon them; and while they endured those things they did not perceive in their mind that for their error those things came upon them.

IX. Let us proceed further to their account of their gods that we may carefully demonstrate all that is said above. First of all, the Greeks bring forward as a god Kronos, that is to say Chiun (Saturn). And his worshippers sacrifice their children to him, and they burn some of them alive in his honour. And they say that he took to him among his wives Rhea, and begat many children by her. By her too he begat Dios, who is called Zeus. And at length he (Kronos) went mad, and through fear of an oracle that had been made known to him, he began to devour his sons. And from him Zeus was stolen away without his knowledge; and at length Zeus bound him, and mutilated the signs of his manhood, and flung them into the sea. And hence, as they say in fable, there was engendered Aphrodite, who is called Astarte. And he (Zeus) cast out Kronos fettered into darkness. Great then is the error and ignominy which the Greeks have brought forward about the first of their gods, in that they have said all this about him, O King. It is impossible that a god should be bound or mutilated; and if it be otherwise, he is indeed miserable. And after Kronos they bring forward another god Zeus. And they say of him that he assumed the sovereignty, and was king over all the gods. And they say that he changed himself into a beast and other shapes in order to seduce mortal women, and to raise up by them children for himself. Once, they say, he changed himself into a bull through love of Europe and Pasiphae. And again he changed himself into the likeness of gold through love of Danae, and to a swan through love of Leda, and to a man through love of Antiope, and to lightning through love of Luna, and so by these he begat many children. For by Antiope, they say, that he begat Zethus and Amphion, and by Luna Dionysos, by Alcmena Hercules, and by Leto, Apollo and Artemis, and by Danae Perseus, and by Leda, Castor and Polydeuces, and Helene and Paludus, and by Mnemosyne he begat nine daughters whom they styled the Muses, and by Europe, Minos and Rhadamanthos and Sarpedon. And lastly he changed himself into the likeness of an eagle through his passion for Ganydemos (Ganymede) the shepherd. By reason of these tales, O King, much evil has arisen among men, who to this day are imitators of their gods, and practise adultery and defile themselves with their mothers and their sisters, and by lying with males, and some make bold to slay even their parents. For if he who is said to be the chief and king of their gods do these things how much more should his worshippers imitate him? And great is the folly which the Greeks have brought forward in their narrative concerning him. For it is impossible that a god should practise adultery or fornication or come near to lie with males, or kill his parents; and if it be otherwise, he is much worse than a destructive demon.

X. Again they bring forward as another god Hephaistos. And they say of him, that he is lame, and a cap is set on his head, and he holds in his hands firetongs and a hammer; and he follows the craft of iron working, that thereby he may procure the necessaries of his livelihood. Is then this god so very needy? But it cannot be that a god should be needy or lame, else he is very worthless. And further they bring in another god and call him Hermes. And they say that he is a thief, a lover of avarice, and greedy for gain, and a magician and mutilated and an athlete, and an interpreter of language. But it is impossible that a god should be a magician or avaricious, or maimed, or craving for what is not his, or an athlete. And if it be otherwise, he is found to be useless. And after him they bring forward as another god Asklepios. And they say that he is a physician and prepares drugs and plaster that he may supply the necessaries of his livelihood. Is then this god in want? And at length he was struck with lightning by Dios on account of Tyndareos of Lacedaemon, and so he died. If then Asklepios were a god, and, when he was struck with lightning, was unable to help himself, how should he be able to give help to others? But that a divine nature should be in want or be destroyed by lightning is impossible. And again they bring forward another as a god, and they call him Ares. And they say that he is a warrior, and jealous, and covets sheep and things which are not his. And he makes gain by his arms. And they say that at length he committed adultery with Aphrodite, and was caught by the little boy Eros and by Hephaistos the husband of Aphrodite. But it is impossible that a god should be a warrior or bound or an adulterer. And again they say of Dionysos that he forsooth! is a god, who arranges carousals by night, and teaches drunkenness, and carries off women who do not belong to him. And at length, they say, he went mad and dismissed his handmaidens and fled into the desert; and during his madness he ate serpents. And at last he was killed by Titanos. If then Dionysos were a god, and when he was being killed was unable to help himself, how is it possible that he should help others? Herakles next they bring forward and say that he is a god, who hates detestable things, a tyrant, and warrior and a destroyer of plagues. And of him also they say that at length he became mad and killed his own children, and cast himself into a fire and died. If then Herakles is a god, and in all these calamities was unable to rescue himself, how should others ask help from him? But it is impossible that a god should be mad, or drunken or a slayer of his children, or consumed by fire.

XI. And after him they bring forward another god and call him Apollon. And they say that he is jealous and inconstant, and at times he holds the bow and quiver, and again the lyre and plectron. And he utters oracles for men that he may receive rewards from them. Is then this god in need of rewards? But it is an insult that all these things should be found with a god. And after him they bring forward as a goddess Artemis, the sister of Apollo; and they say that she was a huntress and that she herself used to carry a bow and bolts, and to roam about upon the mountains, leading the hounds to hunt stags or wild boars of the field. But it is disgraceful that a virgin maid should roam alone upon the hills or hunt in the chase for animals. Wherefore it is impossible that Artemis should be a goddess. Again they say of Aphrodite that she indeed is a goddess. And at times she dwells with their gods, but at other times she is a neighbour to men. And once she had Ares as a lover, and again Adonis who is Tammuz. Once also, Aphrodite was wailing and weeping for the death of Tammuz, and they say that she went down to Sheol that she might redeem Adonis from Persephone, who is the daughter of Sheol (Hades). If then Aphrodite is a goddess and was unable to help her lover at his death, how will she find it possible to help others? And this cannot be listened to, that a divine nature should come to weeping and wailing and adultery. And again they say of Tammuz that he is a god. And he is, forsooth! a hunter and an adulterer. And they say that he was killed by a wound from a wild boar, without being able to help himself. And if he could not help himself, how can he take thought for the human race? But that a god should be an adulterer or a hunter or should die by violence is impossible. Again they say of Rhea that she is the mother of their gods. And they say that she had once a lover Atys, and that she used to delight in depraved men. And at last she raised a lamentation and mourned for Atys her lover. If then the mother of their gods was unable to help her lover and deliver him from death, how can she help others? So it is disgraceful that a goddess should lament and weep and take delight in depraved men. Again they introduce Kore and say that she is a goddess, and she was stolen away by Pluto, and could not help herself. If then she is a goddess and was unable to help herself how will she find means to help others? For a god who is stolen away is very powerless. All this, then, O King, have the Greeks brought forward concerning their gods, and they have invented and declared it concerning them. And hence all men received an impulse to work all profanity and all defilements; and hereby the whole earth was corrupted.

XII. The Egyptians, moreover, because they are more base and stupid than every people that is on the earth, have themselves erred more than all. For the deities (or religion) of the Barbarians and the Greeks did not suffice for them, but they introduced some also of the nature of the animals, and said thereof that they were gods, and likewise of creeping things which are found on the dry land and in the waters. And of plants and herbs they said that some of them were gods. And they were corrupted by every kind of delusion and defilement more than every people that is on the earth. For from ancient times they worshipped Isis, and they say that she is a goddess whose husband was Osiris her brother. And when Osiris was killed by Typhon his brother, Isis fled with Horos her son to Byblus in Syria, and was there for a certain time till her son was grown. And he contended with Typhon his uncle, and killed him. And then Isis returned and went about with Horos her son and sought for the dead body of Osiris her lord, bitterly lamenting his death. If then Isis be a goddess, and could not help Osiris her brother and lord, how can she help another? But it is impossible that a divine nature should be afraid, and flee for safety, or should weep and wail; or else it is very miserable. And of Osiris also they say that he is a serviceable god. And he was killed by Typhon and was unable to help himself. But it is well known that this cannot be asserted of divinity. And further, they say of his brother Typhon that he is a god, who killed his brother and was killed by his brother's son and by his bride, being unable to help himself. And how, pray, is he a god who does not save himself? As the Egyptians, then, were more stupid than the rest of the nations, these and such like gods did not suffice for them. Nay, but they even apply the name of gods to animals in which there is no soul at all. For some of them worship the sheep and others the calf; and some the pig and others the shad fish; and some the crocodile and the hawk and the fish and the ibis and the vulture and the eagle and the raven. Some of them worship the cat, and others the turbotfish, some the dog, some the adder, and some the asp, and others the lion; and others the garlic and onions and thorns, and others the tiger and other such things. And the poor creatures do not see that all these things are nothing, although they daily witness their gods being eaten and consumed by men and also by their fellows; while some of them are cremated, and some die and decay and become dust, without their observing that they perish in many ways. So the Egyptians have not observed that such things which are not equal to their own deliverance, are not gods. And if, forsooth, they are weak in the case of their own deliverance, whence have they power to help in the case of deliverance of their worshippers? Great then is the error into which the Egyptians wandered; greater, indeed, than that of any people which is upon the face of the earth.

XIII. But it is a marvel, O King, with regard to the Greeks, who surpass all other peoples in their manner of life and reasoning, how they have gone astray after dead idols and lifeless images. And yet they see their gods in the hands of their artificers being sawn out, and planed and docked, and hacked short, and charred, and ornamented, and being altered by them in every kind of way. And when they grow old, and are worn away through lapse of time, and when they are molten and crushed to powder, how, I wonder, did they not perceive concerning them, that they are not gods? And as for those who did not find deliverance for themselves, how can they serve the distress of men? But even the writers and philosophers among them have wrongly alleged that the gods are such as are made in honour of God Almighty. And they err in seeking to liken (them) to God whom man has not at any time seen nor can see unto what He is like. Herein, too (they err) in asserting of deity that any such thing as deficiency can be present to it; as when

they say that He receives sacrifice and requires burnt-offering and libation and immolations of men, and temples. But God is not in need, and
none of these things is necessary to Him; and it is clear that men err in
these things they imagine. Further their writers and their philosophers
represent and declare that the nature of all their gods is one. And they
have not apprehended God our Lord who while He is one, is in all. They
err therefore. For if the body of a man while it is many in its parts is not
in dread, one member of another, but, since it is a united body, wholly
agrees with itself; even so also God is one in His nature. A single essence
is proper to Him, since He is uniform in His nature and His essence;
and He is not afraid of Himself. If then the nature of the gods is one, it
is not proper that a god should either pursue or slay or harm a god. If,
then, gods be pursued and wounded by gods, and some be kidnapped
and some struck dead by lightning, it is obvious that the nature of their
gods is not one. And hence it is known, O King, that it is a mistake
when they reckon and bring the natures of their gods under a single
nature. If then it becomes us to admire a god which is seen and does not
see, how much more praiseworthy is it that one should believe in a nature which is invisible and all-seeing? And if further it is fitting that one
should approve the handiworks of a craftsman, how much more is it
fitting that one should glorify the Creator of the craftsman? For behold!
when the Greeks made laws they did not perceive that by their laws
they condemn their gods. For if their laws are righteous, their gods are
unrighteous, since they transgressed the law in killing one another, and
practising sorcery, and committing adultery, and in robbing and steal-
ing, and in lying with males, and by their other practises as well. For if
their gods were right in doing all these things as they are described, then
the laws of the Greeks are unrighteous in not being made according to
the will of their gods. And in that case the whole world is gone astray.
For the narratives about their gods are some of them myths, and some
of them nature-poems (lit: natural: *phusikai*), and some of them hymns
and elegies. The hymns indeed and elegies are empty words and noise.
But these nature-poems, even if they be made as they say, still those are

not gods who do such things and suffer and endure such things. And those myths are shallow tales with no depth whatever in them.

XIV. Let us come now, O King, to the history of the Jews also, and see what opinion they have as to God. The Jews then say that God is one, the Creator of all, and omnipotent; and that it is not right that any other should be worshipped except this God alone. And herein they appear to approach the truth more than all the nations, especially in that they worship God and not His works. And they imitate God by the philanthropy which prevails among them; for they have compassion on the poor, and they release the captives, and bury the dead, and do such things as these, which are acceptable before God and well-pleasing also to men,—which (customs) they have received from their forefathers. Nevertheless they too erred from true knowledge. And in their imagination they conceive that it is God they serve; whereas by their mode of observance it is to the angels and not to God that their service is rendered:—as when they celebrate sabbaths and the beginning of the months, and feasts of unleavened bread, and a great fast; and fasting and circumcision and the purification of meats, which things, however, they do not observe perfectly.

XV. But the Christians, O King, while they went about and made search, have found the truth; and as we learned from their writings, they have come nearer to truth and genuine knowledge than the rest of the nations. For they know and trust in God, the Creator of heaven and of earth, in whom and from whom are all things, to whom there is no other god as companion, from whom they received commandments which they engraved upon their minds and observe in hope and expectation of the world which is to come. Wherefore they do not commit adultery nor fornication, nor bear false witness, nor embezzle what is held in pledge, nor covet what is not theirs. They honour father and mother, and show kindness to those near to them; and whenever they are judges, they judge uprightly. They do not worship idols (made) in the image of man; and whatsoever they would not that others should do unto them, they do not to others; and of the food which is consecrated to idols they do not eat, for they are pure. And their oppressors they appease (lit:

comfort) and make them their friends; they do good to their enemies; and their women, O King, are pure as virgins, and their daughters are modest; and their men keep themselves from every unlawful union and from all uncleanness, in the hope of a recompense to come in the other world. Further, if one or other of them have bondmen and bondwomen or children, through love towards them they persuade them to become Christians, and when they have done so, they call them brethren without distinction. They do not worship strange gods, and they go their way in all modesty and cheerfulness. Falsehood is not found among them; and they love one another, and from widows they do not turn away their esteem; and they deliver the orphan from him who treats him harshly. And he, who has, gives to him who has not, without boasting. And when they see a stranger, they take him in to their homes and rejoice over him as a very brother; for they do not call them brethren after the flesh, but brethren after the spirit and in God. And whenever one of their poor passes from the world, each one of them according to his ability gives heed to him and carefully sees to his burial. And if they hear that one of their number is imprisoned or afflicted on account of the name of their Messiah, all of them anxiously minister to his necessity, and if it is possible to redeem him they set him free. And if there is among them any that is poor and needy, and if they have no spare food, they fast two or three days in order to supply to the needy their lack of food. They observe the precepts of their Messiah with much care, living justly and soberly as the Lord their God commanded them. Every morning and every hour they give thanks and praise to God for His loving-kindnesses toward them; and for their food and their drink they offer thanksgiving to Him. And if any righteous man among them passes from the world, they rejoice and offer thanks to God; and they escort his body as if he were setting out from one place to another near. And when a child has been born to one of them, they give thanks to God; and if moreover it happen to die in childhood, they give thanks to God the more, as for one who has passed through the world without sins. And further if they see that anyone of them dies in his ungodliness or in his sins, for him they grieve bitterly, and sorrow as for one who goes to meet his doom.

XVI. Such, O King, is the commandment of the law of the Christians, and such is their manner of life. As men who know God, they ask from Him petitions which are fitting for Him to grant and for them to receive. And thus they employ their whole lifetime. And since they know the loving-kindnesses of God toward them, behold! for their sake the glorious things which are in the world flow forth to view. And verily, they are those who found the truth when they went about and made search for it; and from what we considered, we learned that they alone come near to a knowledge of the truth. And they do not proclaim in the ears of the multitude the kind deeds they do, but are careful that no one should notice them; and they conceal their giving just as he who finds a treasure and conceals it. And they strive to be righteous as those who expect to behold their Messiah, and to receive from Him with great glory the promises made concerning them. And as for their words and their precepts, O King, and their glorying in their worship, and the hope of earning according to the work of each one of them their recompense which they look for in another world, you may learn about these from their writings. It is enough for us to have shortly informed your Majesty concerning the conduct and the truth of the Christians. For great indeed, and wonderful is their doctrine to him who will search into it and reflect upon it. And verily, this is a new people, and there is something divine (lit: a divine admixture) in the midst of them. Take, then, their writings, and read therein, and lo! you will find that I have not put forth these things on my own authority, nor spoken thus as their advocate; but since I read in their writings I was fully assured of these things as also of things which are to come. And for this reason I was constrained to declare the truth to such as care for it and seek the world to come. And to me there is no doubt but that the earth abides through the supplication of the Christians. But the rest of the nations err and cause error in wallowing before the elements of the world, since beyond these their mental vision will not pass. And they search about as if in darkness because they will not recognize the truth; and like drunken men they reel and jostle one another and fall.

XVII. Thus far, O King, I have spoken; for concerning that which remains, as is said above, there are found in their other writings things which are hard to utter and difficult for one to narrate,—which are not only spoken in words but also wrought out in deeds. Now the Greeks, O King, as they follow base practises in intercourse with males, and a mother and a sister and a daughter, impute their monstrous impurity in turn to the Christians. But the Christians are just and good, and the truth is set before their eyes, and their spirit is long-suffering; and, therefore, though they know the error of these (the Greeks), and are persecuted by them, they bear and endure it; and for the most part they have compassion on them, as men who are destitute of knowledge. And on their side, they offer prayer that these may repent of their error; and when it happens that one of them has repented, he is ashamed before the Christians of the works which were done by him; and he makes confession to God, saying, I did these things in ignorance. And he purifies his heart, and his sins are forgiven him, because he committed them in ignorance in the former time, when he used to blaspheme and speak evil of the true knowledge of the Christians. And assuredly the race of the Christians is more blessed than all the men who are upon the face of the earth. Henceforth let the tongues of those who utter vanity and harass the Christians be silent; and hereafter let them speak the truth. For it is of serious consequence to them that they should worship the true God rather than worship a senseless sound. And verily whatever is spoken in the mouth of the Christians is of God; and their doctrine is the gateway of light. Wherefore let all who are without the knowledge of God draw near thereto; and they will receive incorruptible words, which are from all time and from eternity. So shall they appear before the awful judgment which through Jesus the Messiah is destined to come upon the whole human race.

The Apology of Aristides the Philosopher is finished.

Bibliography

Angus, S. *The Mystery Religions and Christianity: A Study in the Religious Background of Early Christianity.* New York: Charles Scribner's Sons, 1928 (1925).

Anselm. *Cur Deus Homo.* In *St. Anselm: Basic Writings.* tr. S. N. Deane. LaSalle, IL: Open Court Publishing Co., 1962.

Aune, D. E. "Expansion and Recruitment among Hellenistic Religions: The Case of Mithraism." In *Recruitment, Conquest, and Conflict: Strategies in Judaism, Early Christianity, and the Greco-Roman World,* eds. Borgen, Robbins & Gowler. Atlanta, GA. Scholars Press, 1998.

Bainton, Roland H. *Early Christianity.* Princeton, NJ: D. Van Nostrand Company, Inc., 1960.

Barnard, L. W. *Justin Martyr: His Life and Thought.* Cambridge: Cambridge University Press, 1967.

Barnes, Harry Elmer. *An Intellectual History of the Western World, Vol. 1.* New York: Dover Publications, 1965 (1937).

Bloch, Marc. *The Historian's Craft.* tr. Peter Putnam. New York: Vintage Books, 1953.

Brown, Raymond. E. *The Community of the Beloved Disciple.* New York; Mahwah: Paulist Press, 1979.

_____ . *The Gospel According to John (i-xii), Introduction, Translation, and Notes.* Garden City, NY: Doubleday & Company, Inc., 1966.

_____. *An Introduction to the New Testament.* New York: Doubleday, 1997.

_____. *An Introduction to New Testament Christology.* Manwah, NJ: Paulist Press, 1994.

Bruce, F. F. *The Gospel of John, Introduction, Exposition and Notes.* Grand Rapids, MI: William B. Eerdmans Publishing Company, 1984.

_____. "Johannine Studies Since Westcott's Days" in Westcott, B. F. *The Epistles of St. John.* Grand Rapids, MI: Wm. B. Eerdmans Publishing Company, 1966.

_____. *New Testament Development of Old Testament Themes.* Grand Rapids, MI: W. B. Eerdmans, 1977 (1968).

Bultmann, Rudolf. "New Testament and Mythology" in *Kerygma and Myth: A Theological Debate.* ed. Hans Werner Bartsch. tr. Reginald H. Fuller. New York: Harper Torchbooks, 1961.

_____. *Primitive Christianity: In Its Contemporary Setting.* tr. R. H. Fuller. Cleveland, OH: The World Publishing Company, 1965 (1956).

Calvin, John. *The Institutes of the Christian Religion.* ed. John T. McNeill, tr. Ford Lewis Battles. The Library of Christian Classics, Volumes XX and XXI. Philadelphia: The Westminster Press, 1960.

Campbell, Joseph. *The Hero With a Thousand Faces.* Bollingen Series XVII. Princeton, NJ: Princeton University Press, 1973.

Carson, Clayborne, Luker, Ralph and Russell, Penney A. eds., *Volume I: Called to Serve, January 1929-June 1951.* Berkeley: University of California Press, 1992.

Carson, D. A. *The Gospel According to John.* Leicester, England; Grand Rapids, MI: William B. Eerdmans Publishing Company, 1991.

Carson, D.A., Moo, Douglas J. and Morris, Leon. *An Introduction to the New Testament.* Grand Rapids, MI: Zondervan, 1992.

Case, Shirley Jackson. The Historicity of Jesus:A Criticism of the Contention that Jesus Never Lived, a Statement of the Evidence for His Existence, an Estimate of His Relation to Christianity. Chicago: University of Chicago, 1912.

Chadwick, Henry. *The Early Church.* The Pelican History of the Church, Volume I. Harmondsworth, Middlesex, England: Penguin Books, 1977 (1967).

Cheetham, Samuel. *The Mysteries: Pagan and Christian.* The Hulsean Lectures 1896–7. London: MacMillan and Co., 1897.

Clauss, Manfred. *The Roman Cult of Mithras: The God and His Mysteries.* New York: Routledge, 2001.

Cochrane, Charles Norris. *Christianity and Classical Civilization: A Study of Thought hand Action from Augustus to Augustine*. Oxford: Clarendon Press, 1940.

Cumont, Franz. *The Mysteries of Mithra*. tr. Thomas J. McCormack. New York: Dover Publications, Inc., 1956 (Orig. 2nd Ed. 1902).

Daniélou, Jean. *Christ and Us*. tr. Walter Roberts. London: A. R. Mowbray & Co. Limited, 1961.

Daniels, C. M. "The Role of the Roman Army in the Spread of Mithraism." In *Mithraic Studies, Vol. II*, ed. John R. Hinnels. Rowman and Littlefield: Manchester University Press, 1975.

Dodd, C. H. "The New Testament." in *The Study of Theology*, ed. Kenneth E. Kirk, 217–246. New York and London: Harper and Brothers, 1939.

Elliott, Susan. *Cutting Too Close for Comfort: Paul's Letter to the Galatians in its Anatolian Cultic Context*. Journal for the New Testament Supplement Series, No. 248. ed. Stanley E. Porter. London and New York: T& T Clark International, 2003.

Erickson, Millard. *The Word Became Flesh*. Grand Rapids, MI: Baker Books, 1991.

Euripides. "The Bacchanals." In *Euripides III*. The Loeb Classical Library. eds. T. E. Page and W. H. D. Rouse, tr. Arthur S. Way. New York: The MacMillan Co., 1912.

Ferguson, Everett. *Background of Early Christianity*, Third Edition. Grand Rapids, MI: William B. Eerdmans Publishing Company, 2003.

Ferguson, John. *The Heritage of Hellenism: The Greek World from 323 to 31 BC*. History of European Civilization Library, ed. Geoffrey Barraclough. Harcourt Brace Jovanovich, Inc. 1973.

Finegan, Jack. *Myth and Mystery: An Introduction to the Pagan Religions of the Biblical World*. Grand rapids, MI: Baker Book House, 1989.

Fischer, David Hackett. *Historians' Fallacies*. New York and Evanston: Harper Torchbooks, 1970.

Fitzmyer, Joseph A. *Pauline Theology: A Brief Sketch*. Englewood Cliffs, NJ: Prentice Hall, Inc., 1967.

Freke, Timothy and Gandy, Peter. *The Jesus Mysteries: Was the "Original Jesus" a Pagan God?* New York: Three Rivers Press, 1999.

Frend, W. H. C. *The Rise of Christianity*. Philadelphia: Fortress Press, 1984.

Gibson, Richard J. "Paul and the Evangelization of the Stoics" in *The Gospel to the Nations: Perspectives on Paul's Mission.* eds. Mark Thompson and Peter Bolt. Downers Grove, IL: InterVarsity Press, 2000, 309–26.

Glover, T. R. *The Conflict of Religions in the Early Roman Empire.* London: Methuen & Co., Ltd., 1917.

Godwin, Joscelyn. *Mystery Religions in the Ancient World.* San Francisco, CA: Harper and Row, 1981.

Gore, Charles. *Dissertations on Subjects Connected with the Incarnation.* New York: Charles Scribner's Sons, 1895.

_____. *The Incarnation of the Son of God.* The Bampton Lectures, 1891. New York: Charles Scribner's Sons, 1896.

Green, Michael. *Evangelism in the Early Church.* Grand Rapids, MI & Cambridge, UK: William B. Eerdmans, 2003 (1970).

Griffith-Thomas, W. H. *Christianity Is Christ.* Grand Rapids, MI: W. B. Eerdmands Publishing Co., 1955.

Guthrie, Donald. *New Testament Introduction.* Downers Grove, IL: InterVarsity Press, 1973.

Hafemann, S. J. "Paul and His Interpreters." In *Dictionary of Paul and His Letters: A Compendium of Contemporary Biblical Scholarship.* ed. Gerald F. Hawthorne, Ralph P. Martin and Daniel G. Reid, 666–679. Downers Grove, IL: InterVarsity Press, 1993.

Harnack, Adolph. *History of Dogma, Volume I.* History of Dogma: Complete in Seven Volumes Bound as Four, tr. Neil Buchanan. New York: Dover Publications, 1961 (Orig. 1900).

Harrison, Jane Ellen. *Prolegomena to the Study of Greek Religion.* Princeton, NJ: Princeton University Press, 1991 (1903).

Hurtado, Larry. At the Origins of Christian Worship. Grand Rapids, MI / Cambridge, U.K.: W. B. Eerdmans, 1999.

Inge, William Ralph. *Christian Mysticism*. The Bampton Lectures, 1899. London: Methuen & Co., 1899.

Klauck, Hans-Josef. *Magic and Paganism in Early Christianity: The World of the Acts of the Apostles*. tr. Brian McNeil. Edinburgh: T & T Clark, 2000.

_____. *The Religious Context of Early Christianity: A Guide to Graeco-Roman Mystery Religions*. Studies of the New Testament and Its World, eds. John Barclay, Joel Marcus, and John Riches. Edinburgh: T & T Clark, 2000.

Koester, Helmut. *History, Culture, and Religion of the Hellenistic Age*. Introduction to the New Testament, Volume One. Philadelphia: Fortress Press, 1982.

_____. *History and Literature of Early Christianity*. Introduction to the New Testament, Volume Two. Philadelphia: Fortress Press, 1982.

Ladd, George Eldon. *The New Testament and Criticism*. Grand Rapids, MI: W. B. Eerdmans, 1984 (1967).

Latourette, Kenneth Scott. *A History of Christianity: Volume I: to A.D. 1500*. Peabody, MA: Prince Press, 2000.

Lietzmann, Hans. *Volume I: The Beginnings of the Christian Church and Volume II. The Founding of the Universal Church*. A History of the Early Church (2vol.), tr. Bertram Lee Woolf. Cleveland and New York: Meridian Books, the World Publishing Company, 1967.

Lightfoot, J. B. *Essays on the Work Entitled Supernatural Religion*. New York: MacMillan and Co., 1889.

Maier, Paul. In the Fullness of Time: A Historian Looks at Christian, Easter, and the Early Church. San Francisco, CA: HarperSanFrancisco, 1991.

Martyn, J. Louis. *The Gospel of John in Christian History: Essays for Interpreters*. New York; Ramsey; Toronto: Paulist Press, 1979.

_____. *History and Theology in the Fourth Gospel*. Nashville, Abingdon 1979.

McGrath, Alister E. *The Future of Christianity.* Blackwell Manifestos. Oxford: Blackwell Publishers, 2002.

McNeill, John Thomas, Matthew Spinka and Harold Willoughby, eds. *Environmental Factors in Christian History.* Chicago: The University of Chicago Press, 1939.

Metzger, Bruce M. "Methodology in the Study of Mystery Religions and Early Christianity." In *Historical and Literary Studies: Pagan, Jewish, and Christian.* New Testament Tools and Studies, Volume VIII, ed. Bruce M. Metzger, 1–24. Leiden: E. J. Brill, 1968.

Meyer, Marvin W., ed. *The Ancient Mysteries, A Sourcebook: Sacred Texts of the Mystery Religions of the Ancient Mediterranean World.* San Francisco: Harper & Row Publishers, 1987.

Moore, Clifford Herschel. *The Religious Thought of the Greeks: From Homer to the Triumph of Christianity.* Cambridge: Harvard University Press, 1916.

Morris, Leon. *Studies in the Fourth Gospel.* Grand Rapids, MI: William B. Eerdmans Publishing Company, 1969.

Nash, Ronald H. *Christianity and the Hellenistic World.* Grand Rapids, MI & Dallas TX: Zondervan/Probe, 1984.

Nock, Arthur Darby. *Early Gentile Christianity and Its Hellenistic Background.* New York: Harper Torchbooks, 1964.

North, Gary. *The Hoax of Higher Criticism.* Tyler, TX: The Institute for Christian Economics, 1989.

_____. *The Sinai Strategy: Economics and the Ten Commandments.* Tyler, TX: The Institute for Christian Economics, 1986.

Pelikan, Jaroslav. *The Emergence of the Catholic Tradition (100–600).* The Christian Tradition: A History of the Development of Doctrine, vol. I. Chicago and London: The University of Chicago Press, 1975 (1971).

Quasten, Johannes. *The Beginnings of Patristic Literature.* Patrology, Volume I (4vol.), Westminster, MD: Christian Classics, Inc. 1993.

_____. *The Ante-Nicene Literature After Irenaeus.* Patrology, Volume II (4vol.), Westminster, MD: Christian Classics, Inc. 1992.

Quick, Oliver Chase. *Essays in Orthodoxy.* London: MacMillan and Co., Ltd., 1916. Accessed at www.agnglicanlibrary.org/quick/essays/index.htm, as of August 8, 2006.

Renan, Ernst. *The Life of Jesus.* New York: Modern Library, Inc. 1927 (1863).

Ridderbos, Herman. *Paul: An Outline of His Theology.* tr. John Richard DeWitt. Grand Rapids, MI: Eerdmans, 1975.

Rose, H. J. *Ancient Greek & Roman Religion: Two Volumes in One.* New York: Barnes & Noble Books, 1995 (1948).

Rushdoony, Rousas J. *The Biblical Philosophy of History.* Vallecito, CA: Ross House Books, 2000.

_____. *The Foundations of Social Order.* Fairfax, VA: Thoburn Press, 1978 (1968).

_____. *The One and the Many: Studies in the Philosophy of Order and Ultimacy.* Fairfax, VA: Thoburn Press, 1978.

_____. *To Be As God: A Study of Modern Thought Since the Marquis de Sade.* Vallecito, CA: Ross House Books, 2003.

Schaff, Philip. *Apostolic Christianity: From the Birth of Christ to the Death of St. John.* History of the Christian Church, Volume I. Peabody, MA: Hendrickson Publishers, Inc. 1996 (Orig. 1858, 3rd Revision 1890).

Tenney, Merril C. *New Testament Times.* Grand Rapids, MI: Eerdmans, 1972 (1965).

Ulansey, David. *The Origins of the Mithraic Mysteries: Cosmology and Salvation in the Ancient World.* New York and Oxford: Oxford University Press, 1989.

Ulhorn, Gerhard. *The Conflict of Christianity with Heathenism.* eds. & trs. Egbert C. Smith, C. J. H. Ropes. New York: Charles Scribner's Sons, 1912 (1879).

Van Creveld, Martin. *The Rise and Decline of the State.* Cambridge: Cambridge University Press, 1999.

Van Til, Cornelius. *The Great Debate Today.* Nutley, NJ: P& R, 1971.

_____. *A Survey of Christian Epistemology*. In Defense of Biblical Christianity, Volume II. Phillipsburg, NJ: Presbyterian & Reformed, No Date (Orig. 1932).

Vermaseren, M. J. *Mithras, the Secret God*. London: Chatto & Windus, 1963.

Wagner, Günter. *Pauline Baptism and The Pagan Mysteries: The Problem of the Pauline Doctrine of Baptism in Romans VI. 1–11, in the Light of its Religio-Historical "Parallels."* tr. J. P. Smith. Edinburgh and London: Oliver & Boyd, 1967.

Warfield, Benjamin Breckenridge. *The Person and Work of Christ*. Philadelphia, PA: P&R, 1950.

_____. *Studies in Theology*. In The Works of Benjamin B. Warfield, Vol. IX. Grand Rapids, MI: Baker Book House, 2000.

Wedderburn, A. J. M. *Baptism and Resurrection: Studies in Pauline Theology against its Graeco-Roman Background*. Tübingen: J.C. B. Mohr (Paul Siebeck), 1987.

_____, ed. *Paul and Jesus: Collected Essays*. Journal for the Study of the New Testament, Supplement Series 37, eds. David Hill and David E. Orton. Sheffield: JSOT Press, 1989.

Wenham, David. *Paul and Jesus: The True Story*. Grand Rapids, MI and Cambridge: Eerdmans, 2002.

_____. *Paul: Follower of Jesus or Founder of Christianity?* Grand Rapids, MI and Cambridge: Eerdmans, 1995.

Westcott, B. F. *The Epistles of St. John*. (Grand Rapids, MI: Wm. B. Eerdmans Publishing Company) 1966.

_____. *The Gospel According to John: The Greek Text with Introduction and Notes*. (Grand Rapids, MI: Wm. B. Eerdmans Publishing Company) 1954 [Original 1880].

Wright, N. T. *The Resurrection of the Son of God*. Christian Origins and the Question of God, Volume III. Minneapolis: Fortress Press, 2003.

_____. *What St. Paul Really Said: Was Paul of Tarsus the Real Founder of Christianity?* Grand Rapids, MI: Eerdmans, 1997.

Scripture Index

Subject Index